WRITING
IN A
BILINGUAL PROGRAM

Había una vez

Writing Research

Multidisciplinary Inquiries into the Nature of Writing

edited by Marcia Farr, University of Illinois at Chicago

Arthur N. Applebee, *Contexts for Learning to Write: Studies of Secondary School Instruction*

Carole Edelsky, *Writing in a Bilingual Program: Había Una Vez*

Lester Faigley, Roger Cherry, David Jolliffe, and Anna Skinner, *Assessing Writers' Knowledge and Processes of Composing*

Marcia Farr (ed.), *Advances in Writing Research, Volume One: Children's Early Writing Development*

Sarah W. Freedman (ed.), *The Acquisition of Written Language: Response and Revision*

Judith Langer, *Children Reading and Writing: Structures and Strategies*

William Teale and Elizabeth Sulzby (eds.), *Emergent Literacy: Writing and Reading*

IN PREPARATION

Barbara Couture, *Functional Approaches to Writing Research*

Robert Gundlach, *Children and Writing in American Education*

Martha L. King and Victor Rentel, *The Development of Meaning in Writing: Children 5–10*

Anthony Petrosky (ed.), *Reading and Writing: Theory and Research*

Leo Ruth and Sandra Murphy, *Designing Writing Tasks for the Assessment of Writing*

David Smith, *Explorations in the Culture of Literacy*

Jana Staton, Roger Shuy, Joy Kreeft, and Leslie Reed, *Interactive Writing in Dialogue Journals: Practitioner, Linguistic, Social, and Cognitive Views*

Elizabeth Sulzby, *Emergent Writing and Reading in 5–6 Year Olds: A Longitudinal Study*

Stephen Witte, Keith Walters, Mary Trachsel, Roger Cherry, and Paul Meyer, *Literacy and Writing Assessment: Issues, Traditions, Directions*

Writing
in a
Bilingual Program:

Había una vez

CAROLE EDELSKY

Arizona State University

ABLEX PUBLISHING CORPORATION
NORWOOD, NEW JERSEY

Copyright © 1986 by Ablex Publishing Corporation

Printed in the United States of America.

Library of Congress Cataloging in Publication Data

Edelsky, Carole.
  Writing in a bilingual program.

  (Writing research)
  Bibliography: p.
  Includes index.
    1. Education, Bilingual—United States—Case studies.
2. English language—Composition and exercises—Case studies. I. Title.
LC3731.E33 1986   371.97′0973   85-31569
ISBN 0-89391-304-9
ISBN 0-89391-381-2 (pbk.)

Ablex Publishing Corporation
355 Chestnut Street
Norwood, New Jersey 07648

CONTENTS

to Jay, Gail, and Lynn—
the loves of my life

Writing Research

Multidisciplinary Inquiries into the Nature of Writing

Marcia Farr, series editor
University of Illinois at Chicago

PREFACE

This series of volumes presents the results of recent scholarly inquiry into the nature of writing. The research presented comes from a mix of disciplines, those which have emerged as significant within the last decade or so in the burgeoning field of writing research. These primarily include English education, linguistics, psychology, anthropology, and rhetoric. A note here on the distinction between field and discipline might be useful: a field can be a multidisciplinary entity focused on a set of significant questions about a central concern (e.g., American Studies), while a discipline usually shares theoretical and methodological approaches which may have a substantial tradition behind them. Writing research, then, is a field, if not yet a discipline.

The history of this particular field is unique. Much of the recent work in this field, and much that is being reported in this series, has been conceptualized and funded by the National Institute of Education. Following a planning conference in June 1977, a program of basic research on the teaching and learning of writing was developed and funded annually. The initial research funded under this program is now coming to fruition, providing both implications for educational improvement and directions for future research. This series is intended as one important outlet for these results.

PREFACE

Though this is one book, one overall tale, there are actually three stories here. The one that receives primary focus is about elementary school children's writing as it changed during a school-year-long study. Another concerns the continual development, beginning before and continuing beyond the year of the study, of some theoretical notions about writing and reading and about what those imply for practice. And the third, taking place during the same period, tells of part of the life of one program in bilingual education. The three stories are partly intertwined, partly separate. The tales of theory and program could have unfolded independently of these children's development as writers. The history of the children's writing, on the other hand, is intimately connected with what was happening in the bilingual program and indirectly affected by developments in the theory the consultants were using to help shape the program. Relation and separation also characterize the way the stories will be presented in this book. References to theory and program happenings will appear in the story of the writing. But at certain points in the overall account (Chapters 1, 3, and 7 especially), each of these tales will have its own turn in the limelight.

I will spare readers the fourth story—the one about organizing the research and preparing this manuscript. But it is certainly necessary to acknowledge that many people contributed to these efforts. Kristina Jilbert's commitment to the highest quality bilingual education continues to be an inspiration. Sarah Hudelson worked on her own and with me, trying to ensure that children of farm workers in Duncan District would indeed receive that high quality education. Funds from the National Institute of Education (Grant No. NIE G-81-0051) allowed the study to be conducted on a scale large enough to make cross-sectional as well as longitudinal comparisons. Susan Lipp's organizing abilities and good sense allowed the daily affairs entailed by this piece of research to run smoothly and remain in balance. Karin Bergionni was an invaluable informant. Duncan teachers graciously made children's writing avilable. Sarah Hudelson, Florence Barkin, Mary Guerra-Willekens, Nancy Mendoza, and Teresa Rosegrant helped analyze and interpret the data. Homer Baker stored and had the computer sort seemingly infinite numbers of coded bits of data. Ideas that guided major parts of the analyses and organization of the data were provided by Bess Altwerger, Margaret Orr, and Jerome Harste. Transforming the first technical report of the study into a book for a wider audience was aided by Marcia Farr's judgment and Celia Genishi's detailed and thoughtful comments. Merri Schall, Len Cahen, David Lancy, Lou Carey, Carlos Vallejo, Robert Carrasco, and Barbara Flores provided their expertise at key junctures and their support throughout. Jon Englehardt used his good offices to provide crucial help during the preparation of this manuscript. Several thousand miles away, Kathy Ford deciphered and typed from a rough draft, providing amazingly accurate copy. David Lancy, Sarah Hudelson, and Kris Jilbert alternately hollered and applauded in order to prod better revisions. I give deep and heartfelt thanks to all of them.

Chapter 1

BEFORE THE BEGINNING

A skeletal description of the study to be reported goes like this: at four different times during the 1980/81 school year, a team of researchers collected the regular in-class writing of nine first, nine second, and eight third-graders enrolled in an unusual bilingual program in a public school district serving many children of settled migrant farm workers in the Southwestern United States. The research team analyzed the children's writing in several respects in order to acquire some other-than-test-score information on literacy in a bilingual program, specifically to establish a base line on writing development under particular conditions. The team also gathered other data: interviews with teachers and aides, classroom observations, the results of a language situation study, background information on the children's older siblings, past test scores, and notes on observations of administrative, parental, and other community members' responses to the bilingual program. These data were used to help in understanding the contexts of the children's writing.

For readers to appreciate more fully the fleshed-out version, that which constitutes the major story of the three stories to be presented, they should know something of what propelled it into being. The impetus for studying these children's writing at all and for studying it in this particular way came from several sources. The first, at the time the least personally meaningful one, was a need to fill an important gap. While knowledge about children's use of written language was increasing dramatically, none of that new information concerned the special case of bilingual children writing in either or both of their two languages in school programs even minimally aiming at biliteracy. This was not a trivial void. Research on the development of writing in bilingual elementary education could help foster understanding of the relation between important aspects of first and second language acquisition and use. It could also provide a new lens, that of biliteracy, for looking at general and continuing concerns such as the relation between reading and writing or the effect of instruction on the acquisition of written language.

There had in fact been a few studies of some aspects of the writing of other-than-Standard-English-speaking students in the United States. Spelling under test conditions (Temple, 1978; Cronnell, 1979), vocabulary use (Carter & Cuscoe-Lanasa, 1978), and "dialect features" (Mejías, 1978; Amastae, 1982) in compositions had been investigated. Some of Anderson, Teale, and Estrada's (1980) observations captured the social organization of young bilinguals writing at home. Hudelson's (1984) performance analysis of spelling was an inquiry into process and strategy.

The typical approach to research on literacy in bilingual education, however (see Zappert & Cruz, 1977, for a representative sample), was not to look at students' writing under non-test conditions, not to look at writing or students in the act of reading at all. It was to let the static product of reading test scores stand for the dynamic process in varied literacy events, to "operationalize" literacy by means of a score on the standardized reading test and then to strip away the context for reading and writing as human activity.

A host of questions had been rendered non-questions by this prevailing research paradigm. Reading test scores could never say anything, for example, about the nature of text from a child's perspective, about the relation between coming to know the writing system as an object of knowledge (Ferreiro & Teberosky, 1982) and as a medium for creating meanings, about the impact of multiple orthographies in the environment on developing knowledge about written language, about additional considerations in assessing bilingual children's language proficiency. And writing research that examined single samples from any given writer, produced under test-like conditions, or that looked at portions rather than whole texts, would not reveal, much about the nature and development of writing (Donnelly & Stevens, 1980; Emig, 1982; Griffin, n.d.).

Looking instead at particular cases (single settings, single writers) where children's writing was not upstaged by stand-ins (e.g., tests of reading or writing "sub-skills") seemed a more profitable route to getting information on bilingual children's writing development during the early school years. At least it would allow a look at whether "entry" theories would hold up (in fact, ours were modified as a result of this new research) and would ensure that "emergent" theories were grounded.

Clearly, the exciting work from the late '70s and early '80s on writing among monolingual English speakers influenced the present study. That research did not use data from test settings, did not try to investigate writing solely from the researcher's perspective, did not collapse settings. Rather, it could be characterized as naturalistic, guided by broad questions rather than narrow hypotheses, committed to a description of the contexts in which the writing occurred. Some examples are work summarized by Whiteman (1980) and conducted by Bissex (1980), Birnbaum (1980), Calkins (1980), Ferreiro (1980), Giacobbe (n.d.), Graves (1979a,b,c,d), King and Rentel (1980), and Sowers (1979).

As mentioned, there was no comparable research on writing in bilingual education programs. The present study was planned, therefore, to fill a set of definite and related needs: to provide a database that would take a "process" perspective; to expand notions about what constitutes literacy in bilingual education; to use data that are more authentic (i.e., closer to the process being investigated than are one-time, on-demand writing samples); and to begin to provide information about literacy issues peculiar to biliteracy programs (e.g., written code switching and interactions between two written systems).

Filling an information gap, even bucking a prevailing approach to research, was only one prod for beginning this study. Our plans were more directly propelled by some very strong feelings: deep satisfaction mixed with delight, and a sense of urgency. Each requires some explaining—and some story-telling about the development of a theory and the life of a program.

The deep satisfaction we felt was due to evidence that an approach to language and literacy development which we had been wrestling with, evolving, and helping to implement in this bilingual program was having effects recognized as positive by parents, teachers, and some university colleagues. Karin Bergionni, Director of Duncan School District's Bilingual Program,[1] Professor Sarah Hudelson, and I were deliberately and explicitly trying to shape the Program so that it would: provide a curriculum rich in interesting contexts for using oral and written language; refrain from offering a curriculum of artificially separated bits of language; lay a solid foundation for oral and written language development in the first language before introducing instruction in English into these "maintenance" bilingual classrooms (see Kjolseth, 1972, for a fine discussion of nominally maintenance but actually transitional bilingual programs); and reflect some important features of open education (e.g., integrating subject matter, using everyday "stuff" and varied resources for instructional materials, and letting children's interests and questions determine curriculum content). From 1977 to 1983, Hudelson and I were consultants to Duncan's Bilingual Program.[2] We conducted several year-long series of workshops for teachers and aides on

---

[1] To protect the privacy of children, teachers, and administrators, all names of school district people and places are fictitious. My university colleagues and I, however, are identified with our actual names.

[2] When reading the account of our role as "outside experts" bent on trying to change teacher beliefs and practices—an account that is honest if not wholly flattering—I hope readers will not ignore why and how we came to be in Duncan District. If they do, the whole workshop/demonstration/consulting enterprise could be read as inept and arrogant. After all, it was bad enough that we tried to impose our ideas, but we couldn't even make those ideas stand still long enough for all of us (Bergionni, Hudelson, and I and the teachers and aides) to feel the solidarity of sharing an outlook.

There is another way to look at this however. One of Bergionni's responsibilities as Director was to find ways to have her theoretical and philosophical views on language and curriculum implemented in the Program. Hudelson and I could therefore just as well be seen positively as change agents invited by an insider to conduct certain activities that would affect children's education by changing teachers' and aides' activities and conceptions. Rather than providing evidence for our

first and second language acquisition, oral language development, and the reading process. Hudelson taught two graduate courses on language and literacy to Program personnel at one of the District elementary schools. At Saturday sessions, we helped teachers write District-mandated "Goals for Language Arts" and criteria for evaluation that would be least contradictory to the premises and practices we were attempting to have teachers adopt.

Today, these premises and practices, as well as the theoretical approach to language and literacy development, would be somewhat different from what they were then, but even between 1977 and 1980 our ideas were undergoing change. In 1977, we emphasized the primacy of oral language development and the need to devise curriculum that would enable children to use language orally for a variety of their own purposes. One approach we advocated was peer-project work (Edelsky, 1980). The focus of the projects (construction projects, dramatic presentations, book publishing, etc.) was to be on planning, completing, and presenting the project—on function and content—not on language form. We were trying to get teachers to give up desires for a silent classroom, to value appropriate, effective verbal strategies over meager but standard dialect utterances, to abandon "oral language drills" with choral responses or function-less solo utterances. By the next year, we had extended this focus on meaningfulness and purposefulness to written language. Earlier efforts to persuade teachers to stop engaging children in "talk exercises" for oral language development (e.g., to stop demanding full sentence replies, to avoid planning language lessons where children parroted labels for pictures of objects on charts) were based as much on a personal preference for sincerity as on any carefully specified, internally consistent theory. In our later work with teachers in the Program we made the same push for varied, meaningful, purposeful language but this time written language. Therefore, we showed teachers how to use children's literature instead of relying so heavily on workbooks and basal readers. We advocated having children do a variety of kinds of writing (letters, stories, journals, poems, recipes) for a variety of readers. Our interests in eliminating artificial lessons in oral

---

fickleness, the fact that not only teachers' but our conceptions too changed during the process can be understood as evidence that theories are dynamic and humanly constructed.

Still the fact remains that being resources for the Director, our intent to intervene carried with it the message that our theories were "better." It also meant our viewpoint had more official (though not necessarily covert) prestige than did that of the teachers and aides. This may seem like an obvious denial of the egalitarian and relativistic position that everyone has viewpoints, theories, and information—all sensible and valid, merely different. From 1977 on, if we had been in the District for the purpose of discovering the complexities and sense of teachers' and aides' ways of doing things, our attempts to persuade people to adopt our ways would rightly be deemed ill-founded, counterproductive, even arrogant. However, we were not invited to conduct workshops as ethnographers but as advocates for a different way to proceed. Though we took the position that our theories and the teachers'/aides' were all rational (understand-able, place-able, connect-able within a system), we also maintained that ours were justifiable on more and better grounds. In any effort to change educational practice—perhaps in any instance of teaching—that is probably an implicit stance.

language, however, carried over to written language only to the extent of trying to get teachers to eliminate the most workbook-exercise-like examples (filling in blanks on grammar exercises, writing lines of alphabet letters, copying off the board for handwriting practice). We had not yet thought through the issue of authenticity in written language. Thus, we were still showing teachers new techniques with "story starters," new clever gimmicks for getting children to write, and seeing little difference in value between spontaneous child-intended writing with purpose to the writer and contrived teacher-assigned writing. Hudelson, Bergionni, and I believed then that frequent writing for varied purposes to varied audiences, along with extensive interaction with a variety of published print, would be a sufficient way for children to grow as writers. We didn't carefully consider how teacher and peer response might enter into the picture, nor did we look beyond surface form in our efforts to identify purpose or audience. We hadn't yet thought seriously about the fact that whether an assigned, to-be-checked-off piece was a thank you note to the principal or a report written to inform peers, the primary audience in each case was really the teacher, and the child's main purpose in all of these was most likely to comply with an assignment. (So much for variation!)

By 1979 and early 1980 new evidence was fast accumulating that children did not need to practice the separate sub-systems of written language but that they needed to orchestrate all sub-systems during any given written language event (Calkins, 1980; Harste, 1980a), that children developed as writers in school through writing with their own purposes on their own topics (Graves, 1979c) and conferring with interested peers and adults (Graves, 1979a; Calkins, 1980; Birnbaum, 1980; Kamler, 1980). Our classroom and workshop consultations with teachers shifted to reflect the new information.

At the same time, I was becoming uncomfortably aware that fill-in-the-blank exercises and artificially isolated paragraphs were not the only examples of sham writing, that probably most in-school writing fell into that category. The children in Graves's study (1979d) were learning to provide a genuine audience for other children's writing, and their teachers were learning to help them write their intentions rather than simply "teach skills" or correct spelling and punctuation errors. And Graves's children's writing seemed to be profoundly different from that produced for usual school assignments. Regardless of whether the assignment demanded expository writing or fiction, "functional" or "expressive," the classroom writing we were seeing, by contrast, was alike in one way: the authors didn't seem to have their hearts in the pieces in the way Graves's children did. Even though the assigned stories, letters, lists, reports, summaries, recipes, etc. in Duncan District were composed completely by the children, and even though the writing resembled forms used in "real life," there was something wrong. At the time I concluded that the problem was that the writing had no purpose from the child's perspective. Later analyses have in fact confirmed that the writer's perspective is a crucial factor in understanding how a piece of writing takes shape. However, it was too facile to explain away what we were seeing in Duncan District and elsewhere as being due to "purposelessness." On the one hand, it *did* have purpose—but a special kind; on the other, there was more to it than that. It would be a few years before I could begin to offer the explanation which appears in Chapter 7.

Over the course of six years, then, we were changing our emphasis in course and workshop content, in classroom demonstrations with children and demonstrations with teachers from: (1) our early focus on oral language use in the context of long-term projects planned and carried out by children to (2) a focus on varied writing, including varied gimmicks, for supposedly (but not actually) varied audiences to (3) a focus by 1979 on wide reading and writing to serve children's own purposes and (4) by 1980 to one that included extensive conferences aimed at increasing both the range of children's purposes and their ability to achieve them. Despite the movement, we consistently maintained some basic threads. These were our efforts: (1) to decrease a reliance on made-for-school materials (e.g., workbooks, basal readers, graded science or social studies series); (2) to increase the use of local, real world resources and activities that instruct (e.g., children's literature, animals, plants, neighborhood people, interviewing, book making, cooking, constructing); (3) to encourage heavy use of both local and standard dialects; (4) to integrate the teaching of reading and writing with what else is going on at the moment and to base what skills will be taught on which are required by a particular activity rather than by any predesignated sequence of skills; and (5) to infuse the curriculum with content—with projects or units on science and social studies topics so that children might talk, read, and write about thought-provoking substance.

Probably, what allowed the directions we were urging to be tried at all was the administrative artistry of the Program Director. Favoring the same premises and particulars, she demonstrated to Program teachers in countless ways that she would support, help, applaud, and protect them. Winning high regard from the teachers as well as taking the role of instructional leader (a role often advocated for but rarely accepted by educational administrators), Karin Bergionni was able to lend legitimacy to our proposals and to lower teachers' resistance to trying first one then another non-traditional activity.

Underneath our shifts in emphasis regarding classroom practice was a change in our understanding of one basic theoretical position: a "whole language" orientation to written language (Harste & Burke, 1977; Goodman & Goodman, 1981; Edelsky & Draper, in press). That orientation conceives of written language as a super-system composed of interactive, interdependent sub-systems— graphic, syntactic, semantic, and pragmatic. Any instance of written language use taps into each of these sub-systems simultaneously. Even though we were in the whole language camp when Duncan's Bilingual Program began, we barely considered pragmatics as integral to the creation of written texts back then. (We had impressive support here. Goodman (1972), Goodman and Goodman (1979), and Harste and Burke (1977) omitted that system from early discussion of sub-system cues that are used in predicting and creating texts though they sometimes subsumed it implicitly under the semantic system.) Instead we ascribed audience and functional variation to a "context" that was somehow in the background; we missed its centrality. At that time, we thought wholeness was somehow separate from pragmatic concerns. We insisted on the importance of using whole discourses, whole texts, complete units (a complete grocery list, complete story, complete box top instructions), but we did not take seriously the reciprocal relationship between such pragmatic features as boundaries of and sequence in a text and decisions about syntax, semantics, and even graphics. We saw graphic, syntactic, and semantic choices influencing each other, but our consideration of purpose/intention especially and of interrelationships among purpose, audience text sequence, genre, or other contextual factors was separate—probably owing more to a general sociolinguistic stance than to any coherent theory of writing as either process or product. Reading was text interpretation; writing was text creation. We were nowhere near thinking yet of both reading and writing as transactions of texts (Harste & Carey, 1979; Rosenblatt, 1978; Edelsky & Draper, in press).

Other research (Graves, 1983; Kamler, 1980; Harste, Burke, & Woodward, 1982, 1983) as well as work on this study helped us overcome some of our theoretical limitations regarding the pragmatic system (the kinds and extent of contexts and the patterned ways they interrelate with other aspects of written language). By the time the present study was begun, we had greatly expanded our notions of what and how contextual features might influence writing, but at the beginning we still saw context as something writing occurred *in* or against. It took our first data codings to start to suggest that writing (whether viewed diachronically or synchronically) occurred *through* contexts.

Throughout this period, while we three "shapers" were doing our best to have an impact with our ever-changing advice about practice and our evolving underlying theoretical notions, Duncan District bilingual teachers had their own concerns. The Bilingual Program consisted of one or more bilingual sections from kindergarten through sixth grade in each of two elementary schools as well as bilingual sections of selected subject areas at the one junior high and high school in Duncan District. Alongside all of these were non-bilingual classrooms at the same sites. At each elementary school, then, the bilingual classes almost comprised a school within a school. Bilingual Program teachers thus had non-bilingual program colleagues, some of whom ignored, made disparaging remarks about, or explicitly ridiculed bilingual education and its workers and proponents at staff meetings or in the teachers' lounge. Since the Director saw her role in part as being protector and advocate for her teachers, acting as intermediary between them and the principals and other District administrators, and since she was able to argue that the children in the Bilingual Program had language needs which necessitated a different curriculum, she was able to have her teachers excused from certain curricular demands the District placed on the other teachers (e.g., a demand to have all children in a certain grade work in particular English workbooks or a demand to keep records of what English spelling words children could spell on tests). Bilingual Program teachers were not only disapproved of; they were therefore also resented by other teachers for the "special privileges" and sometimes by the principals for their unwitting participation in "management struggles."

Program teachers had to remedy a severe lack of Spanish language materials for science, social studies, general reference, and children's literature. They had to create their own or find ways around the void. They also had to cope with conflicts caused by contradictions between the practices and underlying assumptions Hudelson, Bergionni, and l were promoting as contrasted with those incorporated into State-mandated tests, available instructional materials, and the expectations most lay people and professional educators alike (including themselves) have about how instruction should proceed and how it should be assessed. While our orientation and the ensuing pedagogy denied the legitimacy of separating language into bits, isolating these from other content, and presenting them in a grade-leveled sequence, the "skills" orientation and pedagogy that prevailed then—and still does— (Laboratory for Comparative Human Cognition, 1982; Edelsky, Draper & Smith, 1983a) insisted on all this.

Surprisingly, despite the conflicting and changing demands, teachers still put some of our ideas into practice even if they hadn't shifted theoretical gears (e.g., assignment of a few integrative projects, frequent and regular writing assignments, encouragement of varied language use, extensive use of oral and written Spanish). Whether it was because of dual language instruction, adoption of surface features of what we were urging, or some combination of these or other factors, the Bilingual Program seemed to be having some positive impact. Visitors and principals noted fewer "behavior problems" in Bilingual Program classrooms. The children were attending school more regularly. Parents supported the Program with fund-raising efforts for special equipment and with their presence at District meetings which might have threatened the Bilingual Program. Program teachers with prior teaching experience in that District commented that the children seemed more capable, seemed to know more than they had in years past now that they were writing what looked like whole texts rather than doing workbook exercises. An approach that was supposed to be too loosely structured, with goals too global and long-term for formal education of poor children, seemed to be working with *these* poor children at least.

All of this was a source of deep satisfaction. It was augmented by excitement that now we had more traditional, "school-ish" evidence to counter notions about poor minority language children's educational inferiority. Typical of other poor, semi-rural, non-standard Spanish-speaking children in the United States, Duncan District Bilingual Program children scored badly on standardized tests, were poor achievers with traditional curricula, and seemed to fit the stereotypical language deficit idea of children who "don't know English and don't know Spanish either" and the academic version of language deficit known as semi-lingualism (Cummins, 1979; Skutnabb-Kangas & Toukomaa, 1976). In order to refute the language deficit idea, researchers had used data on code switching (Poplack, 1979) and verbal logic (Labov, 1970) to show the language strengths of speakers of non-standard dialects. They had also analyzed the internal contradictions in the construct of semilingualism (Oksaar, 1983; Edelsky, Hudelson, Flores, Barkin, Altwerger, & Jilbert, 1983b). While such evidence may have convinced some, it mattered little to those who wanted test score evidence for oral and written language abilities and for learning generally, those who saw little theoretical problem with equating responses to test items with reading or inferring abilities in writing and "language arts" from scores on tests which purport to test reading. This constituency seemed to be saying: if children were to be considered as profiting from education, then let them prove their normalcy by scoring well or at least by showing acknowledged signs of being literate.

We could barely contain our glee. When taught by people who asked them to write their own ideas instead of to complete isolated exercises, Duncan Bilingual Program children looked like the normal, language-capable children they were. Their writing could not be dismissed as esoteric, indirect, "ivory tower" evidence of language ability. It was goodol'fashion', basic schoolwork—straight out of the 3Rs. And it contained evidence that countered many of the sub-ideas within the more global idea of language deficiency. When looking at pieces of writing individually, without comparison, positive features leapt off the pages. Much of the writing we were seeing displayed varied and unusual rather than meager vocabulary, both complex and simple syntax, multiple means of accounting for the needs of the reader, cohesive devices and chronological patterns of organization, explicit inferences—hardly signs of deficiency in the written mode. Since individual pieces of writing contained such evidence of language strengths and were charming besides, surely changes over time would be equally stunning. Despite our belief in the importance of program/curriculum/teachers' theories/teaching practice, we let hope take over, expecting to document obvious and continued-through-the-grades leaps in writing acquisition without ensuring more than surface changes in writing instruction. As it turned out, we were both right (over the course of one year) and wrong (over the course of two years for a few children at least) to have such an expectation. At the time of planning the study, however, we saw in Duncan's Bilingual Program an opportunity for examining and describing specific features of writing development. More than that, we saw this Program as providing evidence that would likely be appreciated by a wide audience and that, for once, would allow these children to shine in school endeavors.

That would seem to be reason enough for planning the study. Actually, the whole research enterprise was prodded even more by a sense of urgency. From its inception, the Bilingual Program had had a stormy existence, and never received full support in the District. Various administrators, teachers, and powerful members of two of the three community groups in the District (farm workers, rancher-owners, and the retirement community dwellers who comprised the voting majority in District elections) at one time or another, overtly or covertly, had tried to put an end to bilingual education in Duncan District. By the 1979/80 school year, it looked like the anti-bilingual education, relatively well-to-do Anglo retirement community that controlled the seats on the District Board of Education would soon have its way. Pro-bilingual education demonstrations and the Program Director's behind-the-scene activities had wrangled a year of grace, but it appeared that the following year would be the last one for the Program as we knew it. If there were ever going to be a description of the children's writing development, if there were ever going to be any description of their actual work (rather than test scores), if there were ever going to be a document of historically low-achieving children succeeding in a program that eschewed small, discrete written language objectives and embraced more global ones (producing proficient readers and writers of Spanish and English), it had better happen soon.

And so the present study was planned—with a panicky eye out for Doom, suspected to be galloping up from behind.

Chapter 2

GETTING STARTED

The study began with a perspective on rather than a definition of writing and text and also a set of assumptions. The perspective on writing was that it is a complex, recursive, social, and cognitive process. Others had conceived of writing in a variety of ways. Harste (1980a) presented it as an orchestration of multiple cuing systems to produce a text or partial text which would function pragmatically in a situational context. According to Flower and Hayes (1980), writing was a set of recursive thinking processes orchestrated by a writer during the act of composing. For Smith (1982), it was a juggling and meshing of global and local intentions with global and local conventions during the construction and exploration of possible worlds. Vygotsky (1978) conceived of writing as a second order and then later a first order means of translating the condensed meanings of inner speech. Our perspective included these views. It did not, however, include a linear conception such as think–transcribe–revise or pre-write–write–re-write.

Besides naming a process, the term *writing* also labels both a product and a system, i.e., a piece of writing and the writing system. Though both the piece and the system make use of visual symbols, the cues for interpreting either do not reside totally within those symbols (Harste, Burke, & Woodward, 1981)—and it is just the multimodality of the cues that allows piece, system, and process to be social and cultural as well as psychological and linguistic phenomena. To appreciate the complexity of process, piece, or system, then, one must remind oneself of the following: all three involve inter-related graphic, linguistic, cognitive, and social features.

As for the term *text,* we began by using it synonymously with *sample, piece,* and *written product.* Most simply, this was for the purpose of having a larger repertoire of terms with which to refer to the objects being studied. In Halliday and Hasan's discussion (1976), a text is a semantic unit, oral or written, that is coherent with respect to itself and the environment it is in, an instance of social meaning in a particular context of situation (Halliday, 1978). Whether objectively coherent or not, any passage of language-in-use is likely to be interpreted as a text (coherent in both ways) (Halliday & Hasan, 1976). Thus, with our written data most likely to be *imputed* to be texts, we labeled them as such.

Admittedly this was imprecise. Calling a piece *a text* implies that the piece of paper provided a text boundary and that the texts were either written or oral. In fact, many of the texts certainly exceeded the borders of the page, most likely consisted of both oral and written language, and were composed by more than one participant. To reflect these facts, at least some of the writing should be referred to as partial or even non-texts. However, without observations of the production of each piece, it is difficult to be certain which ones should be so designated; therefore, *text* will most often be used casually to refer to any writing sample in the collection. When text-ness becomes the focus, the meaning will tighten.

ASSUMPTIONS

There were six.

In Order to Understand the Development of Writing In School, We Have to Find a School Where Children Write.   From observing and talking with teachers in numerous bilingual programs in Arizona, Florida, and Texas, it seems that writing is a rare event in bilingual classrooms. To be sure, children fill in blanks, answer questions in writing on basal readers and other textbook selections, and put weekly spelling words in sentences or stories. But the bilingual program at our study site was the only one we knew of then where it was a daily event for children to create their own "possible worlds" in writing. Not only is it necessary to find writing in school in order to study it, but one should at least try to find classrooms where writing is not merely assigned but is supported and nourished.

Examining Piece(s), Process, *or* System Provides Added Insights Into the Nature of Piece, Process, *and* System.   While we shared Harste's (1980a) belief that knowledge of the event is crucial to an understanding of a given piece, we believe his claim is exaggerated that a written piece without an accompanying observation of the production of that particular piece is as totally worthless as an archaeological artifact without the surrounding soil. Just as a written text may be accessed through other cues besides sound/letter correspondences (Goodman, 1977), so the writing process or a writing system can be at least somewhat revealed by something in addition to monitoring the enactment of that process or examining the total system in the abstract. While comparisons of single pieces by the same writer, if written in different languages or for different purposes/ audiences, do not permit statements about the organizing of social resources in the production of any one piece, such comparisons do allow inferences about the salience of different aspects of the two written systems. They can also help support or detract from claims about the process (e.g., that regardless of the language, there are universal characteristics of writing as a process).

To Understand the Product, We Have to Know the Context. Despite the immediately preceding "defense" for not having designed an observational study of pieces-in-the-making, we still believed that, within the limits imposed by another context—the research situation—it was important to know what was happening at the time of composing in order to approach a richer understanding of a piece of writing. This stems from a belief that human processes and activities occur in systems of embedded environments where "the main effect is in the interactions" (Cole citing Bronfenbrenner, 1979, p. x. Cronbach, 1975 makes a similar point.) It is a profound sociolinguistic, language-society-interactionist belief. It assumes that people's language development (written or oral) occurs through interaction in socio-historical contexts, and that the language development is shaped by and affects the contexts and the socio-history as well as the participants. Therefore, we reasoned, if we gathered information from contexts with necessarily fuzzy space and time boundaries (larger and smaller contexts bleed into each other; memories of the past and plans for the future attend present performances), our interpretations of the children's writing development would be more sensible. And so, assuming the interweaving of language (writing, in this case) and context, we planned a study that would collect data from only one program, that would describe that program and the individual classrooms where the writing occurred.

We conceived of "context" as closely-tied-to-text features of the writing event (e.g., genre, audience, code, materials, etc.), teachers' and aides' beliefs and planned classroom writing activities, program philosophy, administrative attitudes, parental attitudes toward the program, school histories of the children's older siblings, the language situation of the community, and socio-politico-economic conditions in the community.

While non-static, some of these contexts change more noticeably and over shorter time spans than others. For instance, variation in classroom activities and conditions for writing is obvious to even the casual observer watching a class for one day. By comparison, the political situation in the community and the pressures exerted by policy-making bodies on programs and classroom events seem much more stable/static. Still, all the contexts change—and all the changes could presumably have an impact, whether direct or tortuously indirect, on the development of writing as well as the writing of particular pieces. Thus, when Bereiter (1979) claims that studies of language use (such as Labov's in Harlem) often take the "best performance" as the norm and explain away the rest through various kinds of bias, he is not only misinterpreting Labov's work. More importantly here, he is opting for the existence of one "essence" of language ability that remains after the situation is removed, a kind of language use that is not

interwoven with context. At base, he is rejecting the very sociolinguistic orientation we are assuming—that language-in-use, including writing, is inherently tied
to its contexts of production. Of course, it is not only Bereiter who rejects this
perspective. Producers of single sample, single setting tests of writing and sup-
porters of uniform, low-level, sequenced writing objectives also implicitly deny
the context/language mesh. In contrast, we have assumed it.

Children Are Hypotheses Creators.   Whether in relation to first language
acquisition (Lindfors, 1980; Peters, 1980), second language acquisition (Hatch,
1978; Fillmore, 1976), early reading (Clay, 1969; Ferreiro, 1978; Barrera, 1981;
Goodman, Goodman, & Flores, 1979), mature reading (Smith, 1978), or beginning writing in English (Graves, 1979b; Clay, 1975; DeFord, 1980; Harste &
Burke, 1980), language users reinvent rather than "copy" the psycho-socio-
linguistic systems they learn. Many of the hypotheses with which they operate
can be inferred from the oral or written texts that they produce. It is especially the
"errors" and the contextually related variations in production which act as
windows through which we can glimpse these internal and tacit hypotheses.

**There Is Some Relationship between the Development of Writing in One
Language and in Another.**   There is some evidence that if children receive
literacy instruction in the first language before second language literacy instruction begins, their reading test scores in the second language are higher than they
are for second language readers who receive no native language literacy instruction (Rosier & Farella, 1976; Skutnabb-Kangas & Toukomaa, 1976). Data from
tests in immersion programs indicate that at least reading test scores, if not actual
reading ability, in the first language are not adversely affected by reading instruction in the second (Cummins, 1979). Investigations of the reading process during
actual reading show certain aspects of that process to be the same regardless of
the language in which one is reading (Flores, 1981). In other words, if there is a
close relation between reading across languages, most likely there is some connection between writing in one language and writing in another.

Writing Is Important Educationally and Worthy of Study.   There has
been a history of artificial separation of writing from reading, yet both are part of
literacy. Even more than both being "part of," writing and reading depend on
and enhance each other (Smith, 1983; Moffett & Wagner, 1976). It is largely
through wide reading that one is exposed to a variety of writing conventions and
through extensive writing that one comes to understand an author's perspective
and problems when one is reading. Further, writing for certain purposes functions as much to help the writer understand and explore various ideas as it does to
communicate those ideas to a reader (Smith, 1982). In other words, writing can
change the writer, help the writer grow conceptually and expressively. Thus it
can be a crucial tool in achieving educational goals.

RESEARCH QUESTIONS

With these assumptions, we carried out a study of the writing of nine first, nine second, and nine third graders over the course of the 1980/81 school year. A week's worth of in-class writing, collected four times during the year, was analyzed in regard to several aspects (code switching; spelling; punctuation and segmentation; structural features; stylistic devices; and subjectively perceived qualities of the content). Classroom observations, interviews, a District-funded language situation survey, District records, and our participation in the District in various capacities during the current and preceding years provided the data for context description.

Three broad research questions guided the endeavor:

1. What happens over time and at any one point in time to several aspects of the children's writing; i.e., their spelling inventions, the structure of their writing (beginning and endings, organizational principles, links between propositions, etc.), their hypotheses concerning segmentation and punctuation, their use of code switching in writing, stylistic devices and content features (characters, settings, etc.), and our subjective impressions of attributes of quality in the content?
2. How is writing in Spanish related to writing in English?
3. From the spotlight that biliteracy beams on literacy in general, what can be learned about various issues related to literacy and literacy instruction (e.g., appropriate sequences in Language Arts, the relationship of literacy learning and teaching, etc.)?

METHODOLOGY

The study officially began in the Fall of 1980 with a core research staff of three. "Officially" contrasts with what seems to be a more accurate but difficult-to-describe characterization of this project's beginning. The core research staff had varying degrees of, but still extensive, knowledge of different circles of contexts. As described earlier, two members of this core (Hudelson and I) had conducted workshops, in-service training, and on-site courses for teachers and aides in the Program. The third, Bergionni, was the Program Director and had worked in the District since 1975. It is obvious then that as kinds of data and means of gathering them are discussed, the discussion must be incomplete. Some of our information on classroom contexts and on relationships among the sub-communities that comprise "the community" came from incidents and interactions which had begun years before. We were privy to this information because we had been involved in the District in non-research ways at the time. In other words, I do not want to give the wrong impression; we did not gather *all* the data for this study during one school year. Some of it came from and all of it was enhanced by a long history of interactions in the District.

CHOOSING THE SUBJECTS TO FOLLOW OVER THE 1980/81 SCHOOL YEAR

In order to be consistent with a wish to situate the data, we decided to choose subjects from a single classroom at each grade level rather than from the grade level at large. (It was more convenient to describe only three classrooms.) We chose those three classrooms based not upon random selection or representativeness but upon our guess about the most likely sites in this Program for such growth in writing to occur.

In order to select the nine subjects per grade, we collected all the writing done the first week of school in September in these three classrooms. Hudelson,

Table 1.   Subjects

Grade	Rating	Subject	Age in Sept. 1980	Sex
1	Hi	Ro	6;9	F
		Se	7;3	M
		Cn	6;5	F
	Med	Ma	6;8	F
		Ro	6;3	M
		Jo.A.	6;10	M
	Lo	Vi	6;10	F
		Ge	7;3	M
		Lu	7;2	M
2	Hi	Pe	9;2	F
		Ed	7;9	M
		Ma.C.	8;9	M
	Med	Ro.C.	7;1	F
		Fr	8;7	M
		Au	8;8	M
	Lo	Jo	7;1	M
		Ma.A.	7;5	M
		Mo	8;0	M
3	Hi	Ve	8;11	F
		Ra	10;2	M
		Ju	9;4	F
	Med	Ma.I.	10;8	M
		Ye	8;1	F
X		Je	9;9	M
		Da	9;9	M
		Ma.S.	11;2	M

Table 2. Summary of Subjects

Grade	Rating	Number	Mean Age in Sept.	Age Range	M	F
1	Hi	3	6;10	6;5–7;3	1	2
	Med	3	6;7	6;3–6;10	2	1
	Lo	3	7;1	6;10–7;3	2	1
	Total	9	6;10	6;3–7;3	5	4
2	Hi	3	8;7	7;9–9;2	2	1
	Med	3	8;1	7;1–8;8	2	1
	Lo	3	7;6	7;1–8;0	3	0
	Total	9	8;1	7;1–9;2	7	2
3	Hi	3	9;6	8;11–10;2	1	2
	Med	3	9;6	8;1–10;8	2	1
	Total	6	9;6	8;1–10;8	3	3
X	Total	2	10;5	9;9–11;2	2	0

Bergionni and I then separately and subjectively evaluated each child as a high, medium, or low writer for that classroom/grade.

We then chose three relatively high children per grade, three medium, and three low writers in order to have a range of abilities and probably, a variety of growth patterns.

After several months, we lost one third-grade "low" subject, who moved out of the District. We also discovered to our dismay that the other third-grade "lows" could not really be considered *bona fide* third-grade participants in the bilingual program. They had just arrived from Mexico at the beginning of the year and thus they had not been enrolled in this program throughout their school careers, as had the other chosen children. Moreover, school records and subsequent conversations with teachers engendered the strong suspicion that these two boys had attended school infrequently in their rural birthplace. (In fact, the estimate was that the older, who was 11 years, 2 months in September 1980, had probably attended school for a lifetime total of 12–20 months.) When we discovered this, we decided to designate these two children as being in "grade X" for the purpose of this research. It seemed more reasonable to consider them as a separate case than as regular third graders. The subjects whose writing was collected throughout the year appear in Table 1. Table 2 provides a summary.

KINDS OF DATA GATHERED

Writing

We defined writing as anything a teacher gave us that she considered to be a child's writing. Graves's (1975) definition, requiring the piece to be at least a sentence in length, while popular, was not used here for two reasons. First, we wanted to be able to include as data the repetitions of names from the first week. More importantly, we adopted the position that social facts are constructed, that if a teacher considered a string of letters and numbers to be writing, the teacher would treat it as such—compare it to later writing, evaluate it, and so on. It seemed sensible for our purposes to use the teacher's category. Our theoretical understanding at the time was also congruent with this categorizing decision. Now, however, that understanding has changed. Although for the reasons stated here, we would still examine and compare all pieces collected, we would now try to distinguish between genuine use (i.e., *writing*) and simulations of written language use (i.e., "writing").[1] This distinction is discussed at length in Chapter 7.

Writing from the first week of school, used for selecting the subjects, became the first of four collections. Teachers were then asked to save all the writing these children did during one week in late November, one in February, and one in April. The collections yielded a total of 556 pieces.

Preparing the writing for analysis consisted of tracing over light pencil marks so they could be reproduced, coding each piece for subject number, collection number, and piece number, and "re-writing" each piece. This last activity was one of putting each piece into conventional spelling, spacing, and punctuation. The rewrites were used separately in the investigation of several aspects of the

---

[1] As noted in the first chapter, our theoretical ideas, including those concerning what counts as writing, have been (and still are) changing. If we were beginning the study today, we would still look at all that the teacher considered as writing for the reasons stated here. However, we would reserve the term *writing* for cases where the *child's* intentions (rather than the teacher's) were what was being graphically displayed, for cases where a text fashioned from inter-related graphic, syntactic, semantic, and pragmatic system options was what was being created. Strings of letters and numbers written as handwriting assignments, messages entered in a journal to meet the teacher's requirements, perfunctory completions of "story starters"—these would not be labeled *writing* even though they would certainly be examined to see how they fit into a child's writing development. Today, we would consider them to be "writing," something that resembles *writing* and makes use of some systems of written language, but either eliminates others (syntax and semantics in the case of letters and numbers written for handwriting practice) or severs or distorts the relationships that would obtain among all systems if the piece were genuine writing. For example, journal genre demands that entries concern content important to the writer written for an audience that is usually the writer. These pragmatic considerations would normally have syntactic, semantic, and possibly orthographic consequences. However, the journals written in these classrooms were produced most often for the teacher and were not vehicles for noting or exploring personal reactions to events of the day. Under these conditions, the pragmatic factor of genre (journal writing, in this case) could not exercise its influence. Instead, other pragmatic factors (audience: teacher; purpose: compliance; stance: get the assignment finished; length requirement: fill the page; etc.) which were not consistent with that genre exerted their own influence but did so while preventing the genre from being what it claimed to be. Further explanation of the distinction between authentic writing and facsimiles appears in the last chapter. Here I simply want to emphasize that although we would still want to scrutinize all the marks a child produced and try to see how different categories of markings were related to each other, we would not define all of them as *writing*.

writing. For example, to analyze invented spellings, we had to know what word was intended; to evaluate the quality of the content alone, we could have been distracted by messiness or unconventional forms.

At first we thought re-writing would be a quick mechanical task, not much more complicated than was tracing over and darkening the childrens' light pencil marks so they could be duplicated for the research team members. In actuality, the process of deciphering semantic and syntactic encodings in the child author's absence was anything but mechanical. It required, from the most generous and sympathetic of adult readers, the use of cues from letter formation, syntax, sense of genre, knowledge of topic, knowledge of the class assignment if there was one, and comparisons with other texts written by the same child on different days and pieces written by different children on the same day. A crucial requirement, of course, was the assumption that the pieces of writing were sensible. Those who had a hand in the re-writing were the children's teachers and aides and members of the research team. Little did we think that some pieces would have to be re-written several times before we arrived at the stage of "Oh, of course! *That's* what that says!" or that on the umpteenth re-reading, a string of letters might suggest a new and better interpretation.

Not quite 6% of the pieces were eliminated from further analysis due to our inability to decipher them. One possible profile of the total collection that was re-written and kept for analysis is shown in Table 3.

Pieces of writing were also obtained from other primary grade classrooms in this District's bilingual program. There was no system to this collection, however. Sometimes samples were requested for particular purposes; other times, a piece would be "donated" because an adult was especially impressed by one of its features.

Classroom Observations

There were two kinds of classroom observations. In the one that was to produce a categorization of the print environments, the intention was to be exhaustive—to observe and record the print available, its type and function, until all the print in

Table 3. Number of Pieces Analyzed

	Grade				
Collection	1	2	3	X	Total
1	9	24	19	3	55
2	57	61	28	17	163
3	78	33	32	11	154
4	45	71	30	6	152
Total	189	189	109	37	524

Table 4. Summary of Types of Methods and Data

Type of Method	Type of Data	Sources of Data	Collection Time	Purpose/Use
Category emergence through coding trials	in-class writing	3 study classrooms, 9Ss per 1st and 2nd grades, 8 in 3rd	Sept., Nov./Dec., Feb., April	to present developmental picture of 6 aspects of writing
coding, using categories				
keeping running lists	in-class writing	other primary grade classrooms in BL program		to highlight relation between context and writing
observation	field notes, map of location of materials, list of materials	3 study classrooms	March–May	to describe print environment
participant observation	field notes	3 study classrooms, 3 others in BL program	April–May	to describe oral code-switching, print used by children, activity during writing
structured interview in school	responses on audio tapes, field notes	3 teachers/aides from study classroom	April	to present self-reported T/A's beliefs about writing, their writing and reading programs
structured interview in home	field notes	S's family members	April	to provide information on older siblings' school completion
record/report collecting	test scores, attendance records, school registration forms filled out by parents, State Dept. records, language situation survey	District records concerned the 26 Ss; others concerned the entire community	May	to describe children's and older siblings' educational histories, language situation in community, socioeconomic situation in community

continued

Table 4   *(Continued)*

Type of Method	Type of Data	Sources of Data	Collection Time	Purpose/Use
participation	anecdotal notes (written after the event)	researchers' memories of School Board meetings, Parent Advisory Council meetings, interactions with other administrators, consultantship and interactions with District personnel over several years	March–June	to describe relations among BL Program, administration, and community

that classroom had been described. Print environment observations were only made in the three study classrooms. The same observer for all observations in one classroom catalogued all print in that classroom by type (workbooks, reference books, etc.). Then the intended (usually instructional) function of the print was noted (e.g., to encourage an awareness of print in everyday life, to promote the idea that print is functional, etc.).

The other kind of observation was meant to sample rather than to be exhaustive. Both the three study classrooms and non-study Bilingual Program classrooms were observed for at least two whole days by two to three different observers. The purposes of these observations were to note oral code switching for comparison with written code switching (inter- vs. intra-sentential, by whom, to whom, on what topics, etc.), to observe children in the act of writing, and to record the kind of language information adults gave children when they interacted about literacy (i.e., does the adult focus the child on graphophonics? on syntax?, etc.). As a follow-up to the print environment observations, these observers were also to note the language of the print the children actually made use of (e.g., the language of the posters they *looked at* vs. those hanging in the room, the language of the library books they read or thumbed through, etc.).

Teacher/Aide Interviews

In the Spring, each teacher and aide was interviewed separately for her perceptions of various aspects of her own writing program, of herself as a teacher of writing, and of her characterization of the reading program in her classroom. (The interview questions appear in Appendix 1.)

Information about the Children

It seems likely that family educational histories affect expectations and interpretations of children's school life. Therefore, we interviewed family members to find out what had happened to the children's older siblings. We also checked school records to find how many of our subjects and their siblings had been referred for Special Education work-ups, and to obtain Bilingual Syntax Measure scores, California Achievement Test scores for our subjects and their older siblings, attendance records, a parental self-report on our subjects' first language, and any indication that the parent was extremely limited in literacy (such as signing a school registration card with an X).

Data on the General Community

Results of a language situation survey, conducted by an anthropologist hired by the Bilingual Program, were made available. That survey included interviews with over 100 families and both in-the-home and community observations (in the fields and at stores, community centers, and other meeting places). The interview schedule asked questions concerning language attitudes, channel and domains of language use, and attitudes about language maintenance or language shift.

The District Bilingual Program Office provided State Department of Economic Security figures on income, ethnicity, and unemployment for families of elementary school children in the District.

Both local newspaper accounts and our own participation over the years in the District allowed inferences about community attitudes toward the bilingual program. The president of the Parent Advisory Council, who happened to be the secretary for the Bilingual Program Office, was a key informant. The fact that one of the research team members was both Bilingual Program Director and researcher made her an invaluable informant; she was quite conscious of local and state administrative behavior toward this program. As Director, she was acutely aware of the demands placed on the program by other administrative units. As researcher, she was able to use this information to help construct the description of the contexts.

The various kinds and uses of data are summarized in Table 4.

ANALYZING THE DATA

The Writing Data

The four collections of writing were analyzed in several ways: (1) they were coded for computer tallying according to various categories within six aspects; (2) they were viewed more impressionistically to trigger hunches about the nature and development of writing; and (3) they were catalogued as counter-examples to various taken-for-granted notions or myths.

Coding for computer tallying was the responsibility of separate research teams. An *a priori* decision had been made to analyze certain aspects of the writing. These aspects were: (1) code switching; (2) spelling inventions; (3) non-spelling conventions such as segmentation and punctuation; (4) stylistic devices; (5) an assortment of structural and content features, such as links between clauses, beginnings, endings, etc.; and (6) quality of the content. Each research team thus had a single focus of attention—code switching or spelling or one of the other chosen aspects.

A team's first responsibility was to "wallow" in the data (decipher the writing, sort and re-sort it, "play" with categories, and so on) so that the data themselves might suggest the coding categories.

The team responsible for coding qualities of the content operated in a slightly different way. Methods of holistic rating that assume children have been given a common prompt/task were obviously inappropriate for these varied pieces of writing. Similarly, holistic rating that allowed spelling and punctuation to enter into the rating decisions seemed unwise since those areas were being treated extensively by other research team members. Therefore, the quality-of-content team did not make use of established schemes for rating, such as are described in Gottesman and Schilling (1979) and Humes (1980). Instead, they devised a way to look only at content and a common means for rating dissimilar genres from different grades at different times of the year.

Three hired raters, instructed and supervised by researchers, were presented with only the re-written versions of the children's writing and asked to generate a list of positive attributes that described the pieces of writing. (See Edelsky, 1982, for further details or development of the attribute list.) This resulted in a list of ten categories (these appear in Appendix 2 at the end of "Categories On Coding the Writing Data"). Group discussions were then held among the three raters and the research team to attempt to attain some uniformity of meaning for category labels such as "originality," "coherence," and so forth. The ten categories were then used to assess each piece of writing in the official collection.

All the categories and subcategories which emerged for coding all six aspects of the writing data, along with a prime example of each, appear in Appendix 2. The major categories appear in connection with Figure 1. There are four points to be highlighted, however, before the major coding categories used within each aspect are presented.

First, since most of these categories resulted from, rather than preceded, the initial analyses, they are both findings and method.

Secondly, 94% of these pieces of writing were assigned; thus type (or genre) was designated primarily on the basis of interviews with the teacher and aide concerning what assignment had elicited the piece. On the rare occasion of conflict between attributes of the piece and the teacher's report of what the assignment had been (e.g., the teacher's instruction had been to write a letter and the child's piece seemed instead to be an expository report), the piece was coded according to the assignment (in this case, a letter), although details of the conflict were noted anecdotally. The reason for coding according to the teacher's assignment rather than in line with features of the writing was that absence of letterness in response to instructions to write a letter, for example, could mean that the child had not yet learned conventions for letter openings or closings. If that piece had been coded as "expository report" instead of "letter," there would have been less chance of noting changes in letter-writing.

A theoretical justification for using the teacher's assignment to determine the type is found in an intriguing discussion by Pratt (1977). She argues that intertwined social conventions, appropriateness conditions, and expectations—the way a piece is treated—rather than textual properties are what makes something "literature." The way a piece of classroom writing was treated then (e.g., was it received as an appropriate response to an assignment) seemed to be a legitimate way to have determined its type designation. Of course it is also possible that the child simply refused to write a letter when assigned to do so. Though we have evidence of topic-refusal, we have no evidence of genre-refusal.

Third, a piece often received several codings under some headings. For instance, under beginnings, there might be such coding entries as *char, stg,* and *frm* (has a character, setting, and a formula at the beginning of the piece).

Fourth, it happened frequently that coding required contextual knowledge. For instance, the following is how one child began his response to an assignment to describe what he did over the weekend.

Yo fui a la cebolla tres días porque el domingo no hay cebolla y el domingo de lo que me saqué en la cebolla me compré en los perros una bicicleta de 15 dólares. . . .
(I went to the onion field three days because Sunday there's no onion field [work] and Sunday from what I earned in the onion field I bought a bicycle for 15 dollars at the dogs [track]. . . .)

To accept "dogs" as a synonym for flea market rather than code it as unusual vocabulary required knowledge of the community (the flea market is held at the greyhound racetrack) and its labeling norms. To code the presence of an explanation for why he worked only three days (there is no field work done on Sundays) as "signals knowledge that there is a reader by clarifying an earlier statement," one must know that the assignment had been to report on a four-day weekend rather than a regular weekend and that the child knew that the teacher was an outsider to the community and might not be expected to know the field schedule.

Each piece of writing was coded by each team, according to that team's responsibility (e.g., spelling, code switching, or some other aspect). With a few exceptions, the coding as well as the category emergence was governed by a search for what was present in the writing rather than what was absent. As mentioned, this was not quite true for the coding of Type. Additionally, the three Quality of Content raters who had generated the list of positive attributes also had to rate each piece from 0 to 3 against the ten final attributes, i.e., as having more, less, or none of some attribute. Oter teams, however, did not generally code pieces as *lacking* in letter closings, character introduction, particular types of organizing principles, or other features.

The fact that many people looked at the same data for different purposes created a many-layered perceptual net. Different lenses (e.g., code switching, spelling, etc.) were used to filter the same data.

What follows is an example of one piece and all the ways it was coded.

A mí me gustó el programa de Mrs. S. y estaba suave y nosotros cantamos suave y nosotros cantamos dos canciones y yo quería cantar otra canción.
El Fin de María M.C.
7 abril 1981
Hoy es martes[2]

(I liked Mrs. S's program and it was nice and we sang nicely and we sang two songs and I wanted to sing another song.
The End by Maria M.C.
April 7, 1981
Today is Tuesday)

---

[2] Throughout, typed versions of children's work appear as initial ''translations'' into conventional spelling and punctuation, followed by English translations.

Code Switching

word code switch	2 (Mrs., Program)
orthography of switch	Spanish, English
word class of switch	address term, noun agreeing in number and gender with surrounding text in other language
fits the flow?	yes
reason for switch	synonym

Spelling Inventions

vowel inventions, Spanish	1 (mi)
consonant inventions, English	1 (Mrs.)
consonant inventions, Spanish	1 (yo)
reason for invention, Spanish	phonics generalization (my/mi; 11o/ yo)=2
reason for invention, English	Spanish orthography (mis/Mrs.)=1

Non-Spelling Conventions

segmentation, any conventional?	yes
unconventional	no space within pronominal indirect object construction (ami/a mí)
	no space within verb phrase (megusto/ me gustó)
	no space between words from different constituents (programde/programa de; finde/fin de)
	space between syllables (canta mos/cantamos)
punctuation	inappropriate use of comma (martes,)
	pattern, capital on certain words (on all but 8)
tilde	appears over a vowel (querĩa, cancĩon)
accent	used appropriately, to maintain stress (María)
handwriting	manuscript

Stylistic Devices

setting	school
dialogue	none
characters	self, school adult, peers
syntax that adds "style"	consistent past tense first person perspective

Structural Features

type	expository, summary of/reaction to media

language	Spanish
unassigned?	yes
number of words	33 (exclusive of name and date)
culturally specific topics?	no
intended reader	general
signal of knowledge that there is a reader?	none
beginning	position on topic
ending	position on topic
	by + name
	date
	explicit end
organizational principle	associative
cohesion: exophoric reference	writer + others
links between clauses	y=4
	none=1 (between *otra canción* and *el fin*)

Quality Attributes (median rankings of three raters)

involvement of the writer	1
originality	2
awareness of audience/purpose	1
organization	1
candor	1
informativeness	1
vocabulary	1
expressive language	2
coherence (understandability)	1
insight	1

All codings were then subjected to various computer tallyings and sortings. Table 5 shows the sub-sets or "runs" made by the computer.

High frequency categories for one sub-set were compared with such categories in another sub-set (e.g., the most frequent "word class for code switches" on the Spanish pieces were compared with "word class for code switches" on English pieces). Sub-categories that were interesting but infrequent (such as endings that were "nice") were not lost however. They were noted on both running lists and in a Myth Hunt.

Running lists were dated notes of impressions, kept during coding sessions. In both use and intent, they bore a strong resemblance to the "theoretical memos" described by Glaser (1978). The lists consisted of unique features of a piece of writing, hunches, future research questions, prime examples of categories, and so forth. They were helpful for interpreting the computer tallies as well as

Table 5.   Sub-sets of Data Tallied by Computer

Language	Spanish
	English
Unassigned	Yes
	no
Grade × Collection[a] × Type[b]	grade 1, collection 2, letters, journals, total types
	grade 1, collection 4, expository pieces, letters, stories, journals, books, total types
	grade 2, collection 1, expository pieces, letters, total types
	grade 2, collection 4, expository pieces, letters, stories, journals, books, total types
	grade 3, collection 1, expository pieces, stories, total types
	grade 3, collection 4, expository pieces, stories, total types
	grade X, collection 1, expository pieces, total types
	grade X, collection 4, expository pieces, stories, total types
Child[c] × Collection × Type	child #3, collection 1, signature, total types
	child #3, collection 2, journals, total types
	child #3, collection 3, letters, journals, total types
	child #3, collection 4, letters, journals, total types

[a]Since the first collection for grade 1 consisted entirely of signatures, the second collection was used for the purpose of comparing same Types over time.

[b]All Types were not tallied because there were not examples of all types from all grades in each collection. The types listed are those that appear in the collection.

[c]The other selected subjects were #6, #11, #15, #20, #22, and #25. (These seven children were designated by all those who had coded data as the "most interesting" children in each grade.) Separate tallies for types within collections and total collections were made for each of these children also.

supplying some assistance in "The Myth Hunt."[3] That is, while coming to know the data intimately through the processes of category derivation and then data analysis, research team members also found and noted in the running lists clear counter-examples of some conventional (or even scholarly) wisdom about writing, reading, biliteracy, and so on. These notations became a list of 29 myths (our term).

The four collections of writing from the three study classrooms were thus analyzed through: category derivation for immersion in the data; data coding using the derived categories; computer-tallied frequency counts of codings and comparisons of the tallies among sub-sets of data; informal running lists of impressions while coding; and examination of pieces of writing for evidence that refuted myths about writing and related topics. (Interpretations and comparisons of computer tallies appear in Chapter 5. Insights from the running lists are presented separately in Chapter 4.

---

[3] It was Jerome Harste who suggested that some of the findings be organized as refutations of myths about literacy.

The writing data collected from other primary grade classrooms in the Duncan Bilingual Program were analyzed in only one way. These were re-written and examined (but not coded) with the coding categories and myths in mind. Again, informal running lists were made of impressions, hunches, and contrasts with the "official" collections of writing. These data were used in describing the contextual circle concerned with classroom practices. Occasionally, they were used to highlight findings from the three chosen classrooms.

OTHER DATA

Community.   Information from the language situation survey conducted by the District contributed to the description of the community context. Demographic data from state government agency figures and notes taken on conversations, school board meetings, and meetings with District administrators all entered into the partial portrait of the community and the administrative contexts.

Teacher/Aide Responses to Interviews.   Interviews with the teachers and aides were tape recorded and also noted in longhand. The interview responses helped uncover both Program philosophy and teacher and aide beliefs, which we considered a factor in classroom practices.

Classroom Observations.   The catalogue of the print available in the three study classrooms was subdivided according to type (workbooks, kits, posters, and so on) and language; then the numbers of each type in each language were tallied. Observers' notes on the language of the print actually used, the type and quantity of oral code switching, the language information provided by adults in interactions focused on literacy, and children's behaviors during the writing of a piece were summarized across observers. The portrayal of classroom practices owes much to these summaries.

Records.   Means of test scores and tallies of Special Education referrals, attendance records, siblings' school status, and parental self-report of the child's language dominance, plus our personal histories over several years with some of the children, constituted the subjects' "educational history" context.

These, then, were the means for gathering and analyzing the data in this study of the development of writing in one bilingual program. The findings on contexts and writing will be presented in separate chapters. However, like the contextual and writing reality they attempt to reflect, the findings on each informed and to varying degrees depended on the other.

Chapter 3

CONTEXTS

At some times of the year, thousands of blooming rose bushes line the road to the District Office. At others, white puff balls of cotton ready for harvest create the illusion that a mischievous Nature has covered the ground with snow while leaving bare the nearby mountain tops. Another season treats one's nostrils to the smell of onions. This is Duncan School District, the largest contextual unit included in this study. Based on the definition of context that follows, the District need not have been the most "macro" of the contexts. Nevertheless, for practical reasons, it was.

In this study, "context" included all factors within the District or at the level of the State Department of Education or below which impinged in some way on the production or interpretation of a piece of writing. No definition was devised or borrowed. Instead, contexts were itemized, including: the politico-socio-economic situation in the District; the community language situation; attitudes of administrators, other officials, and parents toward the Bilingual Program; educational history of the subjects' older siblings and some aspects of our subjects' school histories; Program rhetoric; teachers' and aides' conception of literacy in their own classrooms; and classroom practices and events.

Many scholars have insisted that studies of educational achievement or development of concepts and processes in school must acknowledge contextual features of that achievement or development. Ogbu (1981) criticized educational microethnographies for failing to see that classroom patterns have origins outside the classroom and for consequently encouraging policy makers to think of personal rather than structural change. In Heath's (1981, 1982) descriptions of three communities' beliefs about and characteristics of language interactions, she not only showed how these beliefs were used in children's compositions but she also implied that language beliefs and norms of interaction are always part of a written language user's context and are always used during composing. While Graves lauded the shift in emphasis in writing research away from teacher and classroom and onto writer and writing processes (1980), he also acknowledged, in his admonition to choose research sites with extreme care, the great impact teacher and classroom have on the developing writer as well as the writing

(1979d). Shuy (1981) argued that writing is not writing is not writing, that participant rights and obligations differ in different style levels of writing (and, incidentally, that both educators and researchers erroneously view beginning writing but not beginning speech in relation to the demands of non-interactional, formal, impersonal language use). Woodward too (1980) maintained that writing is not monolithic, that different writing tasks and contexts elicit tests of different hypotheses. Others too, then, have argued that there is a need to at least describe ever-larger contextual units and have explicitly acknowledged them in analyses of writing.

AND NOW TO THE EVER-PRESENT MULTI-UNIT CONTEXT

The District Community

Duncan School District is a small one, serving 3,642 pupils in 1980; 623 of these were in the Bilingual Program in the 1980/81 school year although 1,669 had been identified as having limited English proficiency. The District is in a semi-rural area in a large metropolitan area in the Southwest.

Until a special election in Spring, 1981, Duncan District actually had not one but three district communities within its borders: a small group of primarily Anglo farm owners/ranchers; a large group of Hispanic settled migrants and migrant farmworker families who worked in the onion, cotton, and cut flower fields; and a still larger retirement community developed by a major corporation. As a result of that election, the latter community is no longer within District boundaries.

In the year of the study, according to the latest figures available from the State Department of Economic Security, there was a 23% unemployment rate in the District and 35.9% of the Hispanic families were below poverty level. Most Program students and 1,779 District students qualified for free or reduced rate lunches. Almost all of the children in the Bilingual Program (89%) were from low-income families. A Program-sponsored survey of Bilingual Program kinder-gartners' families found that 77% of these families were supported by field work or gardening. The average amount of schooling for the fathers was 4.1 years; for the mothers it was 3.7 years. None of the kindergartners' parents were high school graduates and only two had finished eighth grade.

The farm work in the area was being increasingly mechanized. Thus many of the migrant adults were twice-migrants; migrating in and out of the District and also spending many of their days within the District traveling from farm to farm looking for places where by-the-day human work was still available. Many children went with their families ''a las cebollas'' (to the onion fields) each day and worked for three to four hours before the school day began.

A Bilingual Program-sponsored language situation survey was conducted with in-home interviews and observations in homes, stores, work, and meeting places (Wellmeier, 1981). According to this survey, Spanish was overwhelmingly the language used in all adult–adult interactions. Children occasionally used English with and received Spanish from adults or used both Spanish and English with each other. Over 60% of the parents interviewed who had kindergarten-age children estimated their children's English proficiency to be poor or non-existent. More than half of the adults interviewed categorized themselves as monolingual Spanish speakers. Of these, two thirds had been born in Mexico.

Parents' initial lukewarm acceptance of but non-involvement with the Bilingual Program had turned into active, enthusiastic support by the 1980/81 school year. By then, they were sending their children to school so regularly that Bilingual Program classes were winning District attendance trophies. Responses to a question on the language situation survey questionnaire showed that over 80% of the parents with children in the Program said they were satisfied with their children's school. (Interestingly, when asked what the most important school subject was, many of these people said "writing." Exactly what was meant, and what relationship this response had to the Program's emphasis on writing is unclear.)

The history of parent involvement for this community within "The Community" is instructive. Prior to the existence of the Bilingual Program, there were no concessions to the needs of the Hispanic parents. Parent Advisory Council (PAC) meetings were held in the daytime and were conducted entirely in English. Only when the Hispanic children were put on stage as performers for entertainment at the meetings did parents attend. Without the enticement of performing offspring, Hispanic parents did not attend PAC meetings. With the advent of the Bilingual Program, a Bilingual PAC also came into existence. From the beginning, Bilingual PAC meetings were conducted in two languages; scanty attendance quickly burgeoned. After two years of meetings held at night and conducted in Spanish and English, PAC leaders realized that many of those in attendance did not speak English. They began to hold meetings conducted only in Spanish unless someone present needed a translation. No longer were children in pageants offered up as gimmicks to attract an audience. Bilingual PAC meetings were simply meetings, yet attendance in the 1980/81 school year averaged 25 per meeting. By contrast, Duncan District PAC meetings for Title 1, a program that also served poor Hispanic children of limited English ability, were held during the daytime and conducted in English. They continued to attract only two or three parents per meeting—unless children entertained.

With much more widespread community involvement through the Bilingual PAC, many more parents knew about school events. That they endorsed what they learned can be seen in the activities leading up to the "disassociation election" of May 1981.

Duncan District voters in the retirement community (which does not admit residents with minor children at home) outnumbered the Hispanic voters and had thus been able to elect a school board that opposed many aspects of bilingual education. Regional editions of the daily newspaper with the largest circulation in the county began printing frequent articles about the conflicts over bilingual education in Duncan District. Retirement community people accused Anglo ranchers of *keeping Hispanics in servitude* through their support of bilingual education. School board members denounced the Bilingual Program and asked, *if my immigrant parents could make it in school without bilingual education, why do these children need it?* Parents who got up at 3 AM to be in the fields by four came to several school board meetings that began at 8 PM and sometimes lasted until midnight. Not just a few, but several hundred Program parents came to show their support for the Bilingual Program. After a few such board meetings, these parents, whose own school histories were short, interrupted, and hardly successful, and who have often been characterized as uninvolved and silent (silenced?), began to speak out in Spanish in favor of bilingual education. The Board's response? To disallow future speeches in Spanish from the floor and to move the next meeting to a spot that would hold fewer than 50 people! Finally, Bilingual Program parents demonstrated, worked with certain ranchers and retirement community people who had their own reasons for wanting new District boundaries, and took part in a coalition that managed to bring about a special election which disassociated the retirement community from the District.

When we planned the study, we had thought that time was running out for the Bilingual Program, that by the end of the 1980/81 school year, the cumulative effect of many single School Board actions (or even some single act) would deal the Program a death blow. That was why the study was designed as it was. We never anticipated that grass roots community activity would manage to grant the Program, its Director, and its philosophy a temporary reprieve.

Administration

Administrators at the State Department, District, and school level had direct and indirect effects on the other adults in the Program, which were most likely incorporated into interactions with children.

Several years earlier, the State Department of Education had mandated that local Districts would implement a uniform and cumulative system for evaluating student achievement. Though each system was local District-designed, each also entailed the use of a list of pre-specified, discrete, and easily testable objectives. The State Department also required annual use of two standardized tests, the California Achievement Test (CAT) and the Comprehensive Test of Basic Skills (CTBS).

The Director of the Bilingual Program as well as various consultants encouraged teachers in the Bilingual Program not to let the tests dictate the teacher's approach to literacy instruction and not to feel that they and the children had failed if scores on the English-only tests were low. Still, teachers continued to voice their anxieties about this throughout the year. It hardly helped alleviate teacher stress when some District administrators told individual teachers they would hold them personally accountable for the students *mastery* of, for example, writing third person singular verb endings or capitalizing proper nouns, while consultants and the Program Director were pulling in the opposite direction, prevailing upon teachers to concentrate on content and to *forget form until the final draft.*

Blessedly, the Superintendent, Owen Dearing, supported the Program. Time after time, either because he trusted Bergionni's judgment or because he believed in bilingual education, he sheltered the Bilingual Program, allowing it to be excused from some "regular" program demands, and thus enabling Bergionni to develop a program that not only offered instruction bilingually, but that aimed, officially at least, for a "whole language" curriculum. Because of the Superintendent's support, other administrators (e.g., the school principals, some District Office personnel) either gave the appearance of outright approval or at least publicly presented a laissez-faire face toward the Bilingual Program. Until Fall 1980, they generally kept "hands off," allowing the Program's philosophy and curriculum to be developed by the Program Director. They did, however, develop certain administrative policies that contradicted the aims of the Program. Had these been implemented as planned (for instance, proposed policies on scheduling and teacher evaluation at one of the schools), there would have been disastrous consequences for the Bilingual Program. Fortunately, the Director was able to drop other activities and spend days explaining the likely consequences so that the policies could be modified before they were implemented. Bergionni also had to plead "special case" in order to exempt the Program from certain curriculum edicts that were in total contradiction to a holistic, purposeful-language-in-use, integrated curriculum. The fact is, however, that most of the time, with implicit backing from Superintendent Dearing, Bergionni's special pleadings were successful.

The administrative context was therefore an ambivalent one. On the one hand, State level Bilingual Education administrators were genuinely in favor of substantively strong (not merely heavily funded) bilingual education, and District administrators either helped or at least did not publicly obstruct the Program. On the other hand, there were mandates for evaluating children and programs that pressured teachers to teach in ways that contradicted Program philosophy. Further, while administrative support enabled the Director to be free to design the Program, administrative statements and policies often kept the Director in a wary state, wondering where the next "brush fire" would be. Moreover, although the principals seemed publicly in accord with or neutral toward the Bilingual Program workings, they sometimes took the opportunity, in meetings with teachers, to impose rules on Bilingual Program teachers that subverted Program goals. Since Bergionni could not have been at every building-level teachers' meeting, she often had to undo damage after-the-fact rather than be able to correct or clarify how Program personnel were excused or held to different demands (e.g., up to 1980 at least, they were excused from having to follow an English-language scope and sequence of Language Arts skills). It should be emphasized here that while the administrative context is presented here as more real than ideal, it was positively utopian in comparison with the "guerilla warfare" that some administrations wage on their bilingual programs (Fishman, 1980)!

The Bilingual Program Director made community organizing an important part of her duties. Over the years, Bergionni had become a part of the networks in the community (regularly attending the local parish church, accepting and reciprocating invitations to family events, establishing close relationships with some of the farmworker families). With the help of her secretary (a community member) and the friends she made, Bergionni revitalized the Bilingual Parent Advisory Council. Formerly reticent parents at first were enticed into working on fiestas sponsored by the Program; they later became members of committees to improve different aspects of schooling for their children. The increasing level of parental participation made it more likely that parents would answer calls from the Director to show support for the Program. Bilingual Program parents did not, then, in one jump go from working in the fields to speaking up at School Board meetings and initiating a petition drive for a special election. Instead, over a five-year period, they responded to the Director's invitations to join groups that took on tasks with increasingly empowering consequences for the group members themselves. Between organizing groups and providing help in negotiating interactions with various bureaucracies (welfare, medical, judicial), the Director was a major force in increasing the power of the farmworker community. When the situation for the Bilingual Program seemed hopeless in 1980, the parents were ready.

The Director was also knowledgeable about current theories in educational linguistics and literacy. She had a "biased" view of Bilingual Program children's language strengths (in contrast to the "biased" view of some curriculum workers elsewhere who assume children's "language deficiencies"). She was overtly enthusiastic about the moves teachers had made toward increasing the "wholeness" of the literacy and language experiences they planned for children, taking every opportunity to praise teachers for such efforts. At the same time, she was an "uneven" teacher evaluator or curriculum supervisor. Lacking funds for additional supervisory personnel, she was unable to provide, by herself, more than sporadic in-class help to teachers who were trying out a new approach to literacy instruction.

Philosophy/Rhetoric

Written documents and interaction with Program personnel revealed that the Program claimed or aimed to have certain characteristics promoted by our in-service training. First, it favored a "whole language approach" to literacy and language development (Goodman & Goodman, 1981). That is, it advocated using whole discourses and focusing on meaning-making by readers, writers, and speech event participants. The use of whole texts that exist and function outside of school (e.g., a newspaper article, a novel, a recipe, grocery lists, a bumper sticker, conversation, etc.) as opposed to pieces defined by analytic units (e.g., a paragraph, a sentence, a word) that exist primarily in schoolish contexts, along with an acknowledgement of the centrality of meaning are key features of "whole language" instruction; they entail writing for real child-held purposes to varied audiences (Goodman & Goodman, 1981; Edelsky, 1983). Second, along with conceptualizing reading and writing as interrelated, the Program also advocated the general integration of curriculum areas. Third, it chose to begin and stay with direct literacy instruction in the native language either until literacy was well-established or until the child was in third grade, rather than concurrently offering initial literacy instruction in two languages. At the same time, it favored choices by the children in regard to which language they would write and sometimes read in.

Classroom Practice

Actual classroom practices and teachers' beliefs regarding literacy, language distribution, writing, and curriculum matched official Program philosophy in varying degrees. In 1980, it was evident that, of all primary grade Bilingual program teachers and aides, some had only begun to put a toe into the waters that wash away "small skills" instruction and fill-in-the-blank writing. Others, however, took our in-service suggestions and allowed children considerable control over their choice of written genre and topics. Some integrated curriculum areas through projects while others maintained clear separations with a twenty-minute period allotted to spelling, fifteen minutes for handwriting, and so forth. In one classroom, it was difficult to find any writing other than that done on dittoed worksheets. There were teachers who consistently engaged children in at least some types of discourse that exist outside of classrooms (e.g., *real* conversation, writer-initiated letters, stories, jokes, interviews, and so on). This was in constrast to other teachers who assigned analytical units (e.g., paragraphs, sentences, words) and classroom-only genres (e.g., impersonal journals, letters-to-no-one, or reports of an event to an audience who was present at the event). There were teachers who, by mid-year at least, believed children could write beyond their knowledge of correct spelling, and in those classrooms children wrote stories, journals, letters. There were others, believing that writing was not possible until children could spell, whose students' rare pieces of writing consisted of close-to-correctly spelled lists of words or phonics-workbook-phrases (*oso soso; amo a mi mamá; sopa popa,* etc.).

Such contrasts provided a good example of an important research and educational issue highlighted by Hymes (1980); i.e., that different speech communities (or classrooms in this case) offer different degrees of fit between people's language abilities and opportunities for their use. In general, then, not only was there no perfect match between practice and rhetoric; there was also no consistency in the mismatch.

What follows is a more detailed picture, garnered from whole-day observations of six classrooms in this Program—first, the three that did not provide the systematically collected writing data for this study and then the three that did. The purpose of these thumbnail sketches of classrooms is to provide more strength to the statement that actual practice varied individually from Program intents.

Ms. A's first-grade classroom had desks in straight rows, and children were told to sit straight, raise their hands, and talk only when it was their turn. Ms. A was a native speaker of Mexican Spanish and lived outside the community. In her whole-class lessons, she tended to ask many questions in succession, often answering them herself before the children could. She organized the curriculum traditionally, i.e., into separate subject matter areas. The only code switching by adults or children that was observed in her classroom was intersentential. Adult switches were mainly translations (e.g., *Ya se bajó del tigre. He's off the tiger now.*) and seemed to be used for language teaching or for ensuring comprehension rather than for emphasis. On the playground, children used both intra- and inter-sentential switches in talk about games. In the classroom when children were addressed in English by either the Chicana or the Anglo observer, they responded in English, although the English responses seemed more slow in coming when they were addressed to the Chicana.

Except for stories read aloud to one group in English and to the other in Spanish (the two groups then changed places), all the print that was used by children was in Spanish in this classroom—books, signs, the teacher's writing on the board, and workbook pages.

Ms. A seemed to have clear ideas about the content of a "lesson" for phonics, spelling, or social studies. In these events, she took charge and directed the children, either in oral work on a skill or a topic or in the procedures or content of written exercises. When it came to following the Program's direction to emphasize writing, however, Ms. A seemed like a different teacher. She often gave children relatively large blocks of time and a single direction. Sometimes the direction was somewhat limiting, such as to write responses to a particular movie. But at other times they were as open-ended as *write*—no topic, no assigned type—leaving the children in control. It was as though Ms. A either had not herself experienced writing in school or had had no instruction in the teaching of writing. Thus, without models to guide her but with a wish to comply with Program directives, she transferred control of that "lesson" time to the children. And it was in her classroom, among the first grades, that the widest range of types of writing and the most unusual hypotheses about how to match conventions to intentions (Smith, 1982) were tried out.

Ms. B taught second grade. She was a native speaker of Spanish and a member of the community. She too put desks in rows and asked that children raise their hands to talk. More peer talk was permitted in this classroom, but there were also many disciplinary remarks from the teacher and aide concerning the "goofing off" that a small number of children frequently engaged in. Most of the children seemed unwilling to respond to the observers' invitations to talk. Ms. B tried to elicit interest in classroom work by instilling a competitive element in many activities; e.g., the best papers would be put up on the wall, the best row of children could get in line first, the best invented recipe would be tried out, and so forth. When a child would read to the class or offered ideas, others did not seem to attend. Children seemed eager to go out for recess.

Ms. B used Learning Centers with topical themes (food, animals, seasons) to organize curriculum. The Director had advised that stories be cut out of basal readers so they could be used in an individualized reading program. Ms. B used them instead for "round robin" reading. Ms. B seemed to speak more English than Spanish to the children, though both she and the children used frequent intra- and inter-sentential code switches (*tienen que decir la palabra* /you have to say the word/ *and then spell the word y decirla otra vez* /and say it again/; *l can touch the suelo* /ground/ *from the board*). When, however, a child asked for the spelling of a word that would have been a code switched item in that piece of writing (e.g., asking how to spell *contest* in a piece otherwise written in Spanish), Ms. B offered *concurso* instead. That is, she seemed to hold different norms for acceptability of code switching depending on whether it was oral or written. Ms. B seemed to delight in recounting the language capabilities she sometimes spotted, such as the time when, *a propos* of nothing, Lourdes asked her to tell the class the story of how carrots got their name. Taken aback, Ms. B had said she didn't know; Lourdes countered with *Well then invent it up!*

Print used in this room was mostly in English (library books, school forms and announcements, packages, textbooks), although most of the children's writing and Ms. B's writing on the board was in Spanish. Writing assignments were frequently related to past activities (e.g., write about what you did during recess) or to Learning Center topics. During writing time, children frequently asked for spelling help. Ms. Q, the aide, would write out the requested word. She would also correct the spelling in the children's journals. Peers too gave information on spelling, sometimes in the form of hints; e.g., pointing to the Spanish alphabet strip in the front of the room, *it's the third one* (the letter c), *the third one!* Children read their writing to Ms. B; at these times, in contrast to other interactions about writing that mainly concerned spelling, she would make a positive general comment about the content or ask the writer to tell a little more about some topic.

Though children greeted writing assignments with a chorus of groans, Ms. B reported *that's nothing compared to what they do when I give them any other kind of assignment.* Her appraisal of their relative enjoyment of writing despite the verbal resistance was probably accurate since her children wrote spontaneously, invented complicated stories, or attempted whole letters in English for the sake of their Anglo recipients.

The other non-research-study classroom that was observed was Mr. M's, also a native Spanish speaker and a member of the community. There were hand-raising norms for fewer situations in this room. There were also few directions given, yet children seemed to be engaged in purposeful school activity. Children, Mr. M, and Ms. H, the aide, seemed to engage in many private, intimate, joking exchanges that often ended in laughter and hugs. The first disciplinary remark heard during any of the observation days (which began at 8:30 AM) occurred at 1:10 PM.

The class day seemed to be separated into grossly divided subject matter areas; i.e., a huge block of time for writing; a time block for math, etc. Within the writing time, children wrote for assignments and also spontaneously (e.g., writing letters and "mailing" them to teacher, aide, or classmates who each had mailboxes in the classroom).

Mr. M seemed to use more Spanish than English with this class he had characterized as *full of monolinguals* (Spanish speakers). Still, code switching was frequent and both intra- and inter-sentential. Not only were codes switched but so too were written styles. When Alicia wrote letters to in-school addressees, she signed them *tu amiga, Alicia* (Your friend, Alicia). When she wrote to her aunt in Mexico, however, she used more elaborate closings such as *su sobrina que quisiera más verla que escribirle* (your niece who would rather see you than write to you), according to Mr. M who had seen some of these letters. Mr. M occasionally code switched in writing, inter-sententially, on the blackboard.

Most of the commercially prepared print that was used in this classroom was in English, although children flipped through library books in each language and even slowed down and read them aloud *sotto voce,* as if for a display of competence, when the observer stood behind them. Many children indicated they did not understand stories when read in English.

Children argued with each other over spelling and gave advice (as did the aide) to *sound it out*. Several proudly shared with another child their own responses to a problem Mr. M had posed for them to resolve in writing. Children asked a child author to clarify the content of what she had written, as did Mr. M when children read their work to him. On one observation day, two boys were involved in a truly collaborative story writing event. Mr. M repeated that the two had worked on a collaborative story the previous week that had taken several days to complete. A few pieces of all the writing produced in the class were "published" during the year; i.e., they were typed by an adult (with most, but not all words spelled conventionally and with a mix of Spanish and English punctuation), bound, and put in the class library. In Mr. M's room, children wrote complaints, threats, and apologies in letters to the teacher and to the aide. That is, as Shuy (1981) advocated, Mr. M had made it possible for children to write interactively and functionally. In this classroom also, the writing events (e.g., letter-to-teacher and response-from-teacher, or creation of an invented story with many episodes) often lasted for several days.

The three classrooms designated as "the study classrooms" were as widely varying as those just described. Variation in writing instruction and other features seemed to stem from a number of teacher-related sources which this study did not sort out. Other researchers (Graves, 1975; Birnbaum, 1980) have looked for contrasting teacher-developed classroom environments to see how these affected children's development as readers and writers. We did not set out with such contrasts in mind. But we found them.

In the first-grade study classroom there was usually a hum of voices and children were busy with school work. The classroom rules of Ms. D, a nonnative speaker of Spanish who lived outside the community, and of Ms. De, her native Spanish speaking aide who was a community member, included license to move around the room and converse with peers. In mid-year, a writing center had been established with a variety of kinds of paper and different writing implements (pens, pencils, colored markers, crayons); children could go there when space allowed and assignments were finished.

At the beginning of the school year, Ms. D reported that mornings were spent with adults taking dictation from children, and children labeling pictures and working in phonics workbooks. By Spring, the schedule had changed. In the mornings, children now wrote in journals for a good part of the morning. During story time, children's stories would be read along with published texts. At such times, Ms. D would comment on particular aspects of the content she wanted other children to begin to use. According to Ms. D, the best way to move children along in writing was to indicate what constitutes progress by publicly praising and identifying a "next step" in another child's piece of work.

Ms. D seemed to use about as much Spanish as English in her interactions with children, though not as much with Ms. De, the aide. Both children and adults were observed code switching frequently. With much delight, Ms. D and Ms. De recounted stories of the children's inventiveness with language.

Most of the print in use in the classroom was in Spanish, including the Spanish phonics workbooks that were used as stories. Occasionally, if a child selected an English book for looking something up, teacher or aide suggested that a Spanish reference be used instead. However, the research team observing the print environment found many more English than Spanish library books.

Ms. D's comments to children who showed her their writing often took the form of requests for more information. With "better students," Ms. D said she gave direct instruction sometimes in the use of certain punctuation marks during conferences about a piece of writing.

In this classroom, certain types of writing were physically differentiated. Journals were always written in stapled together packets of lined paper with a colored paper cover. Books were of pre-stapled rather than loose papers.

Interviews revealed that both teacher and aide believed writing would help teach children to read, that because children would be more actively involved when writing their own material, they would learn more, be *in a learning mode rather than a practicing or pleasing-the-teacher mode.* At mid-year, Ms. D realized she could *take the lid off,* that her children could probably do more than she realized and that her assignments allowed—thus the construction of the writing center and the decreased (but still present) emphasis on phonics workbooks. Ms. D reported that in addition to the writing we had collected, children wrote on *stable spots* on the blackboard—names of who was to go to recess, lists of items needed for particular events, and so on.

Both these adults saw children's writing as having the potential to enhance them in their teacher's eyes. Ms. D and Ms. De took writing development to mean an increase in legibility, a move away from safe topics and safe syntactic frames (*me gusta X, me gusta Y, me gusta Z*), a shift toward being able to write without *talking it all out first,* and an increase in involvement of the writer with the piece.

This teacher believed she was giving children a choice when, after a discussion, she would ask them if they would like to do a story about the discussion topic. Perhaps children took that as a true offer of a choice; perhaps not. But real choice in writing *was* available at the writing center in this classroom—the only one of the three study classrooms to offer children this opportunity with any frequency.

The second-grade classroom was taught by Ms. C, a non-native speaker of Spanish who lived outside the community, and her aide, Ms. G, a native Spanish speaker who lived in the District. This classroom also had a hum of voices. There was very little teacher talk directed to the whole class. Instead, adult and child usually interacted on an individual basis. Like the children in Mr. M's class, these children did not receive any disciplinary comments until almost 2 PM on the days they were observed. Before that, they were cooperative with each other, relatively quiet, and steadily engaged in doing the assignments for the day. They were eager to talk with observers and to read their writing to them.

An incident which was quite revealing of the climate of interpersonal caring that had been established in this classroom occurred when two first graders came in to read a lengthy story they had written. Even after 15 minutes of hearing halting, flat intonation, "first-grade style" reading, without any obvious prompting from the adults, these second graders sat quietly, facing the readers, *so as not to hurt their feelings,* according to Ms. C, even if their attention might have wandered.

Children seemed to prefer to stay in and write rather than go out for recess. Observers' notes frequently mentioned the "non-teacher talk" quality of Ms. C's talk to the children as well as her efforts to make them responsible for solving housekeeping, social, and academic problems.

The adults used more English than Spanish, while children seemed to use slightly more Spanish than English in this room. Both code switched intra- and inter-sententially with great frequency.

On the observation days, there were some children who seemed to only cut, paste, and draw almost all day, with an occasional nod to doing other assignments. The others' interest was sustained all day by writing assignments that constituted the entire day's work. Usually, according to both teacher and aide, the day consisted of time to write in diaries, time to read and do book reports, an "oral language activity" that was connected to social studies or science, reading conferences, and math. It is possible that this teacher tried to please the researchers who were interested in writing by presenting days full of writing and little else. It is also possible that reading conferences and math occurred rarely because the children enjoyed the writing/drawing/pasting so much. In any case, the "usual" schedule, as Ms. C and Ms. G each described it, was not in evidence on the observation days.

In this classroom, children were given dittoed book report forms to fill out. The forms asked for author and title, a check in a box to indicate if they did or did not like the book, a line or two about the book, and a picture about the book. By filling out a certain number of forms, children received an award. What seemed to happen, however, was that children filled out a form without reading the book, that accumulation of forms substituted for interaction with the text. From what was observed, it seemed that despite Ms. C's pleasure in the number of books her children had "read" as evidenced by the number of forms they had filled out, there was very little demand on these children to read anything but their own writing.

Another discrepancy: the Program Director had spent considerable funds in obtaining children's literature in Spanish. These books were placed in the library. The librarian, however, insisted that the children should be reading in English and therefore did not permit checking out Spanish books. Ms. C had circumvented this state of affairs by checking the Spanish books out herself for her classroom. Nevertheless, both the print environment and the print-in-use observations showed that there were more English library books in the room than Spanish and more English books that were flipped through if not actually read.

While children wrote, they also talked with neighbors about what they were writing and other topics, and helped each other sound out words. Occasional conferences in this classroom consisted of a child reading to the teacher and the teacher asking the child for oral elaborations on the content. Ms. C reported that she once asked some children to write down the elaborations; i.e., to revise the content of their writing, but, as she said, *some cried, so I didn't do that again.*

Ms. C believed that writing *got children's minds going,* that children asked better questions (e.g., about subjects rather than procedures) since she started emphasizing writing, that writing *forces them to think.* She and Ms. G saw writing development as a move from *basal reader language* to an individual style, from re-telling to inventing stories, from the writing of fragments to *complete thoughts,* and away from the use of repetitive phrases. By the time these adults were interviewed (during the fourth collection period), each thought children *could go into a slump from too much writing.* Conversations during the second and third collection times, however, revealed that both Ms. C and Ms. G thought at that time that longer was better. Thus they encouraged and received what, by the fourth collection, they called too much writing (e.g., 27-page pieces with nearly 13 pages of repetition). This was the only one of the three study classrooms where a few children appeared to regress in some of the areas of writing that were analyzed. We have no way of knowing if this was related to a dulled interest in a task in which message meaning had less importance than length, to particular attributes of the children, to attention and growth in other aspects of writing for which we had no evidence, to children's considerable lack of involvement with published and conventional print during the year, or to some combination of these. On the other hand, it was also in this classroom that the deepest understanding of social studies and science material shone through in children's writing.

Ms. S, a non-native Spanish speaker who lived outisde the community, was aided by Ms. G, who was native Spanish speaking and lived in the community. While much in Ms. C's second-grade classroom was individually directed, Ms. S conducted lessons with her entire third-grade class. The day was organized to provide for journal writing, "seat work" on social studies or science, a writing assignment, reading groups working in workbooks, math worksheet activities, use of the health textbook, and time for finishing up assignments (which were almost always to be completed in one day). It was observed that children in this class groaned with the announcement of each assignment, that they raced to recess, and that they received many reprimands about both behavior and the quality of their classroom work.

Ms. S used mostly English with the children, though she code switched frequently between sentences. These were almost entirely translations into Spanish, seemingly for the purpose of ensuring comprehension. Ms. S rarely code switched intra-sententially. Ms. G, however, used both intra- and inter-sentential switches, as did the children to each other and to the adults.

Ms. S and Ms. G provided various kinds of information about language as children wrote. As a resource for spelling, they put presumably needed words on the board before children began to write. Many assignments began with an opening paragraph provided by the teacher. Ms. S directed children to stay in one style of script (either manuscript or cursive) and to produce work of a certain length (number of pages were cited).

Some writing was done during group work time. During those sessions, a group of children was also "walked through" the writing each was doing. That is, questions were asked section by section, to direct the sequence of topics in the pieces. After a piece was finished, it was often corrected by an adult for spelling and syntax (if in English) and then sometimes re-copied by the child. The print environment and the print-in-use observations showed that, except for the children's writing, English was the written language of the classroom.

Both teacher and aide believed that writing made the children seem more capable to the adults than children from previous years had seemed, that a great quantity of writing made children take greater care not to make errors in spelling and punctuation, that children now seemed more confident about their own competence and more inclined to relate information from one subject matter area to another. What counted as development differed for each child, according to both Ms. S and Ms. G, but each said it included at least an increasing use of conventional structures (for stories), an increase in the number of different ideas in a piece, and an absence of repetition. It was in this classroom that children wrote the barest-boned facts about social studies material, where pieces from different children were extraordinarily similar in organization and content if not in wording. In this classroom also, however, there were pieces that revealed great expressive capabilities.

In summary, while none of the study classrooms presented a "whole language approach to literacy," each of the three study teachers and aides (as well as many of the other teaching personnel in the Program) must be applauded for the giant strides they took toward practice that was more like that called for in various theoretical statements on writing and language development (see Harste & Burke, 1980; Urzúa, 1980; Lindfors, 1980). Though the three study classrooms were idiosyncratically "imperfect," adults in each:

1. had children writing every day, frequently about personal topics;
2. delivered direct literacy instruction in Spanish (and in English at the third-grade level);
3. permitted children to choose the language they wrote in and read in during "free time";
4. accepted all topics (none were taboo);
5. established journal writing time;
6. sent some letters children wrote;
7. accepted at least some unconventional forms (e.g., some invented spelling, unconventional segmentation, etc.);
8. provided for some sharing of writing with peers;
9. said they believed that content superceded form in what constitutes good/bad writing (e.g., good writing is done by a writer who takes risks, who does not merely repeat, who provides more and better ideas, etc.);
10. believed that an emphasis on writing had improved children's reading, had increased their self-confidence and oral expressiveness (they said the children appeared to question more and act more on their own behalf), had caused them to see these children as more capable than other children had seemed in past years, and had made teaching more interesting for the teacher.

Moreover, some but not all of the adults:

1. had established an environment in which children occasionally controlled their own writing.
2. allowed more invented forms and attended more to content than to form;
3. allowed various physical conditions for writing (the floor, rugs, outside; singly, in pairs; interrupted, at-one-sitting);
4. held occasional conferences during which the content of a piece was praised or some suggestion was made for writing another piece;
5. held occasional conferences with selected children for direct teaching of a punctuation convention;
6. occasionally gave information that cued a child's attention to ways to express both referential and social meaning (e.g., distinguishing between *querido* and *estimado* in letters);
7. could recall and introspect about their growth as writing teachers;
8. unfortunately, presented without any sensitive accompanying discussions, books and audio-visual materials that probably perpetuate racist stereotypes (e.g., *Little Black Sambo*).

However, the teachers and aides did *not:*

1. establish a need and demand for children to interact with a great variety of published (and therefore conventional), whole texts. According to Smith (1982), it is wide reading rather than writing that presents the systems of written language that must be acquired;
2. regularly "publish" selected works; therefore, there was no real need for children to evaluate their own texts to decide what would be published, no need to revise content, and no demands for legibility from an audience—demands which would have provided a genuine reason to edit, to produce a conventional final copy;
3. read aloud *extensively* from children's literature in Spanish. Exposure to written literature is what gives one a feel for the cadence of written narrative (Smith, 1982);
4. hold conferences in which peers or adults questioned the writer on the meaning of a piece in order that children might learn to anticipate readers' needs in relation to the writer's intent.

Print Environment

The available print, what we have called the print environment, was a part of the classroom that deserves separate discussion. Different kinds of print seemed to be present in order to:

1. encourage writing by motivating the writer; e.g., books, pictures, charts were displayed to excite children's interest in a topic; children's work was displayed as a reward for the writers;

2. model certain forms or writing techniques; e.g., using children's work as samples for others to examine;
3. encourage an awareness of environmental print;
4. demonstrate the functionality of print; e.g., displaying lists of needed supplies, office memos conveying information, etc.;
5. promote an understanding that writing can preserve certain processes such as thinking, planning, or organizing for future reference; e.g., brainstorming charts remained from brainstorming sessions;
6. demonstrate that print can designate categories and differentiate space; e.g., classroom signs over particular areas or groupings;
7. display a relation between oral and written language; e.g., printed stories accompanied by taped renditions;
8. promote the idea that written language can be used to entertain others as well as to express one's inner self; e.g., story books, diaries;
9. convey the idea that writing can be shared with others.

Table 6 provides a count of the materials that were found in the three study classrooms. It is important to note at least two points in regard to such a summa-

Table 6.   Types of Materials Constituting the Print Environment

Type of Material	Grade 1		Grade 2		Grade 3	
	Sp.	Eng.	Sp.	Eng.	Sp.	Eng.
Miscellaneous (signs, posters, children's work, flashcards, sentence strips, ditto sheets, games, etc.)						
no. of different types	9	15	9	8	7	11
no. of commercially produced types	3	14	7	8	5	9
Workbooks and Kits						
no. of sets	9	10	2	6	3	10
no. of types of reference materials (atlases, dictionaries, almanacs, etc.)	2	3	2	2	1	2
No. of Books Used for Reference by the Teacher (adult dictionary, sociological texts about Mexican-American children, methods texts, etc.)	0	10	1	1	0	0
Textbook Series (basal reader series, multiple copies of social studies texts, etc.)	17	9	4	8	3	7
Trade Books						
no. of sets	9	1	5	2	1	0
no. of single copies	7	69	16	34	0	2

ry. First, since the table follows on the heels of the descriptions of different classrooms and since it displays classroom differences in quantities of materials, it might encourage readers to infer that teachers were completely responsible for the differences. That there were fewer textbook or basal series in each higher grade and that there were more English than Spanish materials in all grades was more a function of availability than it was of individual teacher choice. None of the Spanish language materials were in these classrooms prior to the advent of the Bilingual Program in 1975. The supply of English materials, of course, had been accumulating since well before that time. Moreover, Spanish language materials were simply not as plentiful or as availalbe even if there had been no budgetary constraints on righting an imbalance. The greater variety of Spanish materials in first than in third grade also reflected a market disparity in supply rather than in will-to-purchase.

Secondly, presence does not mean use, which was the reason for mentioning print-in-*use* in the classroom descriptions. For instance, despite more English print in the first-grade classroom, more Spanish print appeared to be in use. And despite more printed materials in any language available in second than in third grade, more seemed to be used, if grudgingly and for narrow purposes, in third grade.

The Written Context

Here I mean such things as language of the piece, materials used during production, audience and recipient, "genre" or type, and the instigator of a piece. Though for some purposes these factors might be considered part of text rather than context (e.g., red markered vs. black penciled marks; small vs. large letters due to small vs. large paper; letter vs. story), there is considerable justification for considering them as tightly tied-to-text contextual features.

Pratt's (1977) claim—that knowledge that a text is considered "literature" is a *con*text for dealing with that text—is an argument that can also be made for considering "type" a context for the writing of these children. When everyone (teacher, author, researcher) knew a piece to be a letter rather than a journal, that knowledge accompanied the text as *con*-text. Also, Pratt argues that genre in literature is signalled through bookcover, advertising, publishing house, and so on. Similarly, types of writing in some classrooms were signalled by non-text features. Journals, for example, were always written on stapled-together lined 8½-×-11-inch newsprint, covered with a piece of colored paper.

Harste (1980c) and Coles and Goodman (1980) showed that materials affected the print decisions a child makes. (Crayons, for instance, elicited pictures while pencils seemed to call for writing among three 3-year-olds; big pencils with no erasers affected types of early revision.) And Hymes' (1970) proposal for various factors of speech events could be extended to "factors of writing events" where form of the text co-varies with variation in participants, codes, channel, definition of the situation, etc. In fact, different kinds of paper (oversized, small and cut into shapes, unlined vs. lined) was a factor in variation in writing in the first- and second-grade collections; and different writing implements had to be considered in the first-grade samples.

While the typical piece was in Spanish, was prompted by the intentions of the teacher rather than the writer, was expository (and usually a report), and was written for an audience of the teacher in her role of Direction-Giver, there were also pieces of other types, written in another language, prompted by another instigator, and directed to other audiences. Table 7 shows the variety and also the imbalances. Contrasts in features of the pieces varying in these contextual attributes will be presented in later chapters.

Children's Background Factors

And who were the children? Some of the researchers had known some of them and their siblings since they started school. A bit of who these children were can be found in some of their more "institutional" contacts with the school. ("Personal" features of sex and age appeared in Tables 1 and 2 in Chapter 2.) Because we believe a child comes to school with certain expectations based on his or her family's experiences with school, we collected the information that is summarized in Table 8. Means for scores on the Bilingual Syntax Measure appear in

Table 7.   Number of Pieces[a] with Particular Tied-to-Text Features

	Grade 1	Grade 2	Grade 3	Grade X
Language				
Spanish	172	180	75	34
English	8	8	31	2
Assigned				
Yes	159	185	109	37
No	30	4		
Type				
Expository	35	86	76	26
Letter	15	63		
Story	22	26	34	9
Journal	113	21		
Book	6	7	1	
Signature	8	1		2
Caption	1	1		
Poetry		1	3	2
Other				3

[a]The totals for each factor do not add up to 524, the total number of pieces analyzed, because some pieces were coded more than once (e.g., as both letters and expository pieces) and some were not coded at all into these categories (e.g., signatures were not coded as either Spanish or English).

Table 8.   Background Information on Subjects[a]

School Status of Older Siblings (total siblings for 17 Ss = 93)
    younger   28
    older still in school   37
    older, graduated   8
    older, dropped out   20

Special Education Referrals
    on our Ss   1 (4% of 26 Ss)
    on our Ss' older siblings still in school   9 (24% of 37)

Parents' Self-report of Child's Primary Language (18 reporting)
    Spanish   16
    English   2

Number of Ss with Evidence of Minimal Literacy for Parent (e.g., signed   5
    form with X, "drew" first name, got a neighbor to fill out form, etc.)
    (evidence from 17 Ss' forms to be filled out by parents)

Attendance for 26 Ss
    Days absent   0–5   12
                                                                    6–10   5
                                                                    11–15   5
                                                                    16–20   3
                                                                    21–25   1

[a]Complete records on all 26 Ss were not available. For some, there were no school registration forms, for others there was no sibling information.

Table 9. Means on the California Achievement Test, an English test, are given in Table 10.

Children could score from 1 to 5 on the form of the Bilingual Syntax Measure taken by first and second graders, and from 1 to 6S on the form taken by third graders. The Bilingual Syntax Measure is deemed a test of language proficiency; more narrowly, it is also a test of morpheme use under particular conditions. Instructions accompanying the test state the following meanings for the scores:

> level 1—no proficiency, little or no understanding of the language and no ability to produce it;

Table 9.   Means for BSM Scores

	English		Spanish	
Grade	September	April	September	April
1	2.67	3.11	4.33	4.67
2	3.78	4.33	4.67	5.0
3	3.5	4.83	4.83	5.83
X	1.0	1.0	6.0	5.5

Table 10. **Means of *CAT* Scores**[a]

	Sub-Test (in parenthesis is no. of scores available)							
Grade	Reading Comprehension		Reading Total		Language		Math	
1	1.6	(5)	1.4	(3)	0.5	(2)	1.92	(9)
2	1.6	(7)	1.27	(7)	1.36	(7)	1.87	(7)
3	3.18	(6)	2.93	(6)	3.2	(6)	4.02	(6)
X	1.75	(2)	1.65	(2)	1.7	(2)	3.15	(2)

[a]CAT scores should be read as followed by month; i.e., 1.6 = sixth month of first grade, 0.5 = fifth month of kindergarten.

> level 2—receptive only, able to understand some, to repeat short sentences, but not to use the language to communicate opinions;
> level 3—survival use, can make needs known but substitutes first language words for important words like nouns and verbs and omits grammatical markers;
> level 4—intermediate, can communicate ideas without relying on gesture or first language, controls certain grammatical endings;
> level 5 (on the test for younger children)—indicates native-like proficiency (highest level);
> level 5 (on the test for third graders and above)—approaching native proficiency but incomplete learning of some of the more advanced structures;
> level 6N—native-like proficiency along with use of non-standard forms;
> level 6S—native-like proficiency including mastery of broad range of standard syntactic structures.

The range of California Achievement Test scores recorded for Hispanic children who were not in the Bilingual Program, as contrasted with the range of scores for our subjects, appears in Table 11. It should be noted that children were in the Bilingual Program both because of parents' desires and because of evidence of limited English proficiency (including low scores on the Bilingual Syntax Measure).

From the information in Table 8 it is reasonable to infer that these children did not have a family history of success with school or with literacy in particular. Using Tables 9, 10, and 11, one could make a likely guess that, relatively, the children would not succeed well with traditional school tasks which bore a high similarity to the tasks that comprise the tests.[1] Still, with participation in the

---

[1] The test scores are presented here with misgivings because I do not want to increase the legitimacy granted to such scores or the influence they have on educational practices. On the one hand, the tests may or may not predict how well one reads or understands/produces a language in the

Table 11.   Ranges of *CAT* Scores for Children in the Three Bilingual Program Classes and Hispanic Children Enrolled in Non-Bilingual Program Classrooms

| | Sub-Test | | | | | |
| | Reading | | Language | | Math | |
Grade	BL	non-BL	BL	non-BL	BL	non-BL
1	0.7–2.3	0.1–2.6	0.1–1.9	0.1–3.2	1.6–2.3	0.4–1.9
2	0.4–2.3	1.7–3.6	0.1–2.0	0.1–3.9	1.6–2.2	1.7–3.4
3	1.8–3.8	1.7–5.4	2.0–4.1	1.4–5.4	3.0–4.7	1.8–5.9

Bilingual Program, fewer of our subjects than their siblings were seen as "below normal" (i.e., they were not referred for Special Education as often as their siblings). Also, most attended school regularly.

Here then were the contexts for writing development among these 26 children—a socio-economic context, a political one, a community language situation, an administrative context, program rhetoric and actual classroom practice contexts, features that were contextual at a specific text production level, and a context of child and familial educational background factors. It is our sense that some of the contexts were positive and some negative in terms of enhancing children's growth as writers, but the design of the study allows only inferences (even though some can be made with considerable confidence) about which were which. What *can* be said with certainty, however, is that these contexts were always present, impinging in some degree. Moreover, the relationship between writing and contexts was reciprocal in that the children's writing also affected the contexts. For instance, teachers reported that their beliefs and practices changed

---

classroom; prediction can well rest on the congruence of assumptions about reading and language underlying the tests and those underlying practice in specific classrooms (Edelsky, Draper, & Smith, 1983a). For reasons to be presented at greater length in Chapter 7, I believe the tests themselves, however, do not elicit acts of reading, writing, language or whatever the sub-test titles claim. Instead, by eliminating an essential feature of oral and written language use (the interactivity of *four* language cueing systems—graphic or phonemic, syntactic, semantic, and pragmatic), they only *masquerade* as instances of reading, talking, writing. Further, even if these tests could have overcome this major problem, they would have still been beset by the confounding factors associated with any standardized test (Edelsky et al., 1983b) and by those specific to these particular testing sessions. For instance, for some of the means in Tables 8 and 9, over 60% of the subject pool was not included because no scores were available (e.g., some teachers did not insist certain children take certain sub-tests). Moreover, the first and second graders had never been exposed to any workbook exercises in English—and the California Achievement Test is an English-language assortment of workbook-like tests. All of this certainly decreases the amount of faith to be placed in how much these scores reflect what the tests claim—language proficiency, achieved reading ability, achieved "language," and so on. Still, the scores are presented here because they are part of the picture of the children's performance in school.

as they saw the capabilities children diplayed; as teachers scheduled writing rather than skill drills, different administrators either applauded or threatened; some parents reported surprise and pleasure that their children were writing at home; others were horrified by invented spellings. In other words, a reflexive system existed that we saw through the lens of writing development. To have looked at the writing without the rest would have been to miss part of the essence of the object of our investigation—that it occurs in a situation, functions pragmatically, and is affected by and can affect one or more realities.

Chapter 4

MYTHS AND COUNTER-EVIDENCE

People who would never claim to be theoreticians have ''theories'' about the world (Smith, 1975) and ''theories'' about literacy (Harste & Burke, 1977; DeFord, 1981). Even researchers and educators whose main interests are reading and writing or bilingual education may have both less schooled, more informal, less often articulated ''theories'' about reading, writing, and issues related to bilingual education as well as the more formal, academically acknowledged and prestigious THEORIES. Like THEORIES, ''theories'' too are systems of beliefs and knowledge that establish expectancies, shape perceptions, plans, and decisions, and guide action. Unlike THEORIES, however, the particulars of ''theories'' are frequently taken for granted and not subject to critical inquiry. This chapter focuses on the discrepancies between certain beliefs and certain of our data—discrepancies that should encourage a hard look at favorite ''theories'' held by many educational policy makers, educators, and researchers, as well as the lay public.

As categories were derived, as writing was coded and interview protocols were examined, certain data seemed to contrast so sharply with certain taken-for-granted ideas that they highlighted the mythical character of these ideas. As discussed earlier (in Chapter 2 under the topic of maintaining running lists of impressions and engaging in a ''myth hunt''), members of the research team listed the ideas particular bits of data seemed to refute and then went through the data again, purposefully looking for other examples that also countered the taken-for-granted ideas. Here, I will present many of the ''myths'' along with counter evidence. In rebutting, I will present a summary statement of a popular but questionable belief first, followed by a summary statement of what our data would lead one to believe.

Since many of these taken-for-granted ideas may already seem patently false to readers of this book, it could appear that we simply erected ''straw people'' for a contest in which we could emerge victorious. However, though some of these beliefs may seem so ill-founded as to need no refutation, they carry great weight; their influence can be seen in mandates from state departments of education, in recommendations by educational task forces, in curriculum guides, textbooks, and workbook series, and in the teachings of many teacher preparation programs. The counter evidence presented here then may be useful to disbelievers in their discussions with those who still subscribe to these beliefs.

Now it is also possible to substantiate, not refute, many of the same taken-for-granted ideas with data from this study. There are plenty of examples, for instance, that show lack of concern for a reader, that show writing that appears to be speech written down, that reveal similarities in one child's writing across contexts, and so on. But there are also counter examples for every one of these. If examination at close range of a single concrete case can illuminate the adequacy of a theory, then the single contradictory case should at least force the questioning of an assumed "fact." And when there are many contradictory cases, the "fact" should become highly suspect.

Of course, whether a belief is common and prevailing is related as much or more to external historical, political and social factors than to any intrinsic adequacy of the idea. Thus, I am not proposing that myth-questioning will lead to the destruction of certain beliefs regarding literacy and bilingualism or an end to the practices they inspire. Still, thoughtful readers might find these counter examples helpful in their own efforts to change practice and "theory" or even to change THEORY.

MYTHS ABOUT LANGUAGE PROFICIENCY

1. *These Children Are Language Deprived* versus *The Data Show They Had Language Strengths*

Instead of deficiencies, our subjects' writing shows use of varied vocabulary, complex syntax, and a move toward stylistic sophistication.[1]

The children used words that do not appear in primary grade readers—words like *encerrado* (isolated), *autor* (author), *se emborrachó* (he got drunk), *en ese instante* (in that instant), *sorprenderse* (to be surprised), *aplacar* (to calm), *travesuras* (pranks), *lagartija* (small lizard), *apestaba* (smelly), *mugroso* (filthy), and *cachetada* (a wallop of a smack). They used words belonging to "sets" which are often subject to isolated drills with "language development" posters in primary classrooms. For example, there were sets of names of dinosaurs gleaned from Social Studies units, names of animals (*tigre*/tiger, *tecalote*/owl, *gua-*

---

[1] It is important to remember that the examples cited are only a part of the evidence we found to counter any given myth. Space limitations as well as my intent to limit the number of examples of the same point prevent me from providing the full display.

jolote/turkey, *lagartija*/small lizard, *mapache*/raccoon, *chango*/monkey, and so on), direction words or relational terms, and onomatopoetic words.

Children also invented words by using morphological rules. A child who wrote about eating hot chilis and needing to drink cold water explained that *me enchilé la boca* (I chili-peppered my mouth).

Contrary to popular opinion about code switching, the children's *infrequent* written switches often provided evidence that the term in the other language was indeed known by the child. *Sad* and *triste* appeared in the same piece (*estaba muy muy sad*/I was very, very sad; *estaba muy triste*/I was very sad). On other pieces one finds both *loquito* and *crazy*, *engañaba* and *tricked*, *mapache* and *raccoon*.

Another opinion concerning vocabulary, heard in educational quarters, is that poor non-standard Spanish/English bilinguals or non-standard Spanish-speaking children know few nouns and that they substitute *cosa* (thing) for each void in their normal repertoire. In fact, we did not find even one clear example of this phenomenon in over 500 pieces of writing. Most of the pieces contained precise nouns rather than any all-encompassing *cosa*. However, there were times when the children used circumlocutions, often rhythmically symmetrical, in place of what was most likely an unknown word. A third grader used phrases such as *la otra que tenía los huevos mágicos* (the other one that had the magic eggs) and *él que no era mágico* (the one that wasn't magic), describing in order to distinguish between two rabbits and two eggs, helping the reader while reflecting her ability to anticipate potential ambiguities.

Cohesive links between propositions and clauses may reflect both lexical and semantic development. Over 60 different lexical links were found in the children's writing. They could be categorized as additive, adversative, causative, or temporal (Halliday & Hasan, 1976). Though not all were always used with thus-categorized intent, many were (for example, *y*/and was used as a filler as well as a signal that additional meanings were to come).

Simple active declarative sentences were common at the beginning of the year for first graders. However, by mid-year, even first graders were also writing adverbial phrases at sentence beginnings (*en la noche, vamos al cine*/at night, we're going to the movies) and relative clauses (*ahora la maestra trajo una sueter cafe que le hizo a su nieto*/today the teacher brought a brown sweater that she made for her grandson). By third grade, written adverbial and relative clauses resembled (1).

(1)   El Conejo Loco
        Un conejo loco *que vive en un hoyo mugroso y feo adentro del hoyo* apestaba y tenía papeles, basura y libros tirados por todos lados. Había una muchachita *pasando por allí* y *cuando pasó por allí* dijo—¡Ay, que feo huele aquí! Habrá un zorillo.—Y en ese momento *que estaba pensando*, salió el conejo de repente y la

niña se asustó y gritó. *Cuando la muchachita gritó* el conejo se rió y *cuando reía* brincaba y caminaba pero la muchachita le dió una cachetada y se le quitó lo loco.

(The Crazy Rabbit
A crazy rabbit that lives in a filthy and ugly hole inside the smelly hole and it had papers, garbage and books thrown all over. There was a little girl passing by and when she passed there she said, "Oh how ugly it smells here. It must be a skunk." And at the moment that she was thinking, the rabbit came out suddenly and the girl got scared and screamed. When the little girl screamed the rabbit laughed and when he was laughing he was jumping and walking but the little girl gave him a wallop of a smack and he quit his craziness.)

The variety in clausal constructions in our samples was matched by variety in sentence types. In some of the samples, we found questions, imperatives, and exclamations within dialogue (¿qué pasó? mi hija. Dime. Apúrate/what happened, my child? Tell me! Hurry!/ in a first grader's story about seeing a ghost in the house; *el cocodrillo se murió y el Popeye dijo 'yay'*/the crocodile died and Popeye said 'yay'/ in a movie summary by a first grader). In others, questions and exclamations were not couched in dialogue. Second-grader Perlinda used questions as a stylistic device—as an excuse for offering information in (2).

(2)   Yo hice un totem pole y se miraba bien bonito y a todos le gustó y era bien, bien, bien bonito y bien grande y bonito y era café. *¿Y sabes cuántas caras tenía?* Tenía siete caras. *¿Y sabes de qué color es?* Es azul y verde y color rosa y negro y amarillo y café y anaranjado y era bien, bien bonito y me gusta mucho y lo tengo en la escuela y está dentro de mi escritorio y es bien bonito y grande.

(I made a totem pole and it looked really nice and everybody liked it and it was really, really, really nice and really big and nice and it was brown. And do you know how many faces it had? It had seven faces. And do you know what color it is? It's blue and green and pink and black and yellow and brown and orange and it was really, really nice and I like it a lot and I have it at school and it's in my desk and it's really nice and big.)

In (3), her question seems to be a way to interact and signal solidarity with the reader as well as a means to lend exclamatory weight to the offered news item.

(3)   Querida Yolanda,
       A nosotros los gustaron las galletas. Estaban buenas. Quieren a tener un contest para ver quién agarra 1,000,000 popsicle sticks. *¿Y sabes qué?* ¡Yo tengo una mona bien bien grande y mi hermana dice que se parece a mí!
                                                          Tu amiga,
                                                          P.

(Dear Yolanda,
       We liked the cookies. They were good. They want to have a contest to see who

gets 1,000,000 popsicle sticks. And do you know what? I have a really really big doll and my sister says it looks like me!

>Your friend,
>P.)

Not only did the children vary their sentence types for different purposes, they also varied their verb usage, employing both simple and more "advanced" tenses, such as subjunctive and conditional constructions (4).

(4)   Querido Maestro F.

Nosotros le vamos a escribir una historia porque usted está malo y nosotros no sabíamos que usted estaba malo de la pansa o de la garganta. Nosotros queremos que *vuelva* para atrás a la escuela porque nosotros lo queremos mucho porque usted está bien malo. ¿Qué le duele? ¿Está malo? ¿Bien malo? Que (indecipherable) no se puede levantar de la cama. ¿Por cuál calle es para su casa? Yo no sé donde vive. Si *supiera* donde viviera, yo cuando *saliera* de la escuela me iba para su casa con la bike a verlo como estaba malo o poquito. Nomás que no se levantaba. Yo *quisiera* que usted *estuviera* bien bueno y también yo *quisiera*. . .

>Tu amigo,
>A.

(Dear Mr. F.

We're going to send you a story because you are sick and we didn't know that (if) you were sick in the stomach or the throat. We want you to come back to school because we want it a lot because you are very sick. What hurts you? Is it bad? Very bad? That (indecipherable) you can't get out of bed. What street is your house on? I don't know where you live. If I knew where you lived I, when I left school, I would go to your house with my bike to see how (if) you were really bad or a little (bad). Only don't get up. I wish you were really well and also I wish. . .

>Your friend,
>A.)

Syntactic constructions functioning in certain ways (such as the use of a question as a device to "justify" the provision of later information) reveal that children knew how to exploit syntax for its pragmatic and semantic implications. Regardless of the non-standard forms in the examples that follow, the productions show that their authors understood conditionality and the way strings of contingency statements might be used to build up intensity. Example (5) is an excerpt from a long letter about a Social Studies unit on Creek Indians, written to the Program Director—and designed, we believe, to endear the writer to the addressee by exaggerating the importance of the Director's own interests (students, language, school, etc.). In the end, perhaps the pattern overcame the writer, so that he reversed the contingent conditions—or else his estimate of language exceeded that of even the most dedicated linguist!

(5)   Si no hay sol, no hay leña y si no hay leña no hay papél y si no hay papél no hay
       escuela y si no hay escuela no hay estudiantes y si no hay estudiantes no hay
       lenguajes y si no hay lenguajes no hay niños.

       (If there isn't sun there isn't firewood and if there isn't firewood there isn't paper
       and if there isn't paper there isn't school and if there isn't school there aren't
       students and if there aren't students there aren't languages and if there aren't
       languages there aren't children.)

Stylistic devices, such as strategically placed full or elaborated forms, opening and closing formulae, poetic mood setting, humor, metaphor, and a first
person perspective in stories, along with temporally sequenced pieces, also argue
against a language deprivation position.

Many of the children arranged the events in their writing in an earlier-to-later
order, tying the events with adverbs of time (*anteayer, anoche, ahora*/day before
yesterday, last night, now) or sequence (*first, later*), or with linked and "over-
lapped" phrases, as in (6).

(6)   Yo una vez me fui a la tienda. *De la tienda* me voy a la escuela. Me voy a comer,
       de comer a jugar, *de jugar* me voy a dormir, *de dormir* me hago las cosas.

       (One time I went to the store. From the store I go to school. I go to eat; from eating
       to play; from playing I go to sleep; from sleeping I make things.)

There were examples of genre-specific formulae in the samples. For instance,
colorín colorado él que no se pare se queda pegado (untranslatable) appeared at
the end of a story; *el fin* (the end) or some variation ended many stories but no
other genre; *hoy es* (today is) began all first-grade journal entries.

Some writers used metaphor (*un dinosaurio puede a pisarte y te deja como
una tortilla*/a dinosaur can step on you and leave you flat as a tortilla/pancake);
after eating everything in sight *un hueso loco se hizo bien pansón como un
globo*/a crazy bone became big-bellied like a balloon). Others tried to be funny
or even outrageous. The just-mentioned gluttonous Crazy Bone, for instance,
commented at the end of the story that the furniture he had just devoured needed
un poquito sal y pimienta/a little salt and pepper. Another child writing a story
about a crazy bone allowed the bone to blow his nose on his mother—a particularly flamboyant bit of mischief in this community where it was very important to
be well-behaved and to respect one's elders. Of course the bone insisted at the
end that *no más estaba jugando* (he was only playing).

Occasionally, children created or achieved a poetic quality as the following
three first-grade pieces did. In (7), the dialogue conveys urgency and concern.
The description in (8), followed by an understated (and possibly ironic?) quotation from a radio weather report, captures the gloom and frustration of rainy, no-
outside-recess school days. The opening and closing lines of (9) are simple,
hushed, but dramatic.

(7) Hoy es jueves. 12 febrero 1981
El fantasma asustó a la muchachita y gritó muy recio y su papá se levantó y dijo,—
¿Qué pasó mi hija? ¿Qué pasó? Dime. ¿Qué pasó? Dime. ¿Por qué mataron?
Apúrate, dime—ándale.—

(Today is Thursday, February 12, 1981
The ghost scared the little girl and she screamed very loud and her dad got up and
said, "What happened my child? What happened? Tell me. What happened? Tell
me. Why did they kill? Hurry, tell me, go on.")

(8) Caía lluvia del cielo. Charcos en el piso. Dijo las noticias del radio, el señor del
radio, el señor del radio,—Ya no va a llover—. Fin.

(Rain was falling from the sky. Puddles on the floor. Said the news on the radio,
the man on the radio, "It isn't going to rain anymore.")

(9) Todos los días cae nieve en todas las partes. Y también caía lluvia en todas las
partes y un señor se robó y la policía iba. La policía agarría al señor y lo llevó a la
cárcel y allí se estuvo todos los días. Era cuando estaba cayendo nieve.

(Everyday snow falls everywhere. And also rain was coming down all over and a
man robbed and the police came. The police caught the man and took him to jail
and there he remained forevermore. It was when the snow was falling.)

Elaborate endings (one might imagine hearing these read with the flourish of a
swished cape) were particularly evident among the third-grade samples. In a
response to winning an attendance trophy, Ray wrote in English that the trophy
would *stay with us forevermore because we're coming every day, every day*.

There are good reasons for providing so much evidence (more than will be
presented to counter the other myths) to refute the belief that poor children who
speak non-standard varieties of one or more languages are language-deficient or
semilingual (lacking in vocabulary, complex syntax, and ability to perform certain cognitive operations such as inferring, engaging in syllogistic reasoning, or
making analogies). Since it is an idea with such great potential for harming the
children it labels, it deserves a lengthy rebuttal. It is a suspicion turned into
accepted truth by the fact that many poor minority-language children indeed
perform poorly on tests, with test-like curricula, and in tasks designed for research studies (see Cummins, 1979, for examples). However, authors of the
testing instruments, curriculum materials, and research designs have traditionally
ignored the social and pragmatic features of the language performances, whether
oral or written. Moreover, they have defined success *not* as being able to read
and write but as being able to perform in an instructional program or experiment
that conceives of reading and writing as a cluster of isolable skills (Edelsky et al.,
1983b; Edelsky, 1983a). With a different definition and with a set of school
conditions that permitted them to display their language-using/learning
strengths, the children in this study produced ample proof of the error in any
blanket notions of "deficiency" with written academic language.

2. Children's Errors Are Random or Show Deficiencies versus In Our Data "Errors" Were Often Sensible

The fact that the research team could infer reasons for the children's errors strongly implies that they were sensible; they were the result of a child's efforts to make sense of or connect various ideas and systems. The non-random character of some "errors" was seen in spelling inventions. Children made use of visual information in spelling (*Msr* for *Mrs*). No other likely explanation holds for including the *r*. In spelling *también* as *tabien* or *tanbien*, they were using phonetic categorizations that made nasals part of the vowel or that interchanged nasals. Children who spelled *que* as *cue* were using past visual input for the *u* and phono-grapheme information for the *c*. A spelling strategy of elongating a word while spelling it (so-ou-nn-ding it out) probably accounted for the *ll* in *tenilla* for *tenía*.

A third grader made a distinction even college students have difficulty with (Barkin, 1981)—contrasting the spellings of the homophones *a ser* (to be) and *hacer* (to make). In (10), Jorge varied spelling according to meaning, even though he used a stable invention for *hacer* and its derivatives (Jorge's spellings are in parentheses).

(10)   Si yo fuero mágico yo haría muchas cosas y luego yo sacaría un conejo y muchas cosas más. Y yo le enseñaría a unos muchachos *a ser* (a ser) mágico para que ellos les dijeran a sus mamás que podían *hacer* (aser) mágica. Y cuando crecieran les enseñarían a los animales como *hacer* (aser) muchas cosas y todos los animales fueran amigos y mirarán lo que hacía el animal que estaba haciendo el mágico. Y se sentaban a mirar el magic y el animal que estaba haciendo el magic sacará un pájaro.

(If I were a magician I would do many things and later I would take a rabbit out and many more things. And I would teach some children to be magic so they would tell their mothers that they could do magic. And when they grew up they would teach the animals how to do many things and all the animals would be friends and they will look at what the animal is doing who is doing the magic. And they were sitting down to watch the magic and the animal that was doing the magic will pull out a bird.)

If spelling "errors" were not random, neither were invented punctuation patterns such as a carefully placed period at the end of every line or a capital at the start of each line or hyphens between words (the source of periods at the end of each line may well have been basal readers whose sentences are often one line long), and neither was unconventional segmentation that put spaces between syllables (*es ta ba* for *estaba*) or that clustered together pronouns and verbs which are conventionally separated at times (e.g., *megusta* for *me gusta*) but connected at others (e.g., when the verb is infinitive as in *gustarme*). Non-random too was the substitution of *apache* for *mapache* (raccoon) in a story retelling, illustrated with a teepee and three human figures, about two blind men and their conflicts with a mischievous character identified by the child as *un apache*. (In the original, the rascal is a raccoon, *un mapache*.) Since all lived in the woods and since the topic of the Social Studies unit at the time was Creek Indians (who lived in the woods and related to some animals on some occasions as if they were human), it is possible to imagine this second grader assuming that the original story was related to Indians, but Apaches rather than Creeks.

3. *Young Writers Are Insensitive to the Needs of Their Audiences* versus *The Writers in This Study Often Showed Keen Audience Sensitivity*

In fact, many pieces of writing, especially the letters, showed that the children did take account of the audience. There were arrows and marks drawn so that the reader would know a word spread out over two pages was really one word, or so that an insertion would be read in the intended spot. For instance, in (11) a first grader told the reader to look on the back of the page for the rest of the piece.

Example (11)

(11)   Estimada Maestra,
          Nosotros hicimos popcorn y es muy buena para los dientes de nosotros y también hicimos caldo con vegetales y cebolla y ajo con apio
          →   atrás

(Dear Teacher,
          We made popcorn and it's very good for our teeth and also we made soup with vegetables and onion and garlic and celery
          →   over)

Children tried to establish an explicit bond between writer and reader by commenting on what they had in common. Understandably, this happened most frequently in letters. They established that they shared similar interests with their addressees:

(12)   Querido Mr. F,
Yo te quiero decir feliz cumpleaños tuyos y la maestra me dijo que a tí te gusta pescar y cazar y a mí me gusta cazar también y pescar y ojalá que tengas una fiesta.
Tu amigo,
    E.

(Dear Mr. F,
I want to say happy birthday to you and the teacher told me that you like to fish and hunt and I like to hunt too and fish and I hope you have a party.
Your friend,
    E.)

Based on similar past experience, they offered medical advice (in this case, tinged with the self-righteousness of the Healed),

(13)   Querido Señor F,
Yo le mando esta carta con mucho cariño y ojalá que te alivies pronto y que tengas un día bien bueno y que no te salgas de la cama. Nomás cuando te alivies entonces sí te puedes salir de la cama y también ve a mirar un doctor y que tomes medicina. Y yo te mando muchos saludos y también y yo estaba malo también y me dieron medicina y me alivié y ahora estoy en la escuela con mis amigos y la maestra.
Tu amigo,
    E.

(Dear Mr. F,
I am sending you this letter with much affection and I hope you get better fast and that you have a really nice day and that you don't get out of bed. Only when you get well then you *can* get out of bed and also to see a doctor and that you take medicine. And I am sending you many greetings and also and I was sick too and they gave me medicine and I got better and now I'm in school with my friends and the teacher.
Your friend,
    E.

They scolded a pen pal for not writing enough; asked the principal for personal information about his age (*¿cuánto cumpliste ahora?*/how old are you now?) and about details of his illness when he was sick (see example (4) earlier); and instructed Santa Claus on the best way to deliver a motorcycle, as in (14).

(14)   Yo le voy a llevar esta carta a usted, Santa Clos, para que me de una moto. Y la casa tiene un cuartito y allí puede meter la moto para que no batalle mucho metiéndolo por una ventana. Y mi casa es 13574. Gracias.

(I am going to send this letter to you, Santa Claus, so you'll give me a motorcycle. And the house has a little room and you can put the motorcycle there so you don't have to struggle a lot putting it through a window. And my house is 13574. Thank you.

Since they are asides to a reader, parenthetical remarks provided more evidence that children accounted for a co-participant. In reports and summaries they anticipated their assignment-giving reader's desire for precise information they knew they could not supply. Thus, they wrote disclaimers such as the following: (in a report about a school musical program(*Primero cantaron La Bamba. Después cantaron no me acuerdo como se llama la otra canción que cantaron.*(First they sang The Bamba. Then they sang I don't remember the name of the other song they sang.); (in a report of a weekend event consisting of buying a motorcycle trailer) *Mi papá le dijo que cuánto costaba y parece que le dijo que costaba $120. Allí por allí no me acuerdo.* (My daddy asked her how much it cost and it seems that she told him it cost $120. Whatever, I don't remember.); (in a summary of a movie about characters making an escape by boat (*Ellos no querían a tomar agua del mar porque yo no sé que pasa ellos sabían que el agua tenía mucha sal.* (They didn't want to drink the sea water because, I don't know what might happen, they knew that the water had a lot of salt.)

Children seemed to comply with the desires and demands of their first and probably most influential audience, the teacher, even if she was not the named audience. They told her what she already knew in reports of events she too had participated in. They included Social Studies information in what was supposed to be "creative writing," as in (15).

(15)   (The teacher had provided the title and opening event—discovering that nuts being eaten were rotten—as a "story starter" for the whole class.)

La Nuez Podrida

Un día estaba en mi casa comiendo nueces. Yo pelé una y adentro no estaba una nuez. Salió Abraham Lincoln y estaba recien nacido y pasaron años y años y luego él tenía 20 años y luego se casó y él le gustaba leer la Biblia y luego sus vecinos le traían libros para que los leerá y se pasaba toda la noche en la chiminea leyendo los libros y luego era presidente, 16 presidente, y él se parecía a la nuez porque él nació en la nuez. El Fin

(The Rotten Nut

One day I was at home eating nuts. I peeled one and inside there wasn't a nut. Abraham Lincoln came out and he was just born and years and years passed and then he was 20 years old and then he got married and he liked to read the bible and then his neighbors would bring him books so he will read them and he spent all night on the hearth reading the books and then he was the President, the 16th President, and he looked like a nut because he was born in the nut. The End.)

Even if the named addressee of a letter was not a Spanish speaker, letters were written in Spanish—the language the teacher-as-Examiner (not necessarily the teacher-as-Person) wanted the children to write in. When the teacher valued long pieces, children gave her long pieces, even if they had to write big, leave big spaces, and repeat words and phrases (*y era bien bien bien bien bonito*/ and it was very very very very pretty).

Terms of address appeared in the language that was congruent with the ethnicity (and sometimes the language proficiency) of the person being referred to. The monolingual-English Anglo principal was the recipient of many letters written in Spanish, but he was rarely addressed as *señor*—almost always as *Mr*. The bilingual Anglo program director was addressed as either *Sra* or *Mrs*. Chicana teachers and aides were more often addressed as *Sra* in the children's writing, though they too received an occasional *Mrs*. An example of matching language of address term to ethnic identity is found in example (16), an introductory letter to a pen pal in another classroom.

(16)   Querida Sara,
        Yo me llamo Manuel. Me gusta comer carne y a mí me gusta jugar basebol. ¿A tí te gusta jugar basebol? Y mi maestra se llama *Mrs*. Casper y la second maestra se llama *Señora* Gomez.
        Tu amigo,
        Manuel

        (Dear Sara,
        My name is Manuel. I like to eat meat and I like to play baseball. Do you like to play baseball? And my teacher's name is Mrs. Casper and the second teacher's name is Sra. Gomez.
        Your friend,
        Manuel)

It might seem that the children were simply using the address terms that they had heard; i.e., *Mr* might have been perceived as part of the principal's name since no one seriously called him *Señor*. It was indeed the case that the monolingual Anglos' names included an English title. Adult Chicano names in the school were not so unambiguous however. Orally and in writing (e.g., nameplates on classroom doors, school fliers, memos, and the like), Chicano adults' names began with either the Spanish or the English title with the latter choice seeming to be more frequent. Since the children more often chose to write the Spanish title, it is our impression that they were not replicating the frequency of the oral input; that is, it seemed that the input children received was more often English title plus Spanish surname, while their written output was more frequently Spanish title plus Spanish surname. An analysis of actual oral and written title usage would have been necessary to determine if the children were merely writing a name they had heard or were exercising code choice as appropriate to addressee.

Code choice was also sometimes revealed in connection with, but not in, the actual piece of writing. One second-grade girl read a piece written in Spanish to the monolingual English-speaking principal. Her oral rendition, however, was an unprompted translation into English for his benefit.

These young writers differentiated between insiders and outsiders in the amount of precise information supplied. For instance, an invitation to the Program Director, an insider who knew the schools, contained the following (lack of) information:

(17) (long section about Creek Indians) . . . y Señorita yo voy ¿quiere venir a la clase a vernos bailar una canción de los indios y puede ir y que nos vea a jugar stickball y a comer?

(. . . and Miss, I'm going to, do you want to come to the class to see us dance an Indian song and can you go and in order to see us play stickball and to eat?)

The same child's invitation to an outsider included much more information.

(18) Querida Mrs. Edelsky,
Nosotros vamos a tener una comida el miércoles 17 a las 1:00 PM y es muy sabrosa y dígame si va ir. ¿Sí o no? Y pase el día de Christmas y el salón 4 de la escuela S. Y le va gustar mucho.
Tu amiga,
  Rita

(Dear Mrs. Edelsky,
We're going to have a dinner Wednesday the 17th at 1 PM and it's very delicious and tell me if you're going to go. Yes or no? And spend Christmas day and room 4 of S. School and you're going to like it a lot.
Your friend,
  Rita)

Later letters to in-school pen pals were much more informal than first letters. It was not merely that growth, rather than increased familiarity, was what produced the more intimate later letters. The chatty quality of letters to pen pals written during the fourth collection was not an attribute of letters to out-of-school adults written during the same period.

4. *Young Writers Are Insensitive to Demands of Texts and Contexts* versus *Our Writers Showed Evidence of Sensitivity to These Demands*

There were too many refutations to provide examples of each. For instance, if children had not been sensitive to demands of written as contrasted with texts they would have code switched in writing as often as they did or already noted, written code switching was rare. A first grader would n not have translated the Spanish title of a song (La Víbora del Mar) Spanish, into English (*wiseineicadaochen*/we sang a snake on the to have an all-English written text. Nor would another first grad to switch codes to mirror the oral event in a direct written quotation (*el Popeye dijo—¡¡Yay!!—*/Popeye said, 'Yay!').

There were other features of the written texts that were not characteristic of these same children's oral offerings. For instance, third-grade Ray often explicitly introduced his topics or purposes in written reports (*I still remember about yesterday night* in a report on what happened last night, or *I would like to write about the field trip*). Third graders 'set the mood' in written stories. Words and ideas that might have been an embarrassment to express orally to the Anglo teacher appeared in writing. A first grader wrote that some *gabachos* (derogatory term for Anglos) gave his family food and clothing, making that Christmas a good one. A boy penned that he was able to see the underpants of a dancer in the school program.

One interesting example of children's acknowledgement of an oral vs. written vs. oral-rendition-of-writing distinction occurred during an observation. Three second graders were collaborating to invent a recipe. After several oral suggestions, one boy summarized with rising intonation after each item: *le vamos a poner leche, huevos, masa* . . . (we're going to put (in) milk, eggs, corn meal . . .). As the boy repeated his summary, the scribe wrote, inserting *y* between items even though *y* was not being intoned: *le vamos a poner leche y huevos y* . . . (we're going to put (in) milk and eggs and . . .). Before he could add any more, the aide came by and asked the group to read the recipe. The oral rendering of a text that was supposed to be written but had not been finished did not match either what was written or what had been summarized earlier: *Le vamos a poner leche. Le vamos a poner huevos. Le vamos a poner masa.* Gone were the connecting *y*'s and a repeated frame was added. If the marks on the paper revealed only a slight (if unexpected) difference between written and oral text styles, the oral "reading" showed a considerable impact of text modality.

If there had been no sensitivity to demands of different kinds of texts, it would have been impossible to distinguish letters from journals from stories from other types of writing. In fact, it was most often quite obvious. Journals, letters, and stories had different kinds of headings and beginnings. Stories had titles but journals and letters did not. Direct or indirect dialogue appeared in stories or journals but not in letters. Books, but not other types, sometimes included *escrito por* _____ (written by _____). Most authors did not put their names on journals, but they did on letters. Journal entries, but not other types, were sometimes tied to other entries. Examples (19a) and (19b) illustrate the phenomenon of inter-text tying.

(19a)　4 diciembre 1980 (first entry)

Hoy es jueves. Arbolito hicimos de Christmas. La Miss D. no está aquí. Ahora no está. Me compraron zapatos negros.

(Today is Thursday. We made a little tree for Christmas. Miss D. isn't here. Today she's not here. They bought me black shoes.)

(19b)   5 diciembre 1980 (second entry)

      Hoy es viernes. Y también me compraron un vestido (undecipherable).

      (Today is Friday. And also they bought me a dress (undecipherable).)

Despite the encouragement the first and second graders received for drawing pictures along with their writing, there were no pictures on letters.

    A first grader knew that a word strung out across two pages (due to insufficient space on the first page) had to be counted as one word, that the separateness of pieces of paper could not interfere with the unity of a single word. He lined up the straggling letters and encased them with a special mark to attach them to their preceding parts (example 20).

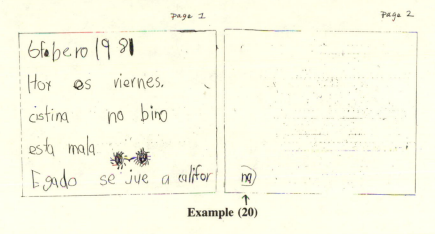

Example (20)

(20)   Hoy es viernes. Cristina no vino. Está mala. Eduardo se fue a California.

      (Today is Friday. Cristina didn't come. She's sick. Eduardo went to California.)

    The youngest children's seemingly random use of upper and lower case letters was not always so random on close inspection. Although many of these first graders did not separate first and last name, they did begin each part of a name with capital letters. (For privacy purposes, the last letters of children's last names have been blocked out in the signatures shown in (21).

    There were other examples of this phenomenon—that the graphic form words took could be affected by the nature of the word itself. First graders often wrote in their journals about going to Circle K (a quick-stop quasi-supermarket) or to K-Mart (a large discount store). They also occasionally wrote about quantities—numbers of days, ages, and so on. They might have abbreviated both store names and number words by writing numerals and ''copying'' K from the store's sign, yet they did not. Instead, they spelled out logos (*ceimart, ceimar* for K-Mart;

Example (21)

circocei, ceircoci for Circle K), but for quantities they either used numerals or numerals combined with words (someone *tiene 12 grado 6/*is 12 years old, 6th grade; someone else received Valentines on *el catorce 14/*the fourteenth). Ferreiro and Teberosky (1982) also found that youngsters differentiated letters from numbers in non-trivial ways in their early concepts about written language. Our subjects extended the distinction to number words and names utilizing letters as words.

5. *Bilingualism Is a Limitation, Especially If the Linguistic Varieties Are Non-Standard* versus *Bilingualism Increased Our Writers' Options for Meaning*

The extent of bilingualism varied from child to child. Still, even what we surmise was minimal proficiency in one of the varieties added to the child's options for interpreting and signaling meaning. Children saw movies or read books in English and wrote about them in Spanish, which provides some evidence that the non-standard dialect of English in which several were proficient was not the only English dialect they knew; they also had some ability to understand the Standard English of movies and books.

By using two codes in writing, the children effectively communicated certain added meanings. For example, by code switching for quotations, a first grader conveyed unambiguously that the quote was direct.

(22)   Un cocodrilo se quería comer a Popeye pero Popeye vió su spinach y la recogió y su
       spinach y la recogió y le pegó al cocodrilo y el cocodrilo se murió y el Popeye
       dijo—¡yay! Y ya se terminó y la pelicula estaba suave, muy suave. El fin. De
       María.

       (A crocodile wanted to eat Popeye but Popeye saw his spinach and he got it back
       and his spinach and he got it back and fought the crocodile and the crocodile died
       and Popeye said, ''Yay!'' And it ended then and the movie was nice, very nice.
       The end. By Maria.)

As already noted, code switching did not necessarily indicate lack of knowledge of the word in the other language; there were pieces of writing that had both *sad* and *triste, raccoon* and *mapache* among other translation pairs. Neither did the use of these pairs provide any evidence for whether or not children knew the switched items belonged to two different languages.[2] What benefit knowledge of the term in each language might have offered the writer, however, was an increase in the number of synonyms for an idea. It may also have allowed another means for expressing emphasis. In (23), completion was an important point to this third grader. Print size increased and two ways of encoding the idea appeared.

(23)   . . . y se fueron afuera y una viejita llegó a la casa de los ositos. Fin. The End.

       (. . . and they went outside and a little old lady came to the three bears' house. The
       End. The End.)

---

[2] Adults who grew up with two languages in the home have reported that they remember being shocked when they discovered that what they had grown up thinking were English words were in fact part of the lexicon of the other language. A graduate student remembered thinking *glorieta* (from Spanish) and *island in the road* were synonymous English phrases. Friends from Brooklyn tell me they did not find out *chaleria* (Yiddish) was not a regional English term for a horrible person or event until college years. I remember thinking *chaloshus* (Yiddish) was simply Yiddish-accented pronunciation of an English word (haloshus) meaning revolting, whose existence I assumed, believing it related to *halatosis*—another disgusting referent!

y se fueron a fuera
y una brejita yego a
la casa de los ositos

FiN The and

Example (23)

6. *Literacy (and Language Proficiency) is Constant Across Contexts, or When You've Got It, You've Got It* versus *Textual Variation Occurred with Contextual Variation*

Evidence has already been cited that young children varied texts to meet demands of different modalities and needs of different audiences. There were additional sources of variation in several aspects of writing.

The main bases for spelling inventions changed when the language of the text changed. That is, while Spanish spellings were often invented on the basis of phonics generalizations (*ll* for *y*) or phonetic features (*tabien* for *también,* with the nasal omitted and presumably categorized as part of the vowel), inventions in first pieces in English were more often based on Spanish orthography (*joup* for *hope*). A change in the language of the text also affected the bases for segmenting language. Spanish words were more often segmented into syllables than English words were; and Spanish verb phrases and noun phrases were more likely than English noun and verb phrases to be unconventionally joined together. Choice of language also affected the existence of lexical links between clauses. English sentences were less frequently joined with *and*.

(24)   We got leaves and put it in the plaster of Paris. There is big bones and little bones. There are big bones bigger than a building. The dinosaurs are big.

By contrast, Spanish texts written the same week by the same child (for instance example 25), typically had *y* or some other link between every main clause.

(25)   Yo ahora vi a una de las señoras de ASU y yo no sabía que ella sabía en ingles y en español y yo voy a estar bien.

   (Today I saw one of the ladies from ASU and I didn't know that she knew how (to talk) in English *and* Spanish and I'm going to be OK.)

Children's own activities could motivate variety in orthographic devices. When first-grade Christina began the next word too close to the preceding one, she inserted a hyphen for separation. Otherwise, she used spaces.

Today is Wednesday.
Today the Ticher brot
a moter sikol and the moteri
col is prite and the
motersikol is now and it kost
alod of mone. Yesterday it
Woz ar program and We.
→ saing [aboutthe] letel rabet
and about the snack And
It Woz fun and i liat
it. Christina

Example (26)

(26) Today is Wednesday.
Today the teacher brought a motorcycle and the motorcycle is pretty and the motorcycle is new and it cost a lot of money. Yesterday it was our program and we sang about the little rabbit and about the snake and it was fun and I liked it.

Materials had an effect. In "shape books" (many pieces of bone-shaped or apple-shaped paper stapled together), children were more likely to supply some character development or to mention a setting than they were when writing stories on regular paper. The availability of colored markers at the first-grade writing center engendered many pieces filled with color words (which were written with corresponding markers—*rojo* written in red, *azúl* in blue, etc.). In attempting to match meaning and marker, several children reverted to earlier spelling for some common words like "and" (e.g., reverting to *i* for *y*).

Type of writing, such as difference in genre or difference between text and signature, also mattered. Children rarely related details or even made any comment about how they perceived the events reported on in journals; they gave "just the facts, ma'am." In expository reports and letters, however, they were more likely to include at least some personal evaluation. When third graders wrote in cursive, they usually did not extend cursive script to their own names. Signatures remained tied to manuscript writing—their earlier resource for signing their names.

Who instigated the piece had an effect on the text. Writing spurred by the intentions of the writer rather than the teacher was often of a different type and purpose than assigned writing. Writing initiated by teachers did not include letters of complaint or genuine thanks, jokes, or songs. Moreover, complaints, jokes, and letters conveying seemingly sincere feeling did not contain tangential ideas strung together like beads, as many assigned letters did.

When children wrote from their own intentionality, they hypothesized about special writing problems, such as how to signal the end of a joke or how to capture the unique rhythm and timing of language when it is sung rather than spoken. A first grader from Ms. A's class tried to graphically display song lyrics as they were sung. Not limited by the calendar, she wrestled with this problem in March, using a song that is part of the Christmas Posadas ritual. She tried out repeated vowels to match the elongation of certain sung words (*tunaaaaaante, mesooooooooon*). Two weeks later, still intrigued by the problem of how to render singing into print but more sure of her solution, she elongated not just a few but many words (example 27).

3-24-81

el nombbe del A *

sieeeeeelo ospidop

osaaaaaada el no

puede aandaaaaaar

no sea un tunaa

aaaaaante.

aqui no es mesooor

sigan adelaaaante

yo no puedo avrit

iiiir no sea un

tunaaaaaaaa aaaaa

aante

Example (27)

(27)   El nombre del cielo
　　　Os pido Posada
　　　Él (Ella) no puede andar.
　　　No sea un tunante.
　　　Aquí no es mesón.
　　　Sigan adelante.
　　　Yo no puedo abrir.
　　　No sea un tunante.

　　　(In the name of heaven

I ask you for shelter
She cannot walk.
Don't be lazy.
This isn't an inn.
Keep on going.
I cannot open up.
Don't be lazy.)

Such hypotheses and struggles never surfaced in assigned writing.

The teacher's presence and questioning was a support in producing some texts. In what may have been an example of the zone of proximal development (Vygotsky, 1978), some children wrote more organized texts, less tied by *y*, when the teacher or aide sat nearby and asked what the child would write next. When the teacher elicited sentences and wrote a group "chart story" in front of the children, she provided a model with a particularly schoolish ring (Santa Claus has a sleigh. The dwarfs help Santa Claus. Santa Claus brings presents. Santa Claus brings sweets, etc.). The children's individual texts based on the Santa Claus chart story were remarkably similar to each other and the model, but were different enough not to have been copied from the board. Absence of links, especially *y*, between clauses was a key feature of these pieces but not others children wrote. Apparently, with the teacher's model in view, the writers were able to and did use her style for this exercise, but it did not appear in any of their other writing.

When both local conventions (e.g., spelling, segmentation, punctuation) and global intentions (e.g., providing an appropriate rendition of a song) varied with context, it is difficult to see the validity of the popular idea underlying the practice of designating a child as reading at a particular "level" or "mastering" certain written language "skills"—as having *one* literacy proficiency. (One *repertoire,* from which alternatives are selected, however, *might* be a reasonable notion.)

MYTHS ABOUT BILITERACY AND BILINGUAL EDUCATION

1. *To Begin Literacy Acquisition in Spanish and Then to Add English Leads to Interference with English Literacy* **versus**
Our Data Indicate Literacy in the First Language Was Applied to, Rather than Interfered with, Second Language Literacy and That the Two Were Kept Separate in Several Ways

Some of the evidence against this myth is not unambiguous. It is possible to interpret much of what follows either as examples showing negative interference or, instead, as examples showing a positive process of application. However, other evidence disambiguates what seems ambiguous.

Krashen (1980) argued against interference and in favor of application when he proposed that second language learners fall back on and use first language rules when their repertoires do not include the appropriate second language rule. That is, rather than being prevented from acquiring a rule in the second language because they already have one in the first language, they use the rule from the first language *until* they acquire the rule in the second. If first language rules interfered with the learning of rules in the second language, then, obviously, no one would ever acquire a second language.

Many of our subjects did indeed use what they knew about literacy in their first language when they wrote in their second language. They used Spanish orthography in English.

(28) nariet   not it
      ai joup llu gou agien   I hope you go again
      tu scull   to school
      baramurosaco   bought a motorcycle
      chi lismi   she lets me
      telebichen   television
      ba llana umen   bionic woman
      stauor   Star Wars

The same child often used similar segmentation types in both first and second language writing. One of the many examples of this appears in (29a) and (29b) where second-grade Arturo used the same bases for unconventional segments in both Spanish and English, segmenting by syllable (underlined once) and also by leaving stranded single non-syllabic letters or joining them to adjacent words (underlined twice).

Example (29a)

(29a) Dear Mr. A.,
       Thank you for showing us the fossils and the telling about the rocks and thank you for giving us rocks. We love you and I love you so much . . .

querido mario grasias
por la canas tita
esta ba mun bonita
y te cero mun ch
por ce tu eres pueno
con mi go i llo
te bo lla ma n da run
can astita

Example (29b)

(29b) Querido Mario,
Gracias por la canastita. Estaba muy bonita y te quiero mucho porque tu eres bueno conmigo y yo te voy a mandar una canastita.

(Dear Mario,
Thank you for the little basket. It was very nice and I like you a lot because you are nice to me and I'm going to send you a little basket.)

Some children used similar syntactic styles in Spanish and English pieces. Many examples of cross-language similarities (in spelling, segmentation, syntactic styles, and so on) provide ambiguous evidence here. That is, one could just as easily say that features of Spanish literacy were *interfering* with English literacy as that Spanish features were being *applied* in English writing.

The disambiguating evidence tilting the scale in favor of an application (vs. an interference) interpretation is *k* spellings and other "sight" spellings. If Spanish orthography had interfered with acquisition of English orthographic rules, all English writing would have been spelled using Spanish orthography. It was not. With the exception of one second grader, no other child used the letter *k* for the Spanish /k/. The letter *k,* which only appears in foreign words in adult Spanish, was reserved for English. Example (30) shows spellings of /k/ by three children; Spanish /k/ on the left and English /k/ on the right.

(30) Child #3   quequis, cecis (quequis)   snack (snake)
      Child #11   cumple anos (cumpleaños)   black
      Child #10   porce (porque)   crikk ingens (Creek Indians)

The following spellings also imply that knowledge of Spanish orthography did not interfere with learning about English orthography and, importantly, that spelling was based on sight as well as sound: *weunt* (went), *MSR* (Mrs.), *the, walkin* (walking).

Cases where the same children segmented differently in English and Spanish will be discussed in the next chapter. For now, the spelling data lend weight to the argument that children were developing separate systems while making use of one system to fill in the holes in the other.

2. *Spanish Spelling Is Graphophonically Regular; Therefore Phonics Instruction in Spanish Results in Consistent Spelling and "Correct" Decodings* versus
These Children Invented Spellings in Spanish and the Inventions Had Multiple Bases

As Natalicio (1979) stated, Spanish diphthongs, consonants, and glides are not at all in one-to-one correspondence with letters. Instead, she gave multiple examples of several spellings for single sounds or sound clusters. In our data, consonant inventions and inconsistencies greatly outnumbered vowel inventions in Spanish pieces while the reverse was true for English. Thus, rather than one regular and one irregular orthography, each of the two are "irregular" in different ways. Moreover, the children's early Spanish phonics instruction may have been what led them astray in some cases. If they learned the lessons in the phonics workbooks that *y* and *ll, b,* and *v, c* and *qu,* etc., "make the same sound," then *llo* (yo), *boy* (voy), and *porce* (porque) were instructionally motivated unconventionalities.

Despite phonics instruction, children used other bases for inventing a spelling in Spanish besides applying generalizations from such lessons. They used the names of letters (*staban* for estaban, *d* for de); phonetic feature categories (spelling all nasals as *n,* for example; substituting liquids for each other, and so on); reversed letters (*b* for *d, q* for *p*), and a variety of other bases (see Appendix 2 for the complete list). That is, like monolingual English-speaking young writers, these children used a variety of kinds of information in order to spell a word. And despite the graphophonic regularity of nuclear vowels in Spanish, they also invented vowel spellings, though these were less numerous than consonant inventions (*casas* for *cosas; puidi* for *pude; feles* for *feliz*).

3. *Exposure to Spanish Print in a Child's Own and Peers' Writing and in a Few Textbooks Provides Sufficient Information About the Nature and Function of Spanish Print* versus
Extensive Interaction with Conventionally Written, Functional Print is Needed for Input and Feedback when Becoming Literate in a Language

Though this study was not designed to compare children's knowledge of the nature and function of print in "writing classrooms" vs. in "workbook or ditto sheet classrooms," it is our subjective impression that the writing classroom children knew more about what writing was for and how to construct a text than did children whose writing consisted of filling in blanks on dittoed worksheets. We wish the myth or at least the operating principle for much of bilingual education was the reality—that a few library books, basal and workbook series, and children's own writing indeed could supply sufficient information about written discourse structures and all the systems of written language (publication norms, genre signals, stylistic devices, written means for accomplishing different intents, spelling and punctuation conventions, and the like) that have to be acquired.

Unfortunately, this was not the case. Exposure to predominantly peer- produced and unconventional print in Spanish may have accounted for the following set of peculiar similarities:

y nios	(indios/Indians)
y la	(y la/and the)
y so	(hizo/he made)

The second-grade child who segmentally and orthographically equated the nominative label for the Social Studies unit, the first syllable of a commonly used verb, and a conjunction and article had interacted with little published print in Spanish.

Despite direct instruction using Spanish print, the print environment and print-in-use data actually showed, in some cases, more interactions with or at least availability of English print. This may have been one reason for first graders' more conventional segmentation of English than Spanish print.

4. *In Order to Read and Write in a Language, One Must Be Orally Fluent in It; the Learning and Instructional Sequence is Listen, Speak, Read, Write* versus
The Different Language Arts Were Not Wholly Used in Any Predetermined Sequence

To some extent, the myth is probably correct. A "completely monolingual" child will be unable to express anything in writing in another language. Though we had no such children among our subjects, the two third graders who had recently arrived from Mexico were barely able to understand or produce any oral English at the start of the year. Most of the other children were also more orally proficient in Spanish. Despite their greater ability in Spanish, many second graders chose library and reference books in English before having reading instruction in English and without speaking much English in class. First graders who did not use much English print and who, during observations, spoke little or no English in class did not refuse or even hesitate to write in English when we requested. Example (31) was produced by a first grader in response to such a request.

today is
Wednesday Mey Memy
Beymy Sem Chiquen
An ay lay quet El et.
An .E y wen Mor chyquen
pet Mey Memy don
Gimi Mor chiquen
pat Ay Cray An
Mey MeMe gimi Mor
chiquen AN May Memy
don limisi da teleBich en
pet Ey Sayat plis
MeMy An chi lismi
Siet de telaBichan
An Eysi da Crtuns

Example (31)

(31)   Today is Wednesday. My mommy buy me some chicken and I like it a lot and I want more chicken but my mommy don't give me more chicken but I cry and my mommy give me more chicken and my mommy don't leave me see the television but I said, "Please Mommy" and she lets me see it the television and I see the cartoons.

It is clear that this first grader used quite varied information sources in order to produce this text. Not just oral English but knowledge of Spanish orthography, Spanish and English word order, English lexicon, knowledge of segmentation, punctuation, journal conventions for her classroom—all this entered into the production of this piece.

Other children too, with less oral proficiency in English, were still able to convey meaning, punctuate, and spell in that language. In fact, an English piece by a given child was often identical on some dimension to Spanish pieces written by that child. A third grader who used an invented punctuation pattern of capital to start the first page, period to end the last, and no other punctuation in Spanish pieces, used the same pattern in English pieces. Similar syntactic styles and pragmatic solutions (e.g., how to end a piece) appeared across languages. In other words, it was not necessary to have "total control" over oral English in order to read and write in English. Nor was it necessary to read English, especially to read it "officially" (i.e., to be assigned to an English reading group), in order to write it (Hudelson, 1984).

MYTHS ABOUT THE TEACHING OF WRITING

1. *Learning Comes from Teaching and Therefore, a Precise, Detailed, Instructional Sequence Must Be Planned* **versus**
Many Features of the Writing Could Not Be Traced to Direct Instruction

Children read and wrote in English without literacy instruction in English. Example (32) is a spontaneous story, written in English in a non-study second-grade classroom in the Bilingual Program.

(32)   Ones supon a time ther livd a good harted lien. He difrent from de adrs. He was good toode adr animoles and de adr animoles wer good too hem. Ande he dident like too fite and he dident like de adr animol too fite. He somtims guen da abr animoles fite gued hime an he liked too play and he livd gapolievr aftr.

   (Once upon a time there lived a good hearted lion. He (was) different from the others. He was good to all the other animals and the other animals were good to him. And he didn't like to fight and he didn't like the other animal to fight. He sometimes when the other animals fight with him and he liked to play and he lived happily ever after.)

Obviously, this second grader used knowledge of Spanish orthography to write this piece, along with use of his own non-standard pronunciation of English. But note the features that had their origin in untaught English orthography—silent *e*, "sight" words, double letters, and the like.

The children invented punctuation that was not taught, such as stars between sentences (33),

1 diciembre 1980.
Hoy es lunes.
papá me da un pato.
asiero un pari.
mecomiandarieeraunafol

Example (33)

(33)   Papá me da un pato. Hicieron un party. Me comí un dari y era un atole.

   (Papa gives me a duck. They made a party. I ate a Dairy (Queen) and it was an atole.)

upright bars at the end of a story, periods at the end of every line, capitals at the start of every page of a multi-page piece, and a hyphen between each word or group of words. No one taught them such punctuation.

Their spelling instruction includes phonics "rules" and attention to visual features (e.g., tildes, accents). The children used more than that information, however. They used phonetic features (spelling according to place or manner of articulation), and a sounding-out strategy (e.g., inserting a sound when elongating the pronunciation as in *mayestra* for *maestra*). Without instruction in any conventional markings for revision, one child used vertical arrows (↕) when he inserted a word after a line had been written. There were no explicit lessons on segmentation, and yet the children's segmentation became more conventional over time.

Even when children were explicitly taught, their own hypotheses were often stronger than the teachings. For instance, first graders were instructed in and provided with several forms which they were to use—letter headings, *hoy es* _____ on journal entries. They did use those forms. But interesting contrasts occurred. Example (34) shows the taught version of *hoy* and the child-hypothesized version.

9 Febrero 1981

Hoy es lunes.

→ oy la mallestra

no bino porce-

es tamala y

bino otra m llesta

Example (34)

(34)   Hoy es lunes. Hoy la maestra no vino porque está mala y vino otra maestra.

(Today is Monday. Today the teacher didn't come because she is sick and another teacher came.)

Although other children too spelled *hoy* unconventionally (usually *oy* or *oi*) immediately after copying the conventional spelling from the board, more children used another word altogether when meaning "today"—*ahora*. Thus both spelling and lexical choice frequently bypassed direct instruction. Similarly, lessons and exercises for third graders on capitals to start and periods to end sentences lost out in favor of children's own hypotheses to begin a *piece* (rather than a sentence) with a capital and to end a *piece* with a period. First-grade teaching of both tildes and capitals to start sentences did not meet with equivalent "success." Tildes were tried out; capitals as punctuation (rather than as handwriting) were not. Not only did children learn more than what was taught, then, but they abstracted from what was taught in order to arrive at their own forms.

2. *Sense of Audience Is a Discrete Skill Which Should be Taught at a Particular Grade Level* versus *Sense of Audience Was a Perspective Our Subjects Developed through Interactions*

When the audience was unambiguous and the intention for the writing came from the writer, the piece was more likely to reflect audience sensitivity. Unfortunately, however, much of the writing in this program, even the writing of letters, was "pretend-functional"—having one ostensible social function, but only superficially hiding its evaluative purpose (e.g., write a letter to Mr. A, thank him, and tell him everything you learned about dinosaurs). The children knew that the teacher was the primary audience. Many wrote in Spanish (the teacher preferred this) even though Mr. A only spoke English. It would have been difficult to develop sensitivity to a named audience in assignments where it was unclear who the audience really was and what purpose the letter really served (politeness? evaluation?).

However the same second graders, whose letters to monolingual English-speaking Mr. A were in Spanish, wrote pen pal letters to unambiguously defined audiences. In these they were able to negotiate relationship issues,

(35) Querida Elsa,
      Yo te voy a decir porque me rayaste poquito pero yo no estoy enojado . . .

      (Dear Elsa,
      I'm going to tell (ask) you why you wrote me (so) little, but I'm not angry . . .)

and could directly address mutual concerns (*will you wear lipstick?*). In Mr. M's class, one of the non-study second grades described earlier, there were mailboxes for each person, and children wrote letters promoted by their own desires rather than by assignment. They were genuinely functional. Some sympathized with the teacher's role (*I knew you didn't want to punish us but we deserved it*), scolded (*why didn't you answer sooner*), and complained, expecting and getting a resolution of the problem. In September, Elisa wrote:

(36) Maestro, yo le mando esta libro de carta. Hoy Eugenio me pega mucho cuando vamos al recreo y a comer y cuando vamos a comer y cuando estoy haciendo la

tarea aquí en la escuela. Me pega mucho y yo no quiero que me pegue porque es muy trabieso conmigo y con los demás no es trabieso. Nomás conmigo y conmigo. Nomás conmigo.

(Teacher, I'm sending you this letter in a book. Today Eugenio hits me a lot when we go to recess and to eat and when we go to eat and when I am doing homework here at school. He hits me a lot and I don't want him to hit me because he is very bothersome with me and with the others he isn't bothersome. Only with me and with me. Only with me.)

Upon receipt of the complaint, Mr. M agreed to allow Elisa to sit near Tony instead of Eugenio. Five days later he received this "follow-up."

(37)   Maestro, ahora sí estoy mejor porque Tony no me pega ni me habla porque él quiere hacer trabajo. Él nomás me dice que si le presto el color café o el borador y él nomás me pide eso porque él no es trabieso conmigo. Su carta escrito por Elisa.

(Teacher, now I *am* better because Tony doesn't hit me. Neither does he talk to me because he wants to do the work. He only tells (asks) me if I (could) loan him the brown crayon or the eraser and he only requests that, because he isn't bothersome to me. Your letter written by Elisa.)

A similar kind of audience sensitivity in letters was found in the non-study first-grade class of Ms. A. Though she directed other subjects extensively, Ms. A gave her children few directions in writing. Some wrote to her, not then as a giver-of-assignments and an evaluator, but as a related-to-Other. One child began her written joke with *Voy a decirle un joke, OK?* (I'm going to tell you a joke, OK?). Another wrote that she was glad Ms. A had returned to school and when it was her birthday, she would invite Ms. A to her party. The rest of the letter contained many signals of graciousness, intended to ensure acceptance of the invitation.

(38)   . . . si puede traer la bebita y su esposo y va ver todos mis amiguitos y a lo mejor mira a mis hermanas. Yo voy a escoger el pastel mas bueno para Ud. y le voy a dar medio de mi pastel para que se lleva para la casa para que se lo coman agusto . . .

(. . . if you can bring the baby and your husband and you're going to see all my little friends and at least see my sisters. I'm going to choose the best cake for you and I'm going to give you half of my cake so you might take it home to eat it at your leisure . . .)

Such sense of audience did not have to wait for lessons in the fourth grade (or whenever it might have been required by a scope and sequence chart). Instead, it occurred with the help of teachers who allowed or actively encouraged the use of written language to pursue and nurture genuine relationships between writer and reader.

3. Writing is Sufficient for the Development of Writing versus What Happened to a Piece During and After It Was Written Was Part of the Developmental Picture

From the variety of classroom practices we observed, along with longitudinal samples we gathered, it seems that not writing alone, but what was done or not done with the writing had great impact on writing development. Each of the three study classrooms had characteristic approaches to treatment of the children's writing.

For instance, the first-grade teacher and aide often asked children for more information; the children's writing remained in folders. The second-grade teacher and aide complimented the child. Some of the writing remained in folders, some in the children's desks. The third-grade teacher and aide corrected spelling, punctuation, and English grammar. Third-grade papers were occasionally kept by the teacher. Most were disposed of as the children desired.

The writing reflected this treatment. First-grade pieces were often in two parts: the original and an unintegrated "addendum." Third graders often crumpled their papers; occasionally, they copied them over to "clean them up." Second-grade pieces showed little evidence that writers had re-read their own pieces either during or after the writing (there were almost no erasures; there were frequent instances of repetition of a word or phrase, as if the writer had looked up, then begun again, forgetting where s/he had left off, repeating the last word or leaving out words that had been originally intended).

Writing, yet no honoring of that writing in a published product, no discussion of content—just writing and lots of it per piece was even destructive in some ways. It encouraged the view that ideas did not need more than superficial corrections, that numbers of pages mattered more than sense.

Though how the children's work was treated had a significant impact (third-grade correction for form resulted in copied-over, corrected pieces; first-grade requests for more information produced two-part pieces; second-grade ignoring of content and an emphasis on quantity resulted in loosely associated pieces full of repetitions), writing alone *did* have some benefits. It must have given children enough confidence in themselves as writers so that almost all tried to write in English, regardless of their oral proficiency, on the one occasion when we asked teachers to make that request. Moreover, the act of writing forced them to cope with several sub-systems of written language at once. Unlike the classes where children only wrote phonics-exercise kinds of phrases or where they only filled in worksheets, these children had to wrestle with syntax, spelling, referential meaning, handwriting, punctuation, and writing for a particular audience, in response to particular task demands which were usually set by someone else. Though it may seem paradoxical, it is the multiplicity of systems supporting each other that eases the burden of acquiring a complex super-system like written language

(Harste, 1980b). In that respect, writing alone was beneficial. But it is our feeling that the benefits could have been augmented greatly if the teachers had used the writing interactively.

MYTHS ABOUT LEARNING TO WRITE

1. *Growth in Writing Is a Linear Accretion of Discrete Skills* **versus** *Growth Seemed Tentatively but More Aptly Characterized as Successive Reorganizations*

The counter evidence here is indirect and tenuous. Taking the view that growth was *reorganization* of a child's literacy knowledge, a reorganization that came about as the child had the chance to orchestrate the demands of multiple systems, it was possible to see how increased demands from one system affected the production of another. The argument against accretion of discrete skills, then, relies on some of the same evidence that denies the assumption that literacy is constant across contexts. If "skills" accumulated in linear fashion, then Christina's several-months-old conventional spelling of *y* would not have regressed to an earlier *i* spelling when she struggled to match color of marker to meaning of word (*rojo i verde*); handwriting would not have improved when syntax was simple and repetitive; and segmentation would not have "deteriorated" with more difficult content. Of course, such variability could have simply meant that the skills had not been "completely mastered" (though surely it should be acknowledged that even highly literate adults also use different spelling and handwriting variants when struggling with difficult ideas in a first draft). To claim that this variability not only reflected the moment-to-moment competition of demands from simultaneous systems (orthographic, semantic, syntactic, pragmatic), but that it also proves reorganization is a big jump. For that, we need data that show multi-sub-system changes.

There were such data, but unfortunately, an incomplete set. These were data that show one view of *text,* at one period of time, with attendant segmentation, clausal links, and spelling, and then later views of *text* with attendant segmentation, links, and spelling. These hint at systemic shifts. Unfortunately, the earliest texts we have are probably too late to show a dramatic difference in what counted as a text to a given child. The earliest texts we have (from first graders written in late Fall) consisted of sentences related sometimes by topic, each having "its own line," segmented only *between* sentences, and containing no (or few) lexical links between clauses, as (39) shows.

(39)   Hoy es miércoles. Puse el arbolito. Hicimos unos angeles. Hicimos unas flores.

   (Today is Wednesday. I put (up) the little tree. We made some angels. We made some flowers.)

3diciembre 1980

Hoy esmiercoles.

bußelabelito.

asimos unángieles.

asimo unasfores,

Example (39)

My suspicion is that there was a preceding time when a piece might have consisted of *un*related ideas, when, to the writers, what made several words a text was their appearance on the same sheet of paper. By early Spring, two months after the production of example (39), this first grader's (and other children's) written system seemed to have undergone a reorganization (example 40).

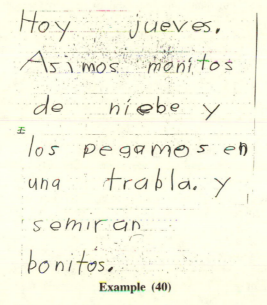

Hoy   jueves.

Asimos monitos

de niebe y

los pegamos en

una trabla. y

semiran

bonitos.

Example (40)

(40) Hoy jueves. Hicimos monitos de nieve y los pegamos en una tabla y se miran bonitos.

(Today is Thursday. We made little snow figures and we pasted them on a mat and they looked pretty.)

A different view of textness is reflected here—one where boundaries were determined by content rather than by the paper a message was written on. Segmentation was now more conventional; a sentence and even a word could appear on more than one line or even one page, periods sometimes marked the end of the text, and main clauses were explicitly bound to each other with lexical links (usually *y*).

According to Harste, Burke, and Woodward (1983), it is through having to cope with all systems simultaneously that a child's system is reorganized (i.e., develops). When children went through drills (such as handwriting exercises where the child's name was written repeatedly) without having to cope with other systems (syntax, semantics, pragmatics), there seemed to be no increased control over what was drilled. Instead, they devised procedural strategies such as writing all the *d*'s and then all the *a*'s.

2. *There Is One Pattern of Writing Development and All Children Go Through It* versus
Within Very General Patterns, Children's Hypotheses and Shifts of Emphasis Were Often Individually Idiosyncratic

To a limited extent, our data could be used to support the idea of a universal developmental pattern. For instance, no child segmented by syllable in September and by clustering whole sentences together in April, although the reverse was true. By and large, however, there was great individual variation in the hypotheses the children created. Using hyphens to separate words was the invention of a few children, stars between sentences the creation of one boy, *k* for *qu* but *c* for *c* in Spanish words was an equivalence for only one child. Additionally, some children seemed loyal to hypotheses concerning spelling, segmentation, beginnings, or endings for the entire year; others were much more fickle.

What did seem to be "universal" was the process of hypothesis-construction and the tremendous intra-individual variation under different writing circumstances. As for "pattern of development," though there were group patterns concerning particular aspects, no child followed the group pattern for all aspects. (This will be discussed in greater detail in the next chapter.)

3. *Writing Is a Solitary Activity* versus
Observation and the Written Pieces Themselves Showed That the Process was Highly Social

Children talked as they wrote—about topics other than what they were writing about and also (occasionally) about what they would write or (more frequently) had written. Not only did the event feature socializing, but pieces of writing sometimes showed the influence of conversations concerning what was being written. Three third graders wrote similar pieces about Sammy Skunk (a made-up character) who stunk. Several second graders were so excited by the idea of a crazy bone who outrageously blew his nose on his mother that they each included the same incident in their own Crazy Bone stories. Several first graders on the same day drew lines on paper at the writing center and then numbered the lines.

"Social" also means child–adult, not only peer, interaction. This too was reflected in the pieces. Adults' questions resulted in second parts of pieces, and adults' corrections were accounted for in edited copies. At this point in their writing development, adult–child interactions influenced a piece of writing obviously and immediately. Presumably, such interactions would later become internalized and their influence would appear more indirectly and less immediately.

4. *Becoming Literate Means Learning Skills to Mastery* versus *The Child's Job Was to Construct, Revise, and Abandon Hypotheses*

Many segmentation hypotheses were based on syntax. For example, there were unconventional segments with no space within a verb phrase (underlined once in (41)), no space within a prepositional phrase (underlined twice in (41)), no space within a sentence or main clause (underlined three times in (41)), a space between but not within a noun phrase and a verb phrase (42). Others were based on phonology or morphology (43).

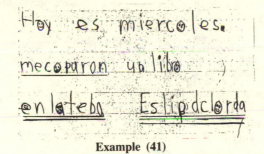

Example (41)

(41)   Hoy es miércoles. Me compraron un libro en la tienda. Es libro de colorear.

(Today is Wednesday. They bought me a book at the store. It's a coloring book.)

Example (42)

(42)   Hoy es jueves. Me gusta el Niño de Dios y los reyes le trajeron . . .

(Today is Thursday. I like the Son of God and the kings brought him . . .)

llo le bolla a lle bar, esto
cantauste san toclos
paraceme de un amoto
y la casea tieneuncuantito
yalli puede meter elamoto
paceno batalle mun cho metiendo
lo poruna ben tanana ymicasa
es 13574 grasias

Example (43)

(43)   Yo le voy a llevar este carta a Ud. Santa Clos para que me de una moto. Y la casa
tiene un cuartito y allí puede meter la moto para que no batalle mucho metiéndolo
por una ventana. Y mi casa es 13574. Gracias.

(I'm going to send you this letter Santa Claus so you'll give me a motorcycle. And
the house has a little room and you can put the motorcycle there so you won't
struggle a lot putting it through a window. And my house is 13574. Thank you.)

Punctuation was accomplished with a variety of invented patterns: periods at
the ends of lines (44), capitals at the start of lines, periods at the end of each page
of a multi-page piece, a capital to start each page of a multi-page piece, a capital
to start and a period to end a piece but no internal punctuation (45), and so on.

(44)   Hoy es martes./Mi papá me/compró el guajolote/y es grande el/guajolote. Es-
taba/frío el guajolote/y mi mamá lo/va a cocinar.

(Today is Tuesday. My dad (me)/bought the turkey/and it's big the/turkey. It
was/cold the turkey/and my mama (it)/is going to cook (it)./)[3]

(45)   Había una vez un fantasma. Andaba alrededor de la casa. Hacía mucho ruido y mi
papá lo mató. No pude dormir. Desperté y le dije que andaba un fantasma.

(Once upon a time there was a ghost. It was walking around the house. It was
making a lot of noise and my dad killed it. I couldn't sleep. I woke up and said to
him that a ghost was walking around.)

Surely "skill learning" doesn't capture what was happening in these examples and others as children segmented and punctuated written language. Neither

---

[3] This translation is presented word-for-word in order to show that the punctuation (period at the
end of each line) was not influenced by syntax or semantics.

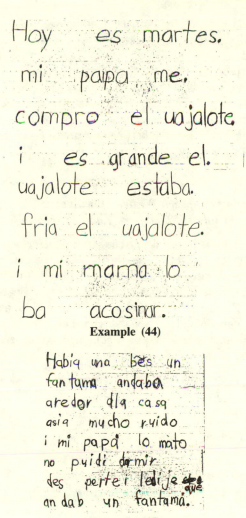

Hoy es martes.
mi paipa me.
compro el uajalote.
i es grande el.
uajalote estaba.
fria el uajalote.
i mi mama lo
ba acosinar.

Example (44)

Habia una bes un
fantuma andaba
aredor dla casa
asia mucho ruido
i mi papa lo mato
no puidi dormir
des peiter ledije que
andab un fantama.

Example (45)

is "skill learning" an apt description for the children's differential treatment of logos and numbers, as described earlier.

Some children developed hypotheses about how to end texts ("nicely" or politely—e.g., *es bueno*/it's good, *gracias maestra*/thank you teacher; or with finality—e.g., *es todo lo que quiero decir*/it's all I want to say, *el fin*/the end). All hypothesized about how to spell words, relying on a variety of bases such as: phonetic features (point of articulation in *eschreya* for *estrella*), Spanish orthography for English (*ai joup llu gou*/I hope you go), and speech community norms of pronunciation (*muncho* for *mucho*). Some temporarily categorized the tilde (˜) as an accompaniment for any nasal (viño) or any /y/ sound (sẽ llama). One child extended his teacher's "rule" for journal beginnings (*hoy es* _____ was to appear at the top of the first page of every entry), to writing in general, putting *hoy es* _____ somewhere on every piece he wrote. A first grader in Ms. A's class struggled with the problem of how to display dynamic singing in static print. She came up with the answer shown earlier in example (27).

It was the creation of hypotheses characterized by invention, abandonment, adaptation, closer approximation, seeming regression, and overgeneralization, that was happening. To call spaces between syllables "skill learning" or to call the final hypothesis "mastery" is to deny the complexity of the child's role and the in-process process.

5. *Beginning Writing Is Speech Written Down* versus *These Children's Writing Differed from Their Speech in Several Ways*

The children's oral narratives did not end with politeness or explicit finality (*gracias maestra*/thank you teacher, *el fin*/the end); written texts did. With the exception of playground rhymes and chants, language not intended for print did not feature a frame repeated in quick succession. For instance, *me gusta X, me gusta Y, me gusta Z* was not a typical structure in an oral monologue, but it was common for written monologues. Even though the children were well beyond the point of using telegraphic speech, some beginners wrote telegraphic-like sentences in both their weaker and stronger languages.

(46)   Today is Wednesday. We play store. We have stuff to play. *Teacher brought motorcycle. We see black.*

(47)   Hoy es lunes. Miramos una novia. Miramos una muchachita. Andaba vestido de blanco. Comimos en el carro. *Soda. Mis hermanos. Comimos.* Mi papá toma cerveza.

(Today is Monday. We saw a bride. We saw a little girl. She was going along dressed in white. We ate in the car. Soda. My brothers. We ate. My dad drinks beer.)

The most striking difference between their oral and written language, however, was the infrequency of written but the prevalence of oral code switching. (This is discussed in detail in Chapter 5.) If their writing had been speech written down, such a discrepancy would not have occurred.

6. *In Considering Direction of Control (or Who Controls What), It Is the Writer Who Controls the Text* versus *Sometimes the Text Seemed to Take Over and Control the Writer*

For instance, a thought in advance about how a piece of writing would look (e.g., the spellings of *queremos* and *que*) may have been the impetus for the spelling of *clase* in (48).

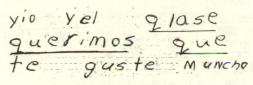

Example (48)

(48)   . . . yo y el clase queremos que te guste mucho . . .

(. . . the class and I want you to like it a lot . . .)

This child spelled all other instances of *clase* with a *c*.

In (49), the sound of the onomatopoetic *miau* may have triggered the association with *miar* (to pee) that then resulted in the out-of-the-blue quotation ''tu miado, yo cagado.'' Although this is interpretable as a verbal assault in the fight scene between the cat and the hen, it still seems likely that it was something about the already-written text (the word *miau*) that influenced the production of what was yet to come.

(49)   Yo tengo un pollito. El pollito hace— ¡pio, pio!—. El pollito se va a jugar y viene. Tiene hambre. El pollito hace—¡pio, pio!—. El gato lo persigue. La madre lo pica y el gato hace—¡miau!—. Y la gallina le hace—*tu miado y yo cagado*—. Por eso la gallina y mi pollito dice la gallina y el pollito estaba escondido. Tenía miedo que el gato lo agarrará.

(I have a chick. The chick says, ''Peep, peep.'' The chick goes out to play and comes (back). He's hungry. The chick says, ''Peep, peep.'' The cat chases him. The mother bites him and the cat goes, ''Meow'' and the hen says to him, ''I peed and you pooped.'' Therefore the hen and my chick say the hen and the chick was hidden. He was afraid the cat will catch him.)

Text controlling (taking over, influencing) writer may be one way to think about similarities across texts by the same author. Sometimes it seemed that a child found a way to say something and was so pleased with the find in one text that s/he used the device in several more. A second grader used *grande no chiquito* (big, not little) in a report on April 9th. On the 10th, he used the idea of opposition in two more pieces.

(50)   4/9/81
       Yo quiero un perro *grande no chiquito*. (Undecipherable) quiero un grande y yo tenía un perro chiquito y estaba creciendo *grande no chiquito*.

       (I want a big dog, not a little one. (Undecipherable) I want a big one and I had a little dog and it was growing, big, not little.)

(51)   4/10/81
       . . . y estoy acabando la letra *grande* (undecipherable) no puedo hacer una *chiquita* y ya acabé.

(. . . I'm finishing the big letter (undecipherable) I can't do a little one and now I finished.

52)   4/10/81
Querida Sonia,
Yo quiero una letra *grande no chiquita* . . .

(Dear Sonia,
I want a big letter not a little one . . .)

¿Bien o no? (OK or not?) was the device discovered by another second grader. He was pleased enough to use it several times.

(53)   4/7/81
Sammy,
¿Estás *bien o no?* Te voy a decir que buscas los palos de los ice cream . . .

(Sammy,
Are you OK or not? I'm going to tell you to look for the ice cream sticks . . .)

(54)   4/10/81
Sammy,
¿Bien o no? Ahora vino un hombre . . .

(Sammy,
OK or not? Today a man came . . .)

In other words, a piece of writing and a writer were interacting with each other—with the writer, at least sometimes, obviously listening to the text, doing its bidding.

DISCUSSION

Although these data have been presented as refutations of specific beliefs, the beliefs belong to prevailing paradigms pertaining to literacy and biliteracy. I use "paradigm" to emphasize that the beliefs comprise a worldview, not just a set of discrete items. Paradigms wield their power by determining how to look at phenomena—where to draw the boundaries, what questions to ask, what to count as answers—which in turn determines what one sees. In this chapter, the paradigms have been unpacked in order to parade their individual, incorrect parts. Such a presentation may have implied that the solution is to replace each erroneous belief, one for one, with an opposing set. However, that would be only a surface improvement. The more profound implication is the need to install a new paradigm altogether for writing, reading, and biliteracy.

New paradigms entail the need for new "organizers" and new issues. Regarding writing in bilingual programs, that would mean throwing out old ones like "skills," "interference," "mastery," "readiness," "four separate language arts." It would mean finding new categories that would illuminate rather than distort the phenomena in research, that would support rather than interrupt the process in instruction.[4]

New units, not just new issues, must also be brought into focus. For instance, our subjects based many of their unconventional segments on the syllable. (Clay, 1977; Milz, 1980; and Ferreiro & Teberosky, 1982 also found the syllable to be an important unit in young children's acquisition of written language.) Yet adult "logic" usually plans for an instructional focus on letters and words. Units that function meaningfully for the learner might warrant more consideration in educational practice. In the final chapter, I will discuss at length the implications of this study for the units of discourse children are expected to grapple with (whole written discourses, akin to speech events, that exist outside of school—like stories, letters, lists, notes, news articles, reports, and the like—as contrasted with artificial, analytic units like sentences and paragraphs).

The myth/reality data presented here also have implications for various aspects of thinking about language proficiency and second language literacy. Since our subjects code switched so frequently in speech, it is easy to understand why they have been considered (by the linguistically unsophisticated) to be speakers of one hodge-podge variety, or (by some with more linguistic sophistication) to be speakers of one variety with inherent variability. It is thus a major finding that the children code switched so rarely in writing. What this means is that under certain conditions they were indeed able to stay in one language at a time. Having written language data not only quells any doubts about the number of systems these children were manipulating, it also provides another piece of a complex picture—a person's language competence. The implication is that it would seem wise to consider using written as well as oral language samples when attempting to ascertain language proficiency.

Based on the evidence in this chapter, the ideas of language interference and language deficit deserve considerable revising (interference) or outright abandonment (deficit). Our subjects' abilities to talk and write Spanish did not prevent them from acquiring English. Instead, they were developing two written language

---

[4] Harste and Y. Goodman have contrasted support vs. interruption of literacy processes (Harste, 1981). My extension of this distinction directs educators first to understand the linguistic, psychological, and socio-historical nature of the *process* of writing, for instance, not of separate writing skills. Then, it means we must look closely at writers' revelations about their own process (by observing their behavior, listening to what they say while they write or talk about their writing, reading journals they keep about their writing), relate this privileged information to what we know about the writing process, and provide help that allows writers to participate in the process of writing and *not* the process of *something that only simulates writing*. Interrupting the process would be to give some direction, lesson, or response that counters and distorts the process by sending the writer off in cross-directions or setting tasks that are not accounting for what the writer is trying to do, for the writer's own pace and rhythms, for the integrity of the written language system the writer must work with.

systems by, in part, applying what they knew about first language writing to second language writing. They applied specific hypotheses, more general strategies, and abstract knowledge about language and literacy. Our data make a plausible case for conceiving of the process of acquiring literacy in the second language as one of application. By definition, that means viewing the children as knowers and doers, as people with linguistic and conceptual strengths. Ultimately, what this implies is the imposition of a precious burden on poor minority language children—the burden of high expectations that they indeed have what it takes to succeed in learning to read and write.

This study's refutation of the children's supposed language deficit emphasizes the need to ask some hard questions. If we cannot blame non-existent language deficits for various problems, then why in fact are these children and their counterparts in other schools "at high risk" educationally? Why are they the targets of "early identification" and "language/concept remediation"? *High risk in relation to what?* I believe they are more likely to meet "educational" failure in schools where literacy exercises and tests of literacy "skills" constitute a closed, coherent, typical but misguided circle of curriculum and assessment. Our data point to the idea that in classrooms where authentic literacy would be the main event—in both instruction and assessment—these children would not be "at risk" in the first place.

The children's ability in their mother tongue should not be the first place to look for the source of their educational difficulties. More likely explanations would be: (1) the powerlessness of their parents; (2) an absence of "trusting relations" between children and school adults (McDermott's, 1977, term for a situation where adults and children can make sense out of each other's interactional work); (3) school definitions (and the institutional machinery and administrative policies stemming from these definitions) that equate literacy with scores on reading tests and school success with scores on achievement tests (so that what is to be made sense of is the playing out of a program based on the idea that writing and reading consist of separate skills); (4) pressure from an assortment of businesses that profit from maintaining definitions of literacy and school success that assure social class-related differences in success. If we are serious about reducing the "risk" to poor minority language children, then a correct analysis is necessary. Solutions to non-problems (e.g., special classes to remedy the children's supposed language deficit) should not be a feature of educational policy.

The data in this chapter also argue against many common school practices. Among them are separating the language arts into reading as distinct from writing as distinct from speaking as distinct from listening; establishing uniform sequences of discrete objectives; assessing literacy on the basis of one piece of writing or one "reading"; assuming a constant literacy "level" regardless of contexts. These practices found no support in our data. Neither did some key ideas inherent in these practices—ideas like "becoming literate means learning separate skills" and "learning comes from teaching."

What we had instead was evidence of changes, leaps, backtracks, and appearances and disappearances of child-generated hypotheses. New hypotheses, revisions in old ones, and reorganization of several could and did occur within any of the sub-systems of written language. It was impossible to predict, for any given piece, which system would be favored with a radical new hypothesis or even a minor revision in an old one. It seems crucial, therefore, to have children be engaged with whole, authentic written discourse—to have to contend with all sub-systems at once so that they have the chance to hypothesize about something as global as audience or as local as a period. The "skills" perspective would have children manipulate other people's language in exercises aimed at particular pieces of sub-systems in artificial assignments that eliminate or distort the connections between some of the interacting systems of written language. When our children were involved in such activity, their products showed it. On the other hand, when the children wrote genuine whole texts, they explored in ways that were never evident in their other writing.

Replacing exercises on separate skills with authentic use of intact written language does not mean the teacher's role becomes less significant. The examples I have presented here, especially those concerning segmentation, punctuation, and spelling, show that children often learned without direct instruction and teachers often taught without immediate evidence of learning. That does not mean that teaching and learning were unrelated, but the connections were often subtle, indirect, and only ascertainable after-the-fact. They certainly did not require the mediation of standard scope-and-sequence chart objectives which encourage teachers to take credit or blame for all learning. Instead, our data encourage teachers to be midwives to hypotheses, stage setters for print environments, coaches of literacy risk-takers, but not managers of input–output pairs.

Most immediately, I hope this presentation of data contrasted with common beliefs inspires teachers and researchers alike to look in two directions: inward—to become aware of their own possibly unacknowledged underlying beliefs about literacy, Language Arts instruction, bilingualism, and language proficiency, and then to hold them up for examination; and outward—to look more closely at children's writing for what it *is* rather than what it is not.

Chapter 5

TALLIES AND COMPARISONS

The preceding chapter concerned various topics related to writing and written language—learning, teaching, proficiency, and so on. It was based primarily on pieces viewed individually. This chapter concerns development; the evidence here comes mostly from comparisons of pieces.

We began with a "sociolinguistic" position—that development always occurs *in* a context. From the findings based on tallies of codings to be presented here and from evidence presented in the preceding chapter, we now believe that it was only *through* contexts that children generated individual and successive hypotheses about different cuing systems of written language; that different combinations of different-sized contexts promoted different hypotheses, highlighted different cuing systems.

As explained earlier, we used the writing to derive the categories that appear in Appendix 2. Then we coded each piece with those categories and computer-sorted and tallied the various sortings. For some tallies, all the writing was used. For example, for more general comparisons, all pieces were sorted according to whether they had been assigned or were written spontaneously. Then particular categories (e.g., invented punctuation patterns) were tabulated for assigned as contrasted with unassigned pieces. For other tallies, we only used certain pieces (e.g., to find changes over time, only two collections were compared, the first and the last. For first graders the second and the last were compared because their initial collection consisted only of signatures and strings of letters.)

Our first research question had been: what happens to several aspects of the children's writing over the school year? The aspects we chose to look at were: code switching, spelling, local non-spelling conventions (segmentation, punctuation, tildes, accents, handwriting), quality of the content, cohesion (links between clauses, exophoric reference), a catch-all we called "structural features" (beginnings, endings, culturally specific topics, organizing principles, signs of accounting for the audience), and stylistic devices (by which we meant features that differentiated letters from journals from stories from other types).

This presentation of tallied codings begins with an answer to that first question. From there, it moves to showing the evidence for the relationship between writing in English and writing in Spanish (our second research question) and on to issues raised by several other general comparisons (our third research question). Because, like pieces of a kaleidoscope, the same codings have been sorted and re-sorted to produce different "designs," there will be some necessary repetition as the different comparisons are discussed. I hope, however, that the separate pictures of each aspect and each comparison, though containing details presented elsewhere, will each have its own coherence and significance.

A LOOK AT EACH ASPECT

Code Switching

Identifying written code switches was not a straightforward task. In much research, oral switches are defined as switches on the basis of phonetic realization. Since these children's spellings were often invented, we could not use orthography as the written counterpart of pronunciation. Sometimes, it is true, spelling helped us determine whether an item was a switch or whether it was integrated into the local dialect. For example, *baica* was not coded as a switch while *bic* (for bike) was. But what about *espinach?* That might have been an invention for Spanish *espinicas* or for English *spinach*. We did not count *espinach* or the few other truly ambiguous examples as code switches.

As can be seen from the crude index shown in Table 12 (a ratio of instances of all code switching to number of words), written code switching was a rare phenomenon. What this table does not show is that only 2 of the 25 children never code switched, yet for even the frequent code switchers the phenomenon occurred on average only once per piece. When it occurred, it was mostly a single word and thus intra-sentential rather than consisting of either intra- or inter-sentential phrases and clauses.

The main reasons for the switches seemed to be having learned the item in the other language (e.g., *field trip, stickball*), using the item as a synonym (the way a monolingual text will alternate *text, piece,* and *written product*), or matching a title (*Mr., Sra.*) with the ethnic identity of the person. There were few written examples of a kind of switch that we heard frequently in these children's oral language—the "translation" switch, used for clarification or emphasis (e.g., *five bucks, cinco pesos*).

In fact, the contrast between children's written and oral usage is instructive. While many if not most oral switches were inter-sentential, written ones were within the clause. Most importantly, although a high rate of oral switching often encourages the perception that the speakers are using neither English nor Spanish, the low rate of written switching here is evidence that writers could and did

Table 12.   Code Switching, Depending on Predominant Language of the Writing

	Spanish	English
Ratio of Code Switching Instances to Total Words	.009	.002
Single Words Switches[a]	64	83
Phrase Code Switches[a]	36	17
Word Class of Single Word Switches[a]		
address term/title	26	
adjective	9	
exclamation	1	
noun + appropriate gender/number	59	14
preposition	2	
verb	4	14
conjunction		29
article		43
Inferred Reason for Switch[a]		
clarification	.5	
direct quotation	.5	
ethnic group identity	15	
emphasis	.5	
learned in that language	54	
lexical variety	30	100

[a]Percentage of code switches (e.g., % of word code switches that were adjectives).

honor the integrity of each language when the situation required it—they were not monolingual in some mixed variety.

Code switching differed depending on the language of the text. There were more switches from Spanish into English than the reverse. Switches in Spanish pieces were longer and were usually "referentially inspired." That is, nouns—packed with referential meaning but less threatening to the structure of the language than pronouns, articles, and prepositions—were the main items that were switched in Spanish texts. Switches in English pieces, however, were more like "slips of the pen." That is, an article or conjunction would "slip out" in Spanish, but the use of Spanish would quickly be brought into check, as in *y es fun, thank you* or *y el dinosaur is gonna be . . .*

The rarity of written code switching can be attributed to children's sociolinguistic sensibilities—perhaps they saw the written channel as more formal, certainly as constraining the use of some typical oral resources. The same dimension—formality—may have been operating to make code switching even less frequent in English than Spanish texts. As noted in the discussion of the print environment, Spanish print was mostly homemade while English print was mainly commercially produced. English print then, not only a written modality but also the "real" language of both school and slick materials, may have seemed doubly inhospitable to informal switches.

Comparing ratios of code switching to total words written by any one grade over time and at the same time for different grades revealed that older children switched less and that switching decreased as the year went on. In an absolute sense, the second graders code switched more, but since they wrote such long pieces to satisfy their teacher's length value, their low ratio of switches to length masks this. Observers reported somewhat more oral code switching by the children and adults in this classroom than in the third-grade classroom. Also, occasional written switches appeared on the second-grade blackboard. Still, it is hard to know exactly why a few of the second graders were the most frequent written code switchers.

Nouns and address terms were the items all children switched most often. The two children in third grade who were the less schooled, monolingual Spanish-speaking immigrants from Mexico (Grade X) wrote very little and, in an absolute sense, code switched the least. Third graders made no switches at all in English texts.

Spelling

Children invented two to five times more vowel than consonant spellings in English than they did in Spanish even though, in a few pages of conventionally spelled published English texts, the proportion of vowels to consonants averaged 0.7; in a few pages of Spanish published writing it was 0.97. Thus sheer frequency in the systems would have predicted relatively more vowel inventions in Spanish. Not some all-encompassing graphophonic regularity in Spanish but the greater regularity of Spanish nuclear vowels (Natalicio, 1979) was probably the reason for fewer (but still an ample number of) vowel inventions in Spanish. Consonants appeared to be an equal problem for the children regardless of the language.

There was much less English than Spanish spelling to analyze (only 49 of 524 pieces were written in English) and thus a relatively small data pool from which to investigate the treatment of multiple inventions for the same word in one piece. Much of the time, whether the piece was in Spanish or in English, children used the same invention for the same word throughout. Treating each instance of a word differently was an early but never a predominant practice. However, depending on the language of the piece, there were different bases for spelling inventions. The earliest bases for inventing spellings of Spanish words were the use of phonetic features (e.g., manner and place of articulation), followed in frequency by the use of phonics generalizations, followed by examples from which we could make no inference and which we simply called "unknown basis." After several months of literacy instruction, and throughout second and third grade, there was a shift—invented spellings were based more often on phonic generalizations. A reliance on phonetic features decreased and the "unknown" basis dropped off.

At the beginning, English spelling inventions sprang from a different source—

a reliance on Spanish orthography. By second grade, given more exposure to English print, children used phonetic features of English as they had done at first in inventing Spanish spellings; and with literacy instruction in English, phonic generalizations became the most common basis for inventions. The application of Spanish orthography dwindled considerably.

Several comments must be made about these sequences. First, it is clear that all "errors" were not equal. Despite an educational propensity "for calling all shades of gray 'black'" (Bissex, 1981), early invented spellings were quite different from later ones, even though all inventions would be equally "wrong" if they appeared on a spelling test. The early inventions were harder to decipher (phonetic feature-based were more difficult than phonics-based substitutions for adult analysts) and to infer any basis for whatsoever. Later inventions based on phonetic features or something we have yet to unravel ("unknown") were far less common. That is, later inventions were more "literate."

Second, in using Spanish orthography for English spellings, the children were not necessarily spelling English words exactly as they pronounced them. They also used conventional spellings (thus spelling contrary to pronunciation) as well as a variety of other bases for English inventions.

Third, the third graders' spelling adds to our claim that the children were developing two separate orthographies. The differential use of *k,* tildes, and accents was augmented by the bases third graders relied on to invent English spellings. With more information about the English written system, they gave up applying Spanish orthography to English and treated the system as one with its own integrity, using phonetic features of English and letter names in English, and finally settling down to rely primarily on English phonics generalizations.

Non-Spelling Conventions

Segmentation.   Though the focus here will be on unconventional segments, it should be noted that only 3 out of 524 pieces had no conventional segments. As indicated in the preceding chapter, there were four bases for children's unconventional segments: syntactic, phonological/morphological, "anti"-syntactic, and "anti"-phonological/morphological. Just as Read (1975) found that invented spelling can reveal children's phonetic categorizations, so our data show that early segmentation revealed syntactic categories.[1] Syntactically based segments were: no space within a main clause; space between but not within a noun phrase and a verb phrase; no space within a noun phrase; no space within a verb phrase; no space within a prepositional phrase; no space between a conjunction and an adjacent word; and so on. (The full list with examples appears in Appen-

---

[1] It was Bess Altwerger who first suggested looking for syntactic units in unconventional segments.

dix 2.) Typical phonologically/morphologically based segments had spaces between syllables or were comprised of a syllable attached to an adjacent word. The two "anti" bases were flagrant violations of syntactic or syllabic boundaries. An "anti"-syntactic segment might group together *para que* (so that) and *no* (NEG), elements from different constituents, to produce *paceno*. "Anti"- phonological segments left single non-syllabic letters stranded or attached them to adjacent words (e.g., *m ela* for *me la*).

In Table 13, the entries enclosed in boxes are those which occurred in over 30% of the pieces during some collection. As these enclosures show, larger and more basic syntactic constituents became conventionally spaced before less central constituents. More verb than noun phrases, however, continued to be joined together. Possibly, the nature of verb phrases in Spanish (where, for instance, object pronouns move and become attached to the verb in certain tenses), rather than something about verb phrases in general, may have accounted for the greater "connectability" of Spanish verb phrases.

Syllables became a leading basis for segmentation even though the totality of all syntactically based unconventional segments combined always exceeded phonological bases.

As with spelling and code switching, segmentation varied with language of the text and with genre. Segmentation was more conventional in English pieces. In Spanish pieces, more conventional segments appeared in first graders' letters (but not their journals or stories) and in second graders' expository writing (but not their letters or books).

The overwhelming majority of syllabic segments were multi-syllabic, fitting either English or Spanish syllabification rules (e.g., *es taba,* where *taba* is multi-syllabic and both *es* and *taba* are acceptable consonant/vowel units in Spanish or English).[2]

We examined the writing of two frequent users of a syllabic segmentation strategy to see if there was a pattern for when bigger (full) vs. smaller (half) spaces were used between syllables. We thought children might have used full spaces between syllables that were morphemes (e.g., *esta mos*) and half spaces between non-morphemic syllables (e.g., *es ta*). In fact, we found no such pattern. All examples of segments coded as anti-phonological/morphological (sylL) were also examined to see if the stranded letter was more often a morpheme. It was not. However, we did find that only five children produced 130 of the 148 codings of sylL. Two of these five produced 100, while 18 others produced none or only one instance. I now believe that the segmentation category of sylL as well as the half space/full space phenomenon may have had as much to do with

[2] I am grateful to Margaret Orr, whose diligence and perceptiveness allowed me to comment on syllabification, half and full spaces, the non-morphemic nature of sylL, and various features of structure and layout which will be discussed under Stylistic Elements.

Table 13.   History of Types of Unconventional Segmentation (Edelsky, 1983b)

		Grade 1		Grade 2		Grade 3	
SEG Type		Coll. 2	Coll. 4	Coll. 1	Coll. 4	Coll. 1	Coll. 4
Syntactically based	xprop	46ᵃ	13	8	2		
	NPVP	7	2	13			
	notNP	38	24	8	4	5	
	notVP	30	41	42	14	5	
	notPP	43	15	29	14	11	10
	conj	29	44	21	20	16	20
	notAdj		2		1		
	notFrm	2	2	4	14		7
	nm	5	15	4			
phon/morph-based	syl	16	61	33	48	32	10
	sylw	18	28	8	8		
anti-syntactic	none	2					
	notCP	7	26	25	8	11	
anti-phon/morph	sylL	7	13	4	20		

ᵃPercentage of pieces that had that type of unconventional segmentation (e.g., % of Coll. 2 from Grade 1 with xprop)

SEG   = segmentation
COLL.   = collection
conj   = no space between conjunction and adjacent word or between a string of function words
nm   = no space between first and last names or name and title
none   = no space within and also none between prepositions
notAdj   = no space between adjective and adverb
notCP   = no space between adjacent words from different constituents (e.g., let me give *youa* kiss)
notFrm   = no space within a formula (e.g., thankyou)
notNP   = no space within a noun phrase
notPP   = no space within a prepositional phrase
notVP   = no space within a verb phrase
NPVP   = no space within but, yes, space between noun and verb phrases
syl   = space between syllables of one word
sylL   = single non-syllabic letter is either standing by itself or is attached to adjacent word
sylW   = syllable of one word is attached to adjacent word
xprop   = no space within a preposition

handwriting, a still undeveloped "consistent hand," as they did with segmentation.

Punctuation.   Early invented punctuation patterns (period at the end of each line, capital at the start of each line, capital or period to start or end every page of multi-page pieces, etc.) were based on units of paper—lines and pages (Table

14). The function of these was usually separation; their use dropped off sharply after first grade. Patterns related to text-ness, however, increased with age (e.g., a capital to start and period to end an entire piece).

The two Grade X boys provided some tantalizing hints at answering the question of whether the segmentation and punctuation developmental trends in these data were due to increased age or increased experience with literacy. These two were older but had fewer months of formal schooling. Their early writing was like the first graders' in segmentation (e.g., they used no-space-within-propositions), but unlike it in punctuation (i.e., they did not use any—neither mundane inventions nor charming ones like stars between clauses or periods at the end of each line). Perhaps their advanced age carried with it a general self-consciousness about writing which worked to prevent their use of extra marks. Segmentation, of course, was not avoidable. Thus their limited experience with print was revealed in less mature segmentation strategies.

Children used no ending punctuation when writing in English or when writing

Table 14. History of Various Patterned, Invented Punctuation (Edelsky, 1983b)

		Grade 1		Grade 2		Grade 3	
	Type	Coll. 2	Coll. 4	Coll. 1	Coll. 4	Coll. 1	Coll. 4
Related to HWT or letter information	invde	11[a]			11		
	pcle	16	13	33	17		
	pcw		13		4	11	3
Related to lines/pages	pnol		7				
	pcp	4	7				
	ppl	14		4	1		
	ppw	8					
	ppp				1		
	pcl	2	7	4	3	5	
Related to text	invend		2		3		3
	ppe	4	4	21	10	11	
	pmsf				7	21	23

[a]Percentage of pieces (e.g., % of Coll. 2, Grade 1 pieces using invde)
HWT   = handwriting
Coll.   = collection
invde = invented design (e.g., stars, curly letters, etc.)
pcl   = unconventional pattern of a capital at start of each line
pcle   = unconventional pattern of capitals on certain letters
pcp   = unconventional pattern of capital starting each page of a multi-page piece
pcw   = unconventional pattern of capitals starting certain words
pmsf = capital at start and period at end, with no internal punctuation
pnol   = unconventional pattern of a number on each line
ppe   = period at end of piece and no internal punctuation
ppl   = unconventional pattern of a period at the end of each line
ppp   = unconventional pattern of a period at the end of each page of a multi-page piece with no internal punctuation
ppw   = unconventional pattern of a period after certain words

spontaneously. Further discussion of variation in punctuation depending on language, assignment, and type of piece will appear in later sections.

Handwriting, Tildes, Accents. It was rare, even for first graders, to fail to supply required tildes. Almost always, tildes appeared where they belonged, except for a few times when they were placed over the wrong nasal (e.g., *ñina* instead of *niña*).

There was no appreciable shift across grades or over time within the year in the use of either tildes or accents. The few children who used accents used them appropriately for the purpose of designating a stressed vowel in what would otherwise be a diphthong. Occasionally, when accents were misused, they appeared when they were not required or on the wrong letter (either a consonant or another vowel).

There was, however, a change in handwriting. In the first collection from the third grade, cursive script appeared in 11% of the pieces. By the fourth collection, it was used in 87%. Obviously, this can be attributed to direct teaching of cursive writing in third grade. However, a small percentage (1 to 2%) of pieces in the first and second grade also contained bits of cursive writing.

"Exploratory graphics" also varied depending on the grade. The youngest children made designs inside letters and lines of stars. Older children's embellishments were more content-related. For instance, one third grader made letters that looked like a skull and crossbones on a title for a pirate story.

Attributes of Quality in the Content

Table 15 shows that children in increasingly higher grade levels wrote pieces rated increasingly better. The group that made the biggest jump in the course of the year was Grade X. The second-grade group appeared relatively unchanged, corroborating the teacher's and aide's remarks about how some children had "regressed" over the year.

The content of English pieces was judged to include more expressive language and be more insightful and original than that of Spanish pieces, while assigned pieces were judged more informative and original than unassigned ones.

It is necessary to know some details about the collections in order to make sense of these findings. Most English pieces (63% of them) were written by third graders, while third graders wrote only 16% of the Spanish pieces. Given that third-grade pieces were judged to be "better" than first- and second-grade pieces, this likely accounts for the "superiority" of content written in English. The same kind of phenomenon accounts for the relatively poor showing of the content of spontaneously written pieces. First graders, who contributed only 32% of the assigned pieces and whose content was seen as least original, insightful, and so on, wrote 88% of the unassigned pieces. Thus "unassigned" and "En-

Table 15. Quality Attributes over Time and Cross-Sectionally

Attributes	Grade 1		Grade 2		Grade 3		Grade X	
	Coll. 2	Coll. 4	Coll. 1	Coll. 4	Coll. 1	Coll. 4	Coll. 1	Coll. 4
Awareness of Purpose/ Audience	0[a]	1	2	2	1	2	0	.5
Candor	1	1	1.5	1	1	2	0	1.5
Coherence	1	1	2	2	2	1.5	0	.5
Expressive Language	0	0	0	0	0	1	0	0
Informativeness	1	1	2	2	2	2	1	2
Insight	0	0	0	1	1	2	0	0
Involvement of the Writer	1	1	1	2	2	2	0	1.5
Organization	0	1	2	1	2	2	0	0
Originality	0	0	2	2	2	3	0	2
Vocabulary	0	1	1	1	1	1	0	1.5
$\bar{X}$ =	.4	.7	1.35	1.4	1.4	1.85	.1	1.05

[a]Median of three raters' assessments on 'awareness' dimension, on scale from 0 to 3, of all pieces for grade 1, coll. 2.

glish,'' in this case, were actually and inadvertently other terms for ''younger'' and ''older'' writers.

Cohesion

Links. There are two general patterns in the use of links between clauses (the possibilities were *none* and some variant of *and, then, so, but,* and *other*). First was a move from ''no links'' to the use of *and* between most clauses to the employment of *and* along with a variety of other links that fall among the categories proposed by Halliday and Hasan (1976), followed by a reappearance of *none* balanced by the total range of links. Rentel (1981) has mentioned the refinement of ''ties'' when the child develops additional resources. The second pattern was an increase with grade level, in the number of different links that appeared in any one collection (from only 4 different ones in the November collection from first grade—*none, y, y también, también*—to 23 in the April collection from third grade—including *pero*/but, *por eso*/therefore, *después*/after, *aunque*/although, and so on).

I suspect that, had we collected data over a long enough time and perhaps more frequently, we would have been able to infer children's changing conception of what constitutes a text from their use of links and certain other written features. The pattern, in exaggerated form for at least some children, that our data hint at was as follows:

(1) A time when topically unrelated clauses or phrases were joined by no lexical links. At this point, what made different phrases into "a text" was their appearance on one sheet of paper. An example, from a classroom where phonics was emphasized and children were not allowed to write anything but workbook exercises until Spring, is (55).

Es una mamá
Es una papá
Es una Tesa
Es una Ano
Es una (Med)
Es una está
Es una Toy
Es una Aidi

Example (55)

(55)   Es una mamá. Es una papá. Es una Tesa. Es una Ana. Es una (Med?). Es una está. Es una Tony. Es una Aida.

(It's a mama. It's a papa. It's a Tesa. It's an Ana. It's a (Med?). It's an is. It's a Tony. It's an Aida.)

(2) A time when clauses were placed one per line, but these were now topically related. Such clauses were often treated to punctuation focused on separation; segments were sometimes whole clauses (no space within a proposition); and there were no lexical links between clauses. Example (56) is such a piece.

(56)   Hoy es martes. Anoche teníamos un conejo. Anoche fuimos a la iglesia. Tenemos un oso.

(Today is Tuesday. Last night we had a rabbit. Last night we went to church. We have a bear.)

A text now consisted of related ideas appearing on one page. (In (56) the relatedness was achieved with time—*anoche*/last night.)

(3) A period when a text was a tight unit, with clauses connected by *and*, the

25 noviembre 1980

Hoy es martes.

anoch tenme nemosunco
nejo
anochejimosu lasoña

tenemo sun noso.

Example (56)

clauses having internal segmentation but probably no punctuation. At this point, texts were held together with the glue of *and*.

(4) A time when the writer could trust readers to make their own connections, when content determined text-ness. At this point, links could be more varied; there could even be sentences that were not explicitly linked. Punctuation concerned text-ness (e.g., a capital to start and a period to end a *piece* rather than a sentence).

To see whether any individual children followed any part of this proposed path, we identified high users of "no links" and high users of *and* and plotted their use of all links over the year. Figure 2 displays this year-long picture for children identified as high users of Ø (no links) in the *second* collection. Figure 3 provides this information for high *y* (and) users.

Those who rarely connected clauses did replace their Ø's with *y*'s during the course of the year. (*We went to the store. We went to church. We went home* became *We went to the store and we went to church and we went home.*) Most who preferred *y* also followed the proposed pattern.

That is, if they had already replaced Ø with *y* (it must be emphasized that this is conjecture), they returned to a more frequent but more sophisticated Ø, a drop in *y,* and an increase in various other links. Child #3, the best reader and writer in her first-grade class, according to the teacher and aide, did follow this pattern, as did the third graders. Child #13's only deviation was in not increasing *so, then, but,* and *other.* Children #11 and #14, however, increased their reliance on *y.* Perhaps it took them longer than one year to go through this sequence, or perhaps this proposed sequence is in error.

There were somewhat different links used within a given collection in different types of pieces. First-grade books, for example, were written one clause to a page (like many published picture books), with no lexical links between pages.

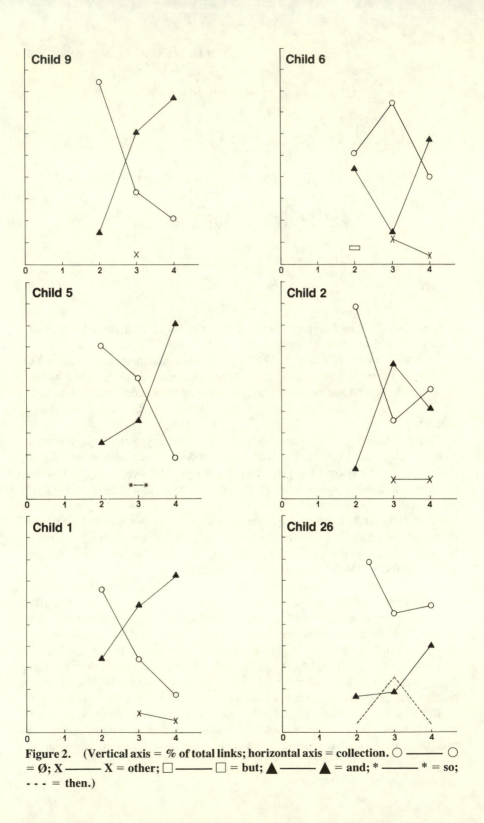

Figure 2. (Vertical axis = % of total links; horizontal axis = collection. ○ ——— ○ = Ø; X ——— X = other; □ ——— □ = but; ▲ ——— ▲ = and; * ——— * = so; - - - = then.)

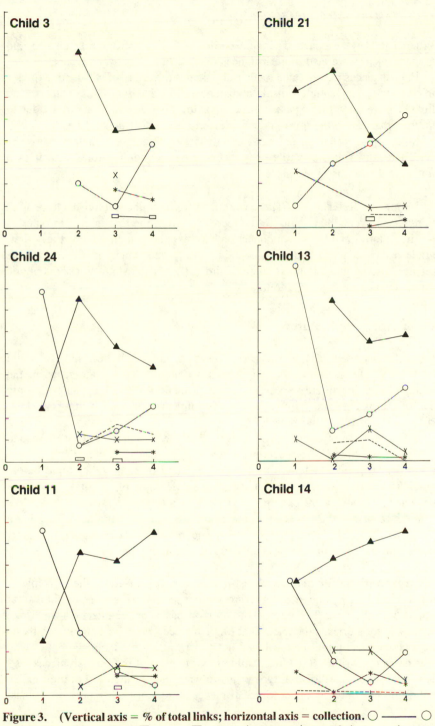

Figure 3. (Vertical axis = % of total links; horizontal axis = collection. ○——○ = Ø; X——X = other; □——□ = but; ▲——▲ = and; *——* = so; - - - = then.)

When letters were coached (in the earlier collections from first and second grades), there were also more instances of "no links" between clauses.

English pieces were treated to clausal linkages (a variety of words for expressing additive, sequential, causal, and oppositional meanings, as well as "no links") more often than Spanish pieces. Again, this was almost assuredly due to the fact that it was the third graders who produced most of the English pieces.

More sophisticated use of links was not always a function of maturity, however. There was a greater variety of links in pieces children wrote on their own initiative than in assigned pieces.

Exophoric Reference.   There were fewer pronominal references to people, things, and events that could not be recovered from the text in certain types of writing. Stories and books contained the least exophera in all grades. Early first-grade letters, coached and often containing only one clause (thank you for the piñata), also contained no exophera. Third graders used slightly less exophoric reference than younger children.

Other Structural Features

Cultural and Bootlegged Topics.   Despite our assumption that we would find many references to culturally specific objects, events, and ideas in the children's writing, there were very few such mentions. They appeared in only 5% of the pieces, and they were single comments about such things as low-riders, chicharrones, and piñatas.

What we did not anticipate, however, was the presence of what we called "bootlegged topics"—outrageous, powerful, or loaded topics that children seemed to slip into their writing under the safety of some other topic before quickly retreating to more innocuous ground. Mentions of drug-taking or misbehavior in school were examples. These topics too were rare ones and, like "cultural topics," did not seem to increase or decrease depending on whether a piece was assigned or not. There was only one instance of bootlegging, however, and no mention of culturally specific topics in English pieces.

Organizational Principle.   Most pieces were organized by the principle of association; i.e., by one idea triggering another so that the last one might rest far afield from the first. The next most common basis for organization was time, especially for stories and books. That English pieces were more frequently based on a chronologic might be attributed not to writing in that language but to who was doing the writing (the oldest children wrote most of the English pieces, as I have mentioned) and to what type or genre was being written (30 of the English collection but only 16 of the Spanish pieces were stories). Importantly, unassigned pieces were also frequently organized according to time despite the fact that these were mostly written by the youngest children. Evidently, determining one's own topic or being able to tap into a schema for stories prompted children to organize by *then* instead of by *this, that, and the other thing*.

Certain principles of organization which were not used frequently were interesting nevertheless. "Big shift" organization, characterized by a sudden switch to a very different topic or function in one piece, was more common for first and second graders than for third graders and seemed to be limited to certain genres. "Big shift" pieces were found among first-grade journals and books (the one phrase per page variety) and second-grade expository pieces. Second graders' sudden organizational shifts were probably attributable to a frequent assignment—describe an object and then tell one's feelings about that object. Few pieces were coded as hierarchically organized around one major super-ordinate theme (a classificatory organization). But of those few, it was books and stories that were the types treated most often to this more sophisticated organizational principle.

The worst "organizational" bases were "random" (a sprinkling of disconnected words) and "repetition" (e.g., *and I like it a lot and I like it a lot and I like it a lot and I like it a lot*). Only three younger children ever used "repetition"; three others we originally designated as "low" writers were the only ones to place words on a page seemingly without regard to syntax (*yo las a yo porque ya si ser y me a la . . .* /I the to I because already if to be and me to the . . .).

Beginnings and Endings. The most common beginnings were what we called "first parts"—starting right off with the first part of an event or story with nothing that might count as an introduction. That statement masks the variety in beginnings that we saw among various genres, however. First-grade journals and all letters also began with formulae in addition to "first parts"; all books and third-grade stories sported titles.

Pieces most frequently ended with a summary statement or a comment on an earlier part (not the whole) of a piece. For example,

(57)   Hoy es martes. Iba al cine con mi hermano y a Tejas con mi mamá. Hicimos guajolote para la Sra. H. (indecipherable) a la tienda con mi mamá comprar cosas para Christmas. Compramos una tela para *mi hermana chiquita. Ella es chiquita.*

(Today is Tuesday. I was going to the movies with my brother and to Texas with my mom. We made turkey for Sra. H. (indecipherable) to the store with my mom to buy things for Christmas. We bought some cloth for my little sister. She is little.)

However, once again, children varied endings with the genre. First graders ended letters with some polite expression and both first and last names. Journals from their fourth collection ended with both names also. I suspect that this was because children were instructed to use full signatures (for identification purposes) in these pieces written in English at the request of the researchers. Stories often ended with a statement that "wrapped up" the whole rather than merely a part. (Again, as with organizational principle, the most sophisticated endings were found in stories.)

Some infrequently used endings appeared more often in unassigned pieces. What children wrote without assignment contained more text markers (explicit endings—*el fin, fin*), more of a dramatic "melody" at the end (elaborated last phrases—*and we're coming every day, every day*), more marks of authorship (*by* + name), and were less polite (fewer instances of "something nice" at the end). Perhaps these were some of the cues for our impressions that children were more involved with their spontaneous writing.

Accounting for an Audience.   The first thing that must be pointed out is that much "accounting for the audience" in these pieces is simply an artifact of the way we coded. That is, we judged that the audience in most cases was the teacher-as-giver-of-the-assignment. Referring to the teacher in the third person, for instance in journal entries which frequently concerned school activities, was coded as acknowledging the audience. (It could also be argued that the use of the third person for mentioning the teacher in fact ignored, rather than acknowledged, that the teacher was the reader.) We also included second person references in this category as well as naming the audience in a heading. Thus, not surprisingly, letters were the genre in which children took most account of the reader and journals were second highest in this regard—at least according to the way we coded.

Sub-categories that seem to be more genuine reflections of accounting for an audience were: "makes marks for the reader" (arrows, notes such as *turn over*), "provides precise information," and "explicitly relates own life to reader's" (e.g., *I know you like to fish and I do too*). There were no differences between assigned and unassigned or English and Spanish pieces in the use of these ways of accounting for a reader. However, letters and books contained more arrows, notes, and other marks for a reader. The second graders, whose teacher gave them so much respect as thinking human beings in her interactions with them, were the only ones who "related own life to reader's"—and they did that in letters.

The most frequent coding for "acknowledgment of the reader," however, was "none." Most pieces showed no sign of any of our sub-categories. Interestingly, pieces children seemed most involved with (stories, books, and unassigned writing) were least likely to contain any sign that there might be a reader; they were most likely to evoke, in us as analysts, a sense of a writer–object relation than one of writer–object–reader. We have some evidence, however, from observations as well as from commonalities among pieces themselves, that there were other authors, writing at the same time, who would look at the text as an object and giggle over some of its daring attributes, as when several children wrote books in which the main character was disrespectful to his mother. If readers could be present-with-the-writer, not just distant or solitary, then perhaps there was no need to account for the audience with notes and arrows. Perhaps outrageous content was not just for the pleasure of the writer but for gaining prestige among fellow writers/readers.

Stylistic/Structural Elements

Most settings were imaginary or school-based. Very few pieces contained dialogue. The most frequent characters were the author, fantasy characters, and school adults. Most pieces were written in the first person and contained either inconsistent tenses or consistent past tense.

All pieces categorized as book, journal, letter, or story were also examined to see if they contained gross features of structure and layout usually associated with those types. Almost all books, regardless of the author's grade level, had a title and a text, read from left to right and front to back, and had title/author information on a different page from the opening line of text. Second-grade books frequently had numbered pages, and first-grade books sometimes had a separate page for *el fin*. The children seemed to know the physical essentials of books.

Adult journals usually have some signal of datedness, and to the outside reader, the events or problems with which they are concerned may seem either ordinary or extraordinary. Sometimes, they merely cite the event (*went to Marge's today*); sometimes they comment (*her kids are driving her nuts*); sometimes there is explicit mention of what is problematic or noteworthy for the writer (*was I so harried when mine were little?*). Though we have no idea how often "sometimes" is in adult journals, we now have some notion regarding these children's journals. They more frequently concerned out-of-the-ordinary (for the child) events (a birthday party, getting new shoes, moving). Most often, these were simply reported or briefly commented on. Rarely was there explicit mention of how the writer was affected. If the event was out-of-the-ordinary, it was more likely to receive the more elaborate commentary. (It must be remembered that these were not interactive journals—Shuy, 1981; Edelsky & Smith, 1984—where child and teacher engaged in written dialogue.) As for layout, almost all journals had the date on a separate line from the text; most used running text (clauses continued onto the next line(s)).

Letters were less like their adult counterparts than journals and books were. Most had headings and all had texts. More second graders used a closing formula, but more first graders signed their names. Headings were almost always on a separate line from the body of the letter, but both closings and signatures were often connected to the body rather than on separate lines.

There were several "unusual features" in some letters that indicate they may well have seemed more like schoolwork than genuine letters (writer's name at the top of the page, *hoy es* on some first-grade letters). Also noteworthy was the commonly used closing, *tu amigo*. We wonder if the translation of school-ese *your friend* was common in this speech community or if children used it only because the teachers were unaware of the more elaborate closings used in Mexico (and in this community?) and offered the children only this translation.

According to Stein and Glenn (1979) a story must have at least one episode consisting of an initiating event or an internal response, an attempt, and a consequence to be complete. Among these children's stories, the proportion of complete to incomplete stories increased with an increase in grade level. There were also more multi-episodic stories in the higher grades.

SOME GENERAL CONTRASTS

As has been explained, this study conceptualized writing as developing in various simultaneous interacting contexts. That is, written products and hypotheses about writing could come about through interaction with any number of co-occurring conditions. Three that will be presented here are: the language of the text, the instigator of the piece, and the influence(s) of the teacher. Differences co-occurring with shifts in genre will be presented in the following section.

Spanish vs. English Pieces

Most pieces from all grade levels were in Spanish; most English pieces were written by third graders. This accounts for many of the Spanish/English differences that were tallied by computer. That is, more mature writers contributed a greater proportion of the English than the Spanish pieces.

In some respects, English pieces seemed "better." More were organized on the basis of time; fewer were based on loose association. No English pieces consisted of an assortment of random words. (The Grade X child who produced these in Spanish did not even try to write in English.) There were fewer unconventional segments in English pieces, and these were either syllable-based or chunkings of low-level syntactic units (e.g., run-together formulae, conjunction + adjacent word).

The segmentation findings are probably explained by the fact that the youngest children did not write in English at all at the point when they were using the least mature segments (e.g., no spaces between or within propositions). Thus, these types did not appear in English.

There were also fewer hard-to-read spelling inventions based on phonetic features or some unknown basis. The source of the children's language proficiency might help explain both this finding and some of the segmentation findings too. The children had acquired Spanish through oral language interactions. Part of their English proficiency, however, may have come from English print, since school records revealed that many were monolingual Spanish speakers prior to entrance to school. Thus, some of their knowledge of spelling and word boundaries in English may have been less susceptible to influence from oral elisions and phonetic categories and more tied to visual images.

The mean of ten attributes of quality of the content was also higher in English pieces.

In other respects, Spanish pieces were "better." They had a larger variety of lexical links between clauses. Punctuation for English pieces was more related to letter formation; in Spanish pieces it was related to marking the start and finish or simply the ends of texts. Third graders tended to revert to manuscript writing for English; for Spanish they wrote in cursive.

Other differences that signal neither "better" (more mature) nor "worse" are the earlier mentioned findings on type and amount of code switching (less in English, switching nouns and address terms in Spanish but slip-of-the-pen switches in English) and differences in settings and characters. In English pieces, there were no settings coded as "community" and no characters coded as "family." The children were apparently making some topical division according to language.

Several impressions garnered during coding, noted in dated running lists, but not necessarily reflected in the tallies, concerned comparisons of first and second language writing. The most important was that seemingly there were no cases where the writer was very involved with a piece of writing in the second language; while there were writer-involved first language texts, there were no comparable pieces of second language writing.

If impressions favored first language writing, tallies produced an ambiguous answer to the question of which was better. Another question, however, concerned "same" and "different." Looking at Spanish and English pieces written by the same child (and ignoring the tallies), we found the following cross-language similarities. Some children used the same type of unconventional segmentation for each language. A third grader whose first written language was English provided wonderful examples here. This boy always clustered together *and* and *then* as *enthen,* but not other strings containing *and* (58).

(58)   One day I was walken *enthen* I found a plane *and* I ternd it on *and* I took off very forn from home *enthen* I came back home *and* I kept that plane *and* I made my self a air port *enthen* I had 2 air planes *enthen* 9 *enthen* 10 *enthen* my air port got biger *and* biger *and* biger that I cood fit 5000 air planes in it it had everything for than sky horber air port *and* all the people came ther *and* that is the end.

In Spanish he did the same thing, grouping together *y luego* but keeping *y* separate from other words (example 59).

Una vez yo estava
andando idlego
stava lloviendo
gatos ⅃ peros ⅃ me
meti en mi casa
idlego cuand paro
yo gare 20 peros
⅃ 30 gatos Idlego
yo teni todos los
gatos ⅃ pero Idlego
vendi ⅃ gare
munch ninero

Example (59)

(59) Una vez yo estaba andando y luego estaba lloviendo gatos y perros y me metí en mi casa y luego cuando paró yo agarré 20 perros y 30 gatos y luego yo tenía todos los gatos y perros y luego vendí y agarré mucho dinero.

(One time I was walking and then it was raining cats and dogs and I got into my house and then when it stopped I got 20 dogs and 30 cats and then I had all the cats and dogs and I sold and I got a lot of money.)

Children applied Spanish orthographic knowledge to English pieces. Some children used a similar syntactic style (strings of *para*'s/in order to's) in each language or a similar way of filling up space to satisfy a teacher's requirement for long pieces or a similar solution to the pragmatic problem of how to end a piece (*y gracias maestra* in Spanish, *thank you* in English; *y es todo* in Spanish, *that's all* in English).

Other children, however, wrote Spanish and English pieces which exhibited the following differences. A few segmented heavily by syllable in Spanish but not English. Almost all spelled the /k/ phoneme with a *c, cu,* or *qu* in Spanish but with a *c* or a *k* in English. Several children used much greater syntactic complexity in Spanish (many embeddings, strings of adverbial clauses). One child consistently ended Spanish pieces explicitly and English pieces implicitly, which was the way he had ended Spanish pieces earlier in the year. Code switching and script for handwriting was different, as has already been explained.

To interpret the "better" and "worse" tallies requires at least a guess about the factors that were involved in claiming language of the text influenced writing hypotheses. The differentially heavy demand on certain cuing systems when langauge shifted (e.g., on syntax) that was compensated for by other systems (e.g., graphic—script), language proficiency (e.g., assymetrical knowledge of a variety of lexical links), and the source of language proficiency (e.g., oral interactions vs. oral and written sources) were all part of the context called "language of the text" which was reflected in the tallies.

What the "same" and "different" piece-by-piece comparisons reveal is that children *applied* (not a passive transfer, but an active application, adaptation, and modification) what they knew about first language writing to writing in the second language. While the "differences" produced by the same child might look like non-application in a linear, discrete-skills, a-contextual model of writing, they are clearly evidence of application in a model that captures both the recursiveness of accessing and juggling multiple cuing systems and the highly contextualized character of the writing process. When children applied "what they knew about first language writing," they were applying everything from specific hypotheses about segmentation, spelling, and endings to general strategies for literacy acquisition (e.g., use the input—Spanish print does not have k's; English print does not have tildes and accents), to high level knowledge (that texts are contextually constrained), to a crucial process (orchestration of cuing systems).

Language of the text, with all attendant factors, certainly affected the children's writing. The nature of the relationship between first and second language writing was not one of interference (early use of Spanish orthography in English did not prevent children from coming to know English orthography on its own terms). Rather, it was one of application, of using and adapting what was already known in order both to fill in for what was not yet known and to push the limits, to go beyond what had been done before.

Assigned vs. Unassigned Writing

Only the first graders had many opportunities to initiate and control their own writing. Such opportunities were also available in two other non-study classrooms. This discussion then will present both tallied findings and contrasts between individual pieces written by children other than our 26 subjects.

The tallies show that when children wrote out of their own intentionality in the three study classrooms, they did not write journals or letters. (In Mr. M's class, they did write unassigned letters.) Except for one child, neither did they write in English. Unassigned pieces were shorter. (However, assigned pieces included the motley genres from the second grade that went on for over 20 pages.) Endings in child-instigated writing were not only more elaborate—marked and so on, as already discussed—they were also more sophisticated (wrapping up the totality; less likely to lack closure.) Fewer unassigned pieces had the writer as a character; more concerned peers. Probably this can be attributed to assignments that made the writer the central figure (tell what *you* like, what *you* do, where *you* went, etc.) rather than to a spontaneous preference for peers. Settings were more likely to be home and community in unassigned pieces. Children seemed to be more taken with numbering the lines they drew on oversized unlined paper than with punctuating the text or accounting for a reader in the pieces they wrote on their own initiative. Despite what seemed to be slightly more tallied differences favoring unassigned pieces, subjective ratings of quality of the content slightly favored assigned pieces. Again, the differential contribution of first grade to unassigned and third grade to assigned collections probably accounts for this discrepancy.

A more convincing picture of the value of allowing children to control their own writing comes from looking closely at individual pieces written in several different classrooms. Readers might recall from Chapter 3 that while Ms. A controlled and parceled out other lessons, she allowed children considerable responsibility for writing. And in her classroom, a wider variety of genres were written, including jokes, songs, and pleas. Examples(60) and (61) are excerpts from pieces from Ms. A's classroom.

(60)   Ms A, le voy a decirle un joke ¿ok? ¿Ud. conoce a los Polacks? Pues, había tres Polacks y uno estaba cargando una jarra de agua y el otro Polack estaba cargando una canasta de comida y el otro estaba cargando una puerta de un carro . . .

(Ms A, I'm going to tell you a joke, OK? You know about Polacks? Well, there were three Polacks and one was carrying a jar of water and the other Polack was carrying a basket of food and the other was carrying a door from a car . . .)

(61)   El nobre del cieeeeelo (a song being *sung*) os pido posaaaaaada . . .

(El nombre del cielo
Os pido posada . . ./In the name of Heaven, I ask you for shelter . . . /)

In the first-grade study classroom, several pieces of unassigned writing were more poetic than anything written by the same children for assignments.

(62)   (unassigned; beginning and ending)
Todos los días cae nieve en todas las partes y también caía lluvia en todas las partes . . .
. . . Era cuando estaba cayendo nieve.

(Every day snow falls everywhere and also rain was falling everywhere . . .
. . . It was when the snow was falling.)

(63)   (assigned writing by same child during same collection period)
Hoy es jueves. Hicimos monitos de nieve y los pegamos en una tabla y se miran bonitos.

(Today is Thursday. We made little snowmen and pasted them on a board and they looked nice.)

(64)   (unassigned beginning)
Siete naranjas se caeron y el árbol está triste en lágrimas . . .

(Seven oranges fell and the tree is sad to the point of tears . . .)

(65)   (assigned writing by same child during same collection period)
       Estimado amigo,
          Hay muchas reportes y jugamos yo y mi hermanito.

       (Esteemed friend,
          There are a lot of reports and my little brother and I played . . .)

Example (65) was a "pretend-functional" piece of writing, an assigned letter, written to no one. This is certainly not the kind of interactive, intimate writing that Shuy (1981) advocated as necessary for writing development. Contrast this with excerpts from letters from Mr. M's class. These letters were written because the children had something to say and because they wanted (and would receive) written answers from Mr. M. They were genuine queries, threats, complaints, excuses, and clarifications.

(66)   Querido Mr. M,
          ¿Quién son las señoras que vinieron y yo lo he visto a la Sra. que tiene anteojos en la tienda . . .
       (Dear Mr. M,
          Who are the ladies who came? And I've seen the woman who has glasses at the store . . .)
       Mr. M,
          Se me olvidó decirle mi perro tiene 6 dedos y no estoy diciendo mentiras . . .
       (Mr. M,
          I forgot to tell you my dog has 6 toes and I'm not telling lies . . .)
       Querido Mr. M,
          ¿Porqué no me ha mandado mi carta? Dígame en la carta cuando me va a mandar la carta porque si no me dice yo me voy a enojar con Ud . . .
       (Dear Mr. M,
          Why haven't you sent me my letter? Tell me in the letter when you're going to send the letter because if you don't tell me I'm going to get angry with you . . .)

Whether looking at the actual pieces or at the tallies, it is clear that children made different decisions about content, form, and reader/writer relationships depending on whose motives had instigated the piece. The message here is obvious: if classroom practice does not establish means for and encourage children to write out of their own intentionality then it substantially distorts their experience with written language. It deprives them of truly *intending,* of matching intentions to conventions, of finding ways to have an effect *they* want to have.

The Role of the Teacher

There were no tallies to help us here; still, observations, anecdotal runnings lists, and writing collected from a variety of classrooms throughout the program suggest important connections between teacher activity and children's writing.

Though this Bilingual Program claimed to be using a "whole language" approach to literacy, in actuality it did not (as discussed in Chapter 3). To be fair, it must be noted again that teachers in this Program *did* have children writing every day; they did emphasize content over form; they did send many letters that were written; they did provide for some sharing of writing with peers. Thus, although these were not "whole language" classrooms, they *did* provide children with many advantages not often available in school.

Still, deviations from the claim that a "whole language" program was being offered were all too obvious. There were teachers in this Program who gave children only artificial pieces of someone else's language to manipulate. All asked children to write about what they often did not care about. Many created artificial school genres and required children to write for no purpose other than to comply with an assignment. Occasionally, they even asked them to write letters to no one in particular. They did not establish a demand for wide reading or procedures for publishing children's writing. They saw revision as related to errors (in spelling, punctuation, or amount and type of information) rather than as related to intention.

Such practices and their underlying beliefs certainly had consequences in the children's writing. Many pieces showed no involvement of writer with writing. Where children were offered only artificial pieces of language to read, their writing resembled workbook exercises. We saw no evidence of revision other than erasures at the word level, addenda prompted by Ms. D, or an occasional recopying at the request of Ms. S. On the other hand, we had much evidence that children rarely re-read their writing, let alone revised it. Only a few stories resonated strongly with the melody of written narrative. But we did have some data that showed that the more children were asked to engage in real writing, the more systems of written language they had to cope with simultaneously, the better their writing seemed; they were learning different things from working with a sentence vs. a purposeless text vs. a text-with-intent.

In presenting these data, the concrete details that show the teacher's influence on her students' writing, I have categorized those influences as either direct or indirect. They were direct if the teacher intended them to have a specific effect. Indirect influences were those that occurred when the teacher was not aware of the effect of a particular action, when the teacher intended to have only the most general effect (such as "to make the children want to write"), or when the teacher's direct attempts at impact had additional unintended consequences.

Direct Influence.   Obviously, teachers' assignments, shaped by their beliefs, had a direct impact on genres written. When Ms. D thought children could only write their names, that is all she assigned, and that is all children wrote officially. When she thought they could write journals, they wrote journals. In another first-grade classroom where the teacher had little confidence in children's writing ability, at the end of the year children were just beginning to write captions and "stories" that resembled worksheet language. Meanwhile, Ms. D's class had been writing a variety of both assigned and unassigned genres for the past several months.

The writing center, provided by Ms. D with the express purpose of "unleashing creativity," did seem to elicit pieces that were more poetic.

Ms. C's articulated belief that longer pieces benefited development must have been related to her students' production of 27-page pieces, while the longest non-book pieces from the other second grades were 5 pages.

Teachers believed that sound was the basis for spelling. They intended to influence children to appeal to sounds while spelling a word—they gave phonics lessons as well as advice to "sound it out." Spelling inventions traceable to phonics lessons ("*y* and *ll* make the same sound"; probably related to spelling *yo* as *llo*) or the addition of letters, usually glides, from elongating words while sounding out (*mallestra*) were likely teacher-influenced or at least teacher-strengthened strategies.

On a few occasions Ms. C tried to model "composition" so that children would not connect all sentences with *y*. She elicited single sentences from the children and made a chart story. Then she asked them to write their own. In fact, they did write pieces in "chart story style" (*Santa Claus brings presents. Santa Claus brings cars. Santa Claus goes out at night,* etc.). Though this syntax and text organization was not typical, children could and did produce it when the teacher supplied the eliciting conditions.

Indirect Influence. Indirectly, non-deliberately, what teachers did nevertheless had an influence on many features of children's writing. For instance, one characteristic of the print environments in the classrooms was that, because they had to, teachers made more of the Spanish print themselves (posters, dittos, displays of children's work) while, because it was available, they used commercially produced English print. Without intending it, teachers may have made Spanish print seem less formal and more hospitable to code switching. More frequent code switching in children's Spanish texts may therefore have been related to the character of the print environment the teacher created.

Though Ms. D intended for colored markers at the writing center to entice children to do more writing, she did not intend to sway topic choice. Still, color became a topic so that pieces could be full of color words written in matching markers.

Teachers' beliefs about children's abilities and about appropriate assignments had unintended consequences for text structure. Assignments to produce "motley genres" (teacher-created juxtapositions of several topics or functions, such as directions to make a social studies report and extend an invitation, all rolled into one letter), coupled with a premium on length, produced pieces with big topic shifts full of repetition (some of it nonsensical), oversized handwriting, and empty spaces. As Smith (1982) indicated, sheer quantity does not necessarily promote growth because children are better at "furthermore" than "on the other hand." When they are pressed to write more and more, they are likely to merely repeat.

Teachers' beliefs about children's capabiliites as writers (or perhaps about their own as teachers of writing) were evident from the beginning. The first-grade teacher who believed children could not write until they could spell and who felt children's writing had to be carefully controlled spent much time on phonics lessons and occasionally took dictation from the children. Though children in her class began the year like children in the other first-grade classes, just writing their names or strings of letters, by January the only "texts" they wrote were single phrase captions for pictures, accompanied by a sentence dictated to and transcribed by the teacher or aide. By June, these children's pieces contained more phrases, but most of these were disconnected, resembling the "controlled vocabulary" of phonics workbooks. In fact, only 15 of the 50 pieces this teacher had saved as "good examples of writing" consisted of coherent texts, and all of these were flat, general reports (*I have a teacher. I go to X school,* and so on). In other words, though this teacher's intention was to teach conventional spelling and elicit "correct" pieces of writing, her practice (stemming from her beliefs) encouraged children to hypothesize that texts they produced for her should have no topical theme but should be structured around, for example, repetitions of short or long vowels. This was an extreme example of Graves' (1979c), Harste et al.'s (1981), Boiarsky's (1981), Lindfors' (1980), and many others' admonitions about a focus on form detracting from and distorting content.

By contrast, most of the time Ms. A, who either believed children could control their own writing or that she could not teach writing, let the first graders write whatever they wanted. While the "phonics classroom" children were writing *amo a mi mamá, papá oso casa,* Ms. A's children were writing texts with complete joke structures (see example (60)), coherent summaries of movies they had seen, and a variety of other types.

Teacher activities intended to capitalize on children's own intentions also seemed to enhance writers' involvement in their writing. The excerpts shown in example (66) are from pieces written because the teacher wanted to give children an opportunity to write "authentically." They were not part of lessons to "develop a sense of audience" (Kroll, 1978); they were a *result* of relationships that were developed through both oral and written language. By providing mailboxes and genuine responsiveness, Mr. M also gave children the opportunity to "own" and "own up" in their writing.

WITHIN GRADE DIFFERENCES AMONG TYPES OF PIECES

Teachers' beliefs and classroom practices, language of the text, instigator of the piece—these were not the only contextual vehicles for writing development. Administrative policies and occasional threats regarding evaluation strengthened teachers' beliefs about the need for skill-drilling and their fears about their own status in relation to children's scores on skills tests. This in turn affected how far teachers were willing to venture in the direction we had been urging in in-service courses, which in turn affected children's writing.

Cultural values (children should behave in school; home and school are very separate domains) most likely influenced topics that were not mentioned as well as those that were. Culture and socio-economic class together probably affected which books, magazines, and newspapers were in homes and stores and which were not, while the relative power positions enjoyed by two languages could be seen in the negligible number of Spanish books in the neighborhood library that served many monolingual (and monoliterate?) Spanish speakers. Speech community norms were seen in children's written non-standard syntax and morphology. Our analyses do not permit more than this mention of these effects. However, the relation of one more "context"—type or genre—to features of writing will be presented below.

Only the first and fourth collections (the second and fourth for Grade 1 because the first collection consisted only of signatures) were used to compare differences among types of writing for a given grade at a given time. Although spelling did not vary according to type of piece (except for the earlier collection from first grade), other features of the writing did in all grades. The differences related to:

1. notions about the structure and organization of different genres
2. reflections of the writer's involvement
3. judgments of quality
4. the settings for writing (what else was happening)

Genre Sense. The children had a "sense" about different genres. They accounted for the audience in different ways in letters (headings, direct speech acts, referring to the audience in the second person, politeness, appropriate closing pronouns) and in journals (by referring to the teacher/audience in the third person) and not at all in stories, books, and expository pieces. Tied to audience was second graders' differential use of code switching in different genres. Address terms were frequently switched items in letters, which were more likely to provide such opportunities. Nouns, especially those learned in school (e.g., field trip), were more often the items switched in journals and expository pieces, which often concerned school topics.

The various genres began and ended differently. Letters, stories, and journals began with distinct formulae (*hoy es* for first-grade journals, "Dear X" for letters, a Spanish variant of "once upon a time" for stories). By third grade, stories began with titles, as did books as early as second grade. Expository pieces had no formulaic beginnings. Instead, they started with the first part of some event, a statement of the topic, or the writer's position on a topic or his/her goal in writing. First parts of events were also common beginnings in journals, stories, and second-grade letters and books. The writer's position on a topic was a favored beginning for letters. (Grade X's beginnings were an exception. I have categorized them as relating more to what else was happening at the time of writing than to some sense about genre.)

Endings were genre-tied also. Letters ended with politeness, formulae, and full signatures or first name only. Other genres did not end in these ways. However, letters shared with other types the closing summary of or comment on a part rather than on the whole. First graders ended journals by providing no closure—simply stopping; second graders neglected to wrap up expository pieces. In the second and third grade, explicit endings began to appear on stories but not other genres, as did summaries of entire pieces.

Organizational principles varied. "Big shifts" appeared in first-grade journals and books and second-grade expository pieces. The most hierarchical organization was found in stories. Time was the organizational basis for many types, but especially for stories or books at any one grade level.

Presenting a problem and a resolution in second-grade stories but not in other types, using the third person for stories and books and the first person for letters and journals—these too were evidence of a sense of genre.

First graders punctuated journals but not letters with invented designs—a signal that they may have understood something special about letters (that letters meant business, that letter writing was not to be playful). Third graders' underlining of titles and embellishing of handwriting in stories, on the other hand, probably reflected their experience with printed stories themselves—that these but not other types could be illustrated and designed physical objects.

Writer's Involvement.   Stories and books were not punctuated as often as other types until the third grade. This finding is being categorized as "involvement" because it seems that if writers were excited about writing (teachers reported this to be the case with books) or had a sequence of events to unravel (if pre-planned) or assemble (if one event triggered the next "on the spot"), they paid more attention to content and less to graphic form. At first children seemed to treat punctuation as graphic form, pertaining to lines, pages, or word boundaries. When they began to treat it as text-related, they began to use it in story, the type of writing where content seemed to hold the writer's attention.

According to their teacher, second graders loved writing books; and it was only books (and stories to a slight extent) that contained any risky bootlegged topics.

First-grade letters from collection 2 were judged better because they showed more audience awareness (letter form and function predicts that) and more organization (these letters were often coached). Journals, being relatively more revealing than thank you letters, were judged as more informative. However, fourth collection journals written in English received low marks on unusual vocabulary and candor. Stories, letters, and books, the types most likely available for schema-tapping, were rated highest overall.

Early Grade 2 letters were also judged better than other genres on audience awareness, coherence, and organization (attributes possibly related to teacher-coaching), and on writer involvement and expressive language. In the final Grade 2 collection, letters, stories, and books were judged to show most awareness of either purpose or audience. To raters (and probably to writers too), journals and expository pieces apparently seemed to lack purpose.

In the third grade, stories elicited more imaginative vocabulary and language devices (onomatopaeia, dialogue). While dialogue fits more "naturally" into stories, the pedestrian nature of most assignments for expository pieces probably also contributed to duller language use in that type.

Grade X stories were rated much lower than expository pieces. My only hunch here is that these children were coached or provided with partial models on the blackboard for expository pieces.

Settings for Writing. Several of the differences between early first-grade letters and expository pieces were due to the fact that the letters were coached and were mainly one sentence or even one line long. Thus, there were fewer opportunities for multiple instances of one word and therefore fewer chances to invent different rather than stable spellings of the same word. Probably minimal length, along with coaching from the teacher, was also behind the absence of use of *and* as a link (with one clause, what need for links?), the absence of exophera, and the absence of invented punctuation patterns in letters.

Second-grade letters from the first collection were also monitored and coached. These letters were longer than the first graders' and thus had possibilities for the use of links between clauses, but adult coaching could easily have been responsible for children's avoidance of explicit links.

Grade X expository pieces began with titles; surprisingly, stories did not. In this classroom, writing assignments were written on the board. It is conceivable that assignments for expository pieces were titled by the teacher more often than story assignments and were copied off the board by these less able writers.

That first and last name appeared as an ending on journals (as opposed to other types) from the fourth collection (but no other) was likely a function of our request for at least one piece of writing per child in English. Knowing these pieces would be used for this study and wanting us to be able to clearly identify the writer, Ms. D asked the children to put both their names on the journal entries she requested in English.

The "punctuation" pattern of a number on each line appeared in expository pieces because that was the type written at the writing center on oversized, unlined paper. It was the material, and probably the model of one child, rather than anything about the genre, that prompted the production of numbered lines.

Although some features of writing probably differed as a result of constraints exerted by the demands of the genres, at least some others then were more likely caused by what else was going on at the time.

In sum, type or genre was both a ''front'' and an influence in its own right. Different types were written under different circumstances. These contextual circumstances were what was behind the variance in many of the features found among different types. However, the types also exerted their own demands. ''Type,'' therefore, deserves to be ranked with teachers and classroom practice, instigator of the piece, and language of the text—all more or less local contexts through which children wrote and grew as writers.

Differences over Time

We compared total collections written by each grade at the beginning and at the end of the year to see how the frequency of different codings changed. In order to eliminate the impact of type on these differential frequencies, we also made separate comparisons of start- and end-of-the-year journals, early and later letters, stories, and whatever types we had from a given grade with sufficient examples in different collections to make that kind of comparison.

Even controlling for type, teachers' assignments and directions changed from the first to the last collections; researchers made requests at the end of the year that they had not made at the beginning; different materials were available in February than in November. Therefore, the findings on how the writing changed over time will be divided into those that seem heavily in debt to such contextual influences (like many of the differences noted among the varied types or genres) and those that seem to reflect ''development.''

Changes over time in context might well be seen as examples of the reflexivity of writing and context. As children's writing changed, teachers' perceptions of what they were able to do also changed, which in turn led to changes in favored assignments, in assigned audiences, and in materials offered, which in turn led to other changes in children's writing. Changes in writing that I have assigned to the category called ''development'' seem to have been less directly tied to the activity of others.

Differences over Time Influenced by Teachers and Researchers.

For the first grade, greater variety in types written in April was due to Ms. D's changing perception of her students' abilities. Because she believed them capable of it, she gave more expository assignments as the year went on. Thus the last collection had fewer formulaic beginnings because there were relatively more non-journal types. By establishing the writing center, she encouraged the production of more spontaneous pieces; therefore, there were fewer pieces written for an audience of teacher-as-direction-giver.

Comparing only journals, and therefore eliminating the influence of other types, still shows the effect of teachers' and researchers' activities. There was more writing in English later in the year, but that was undoubtedly due to our request. More English occasioned other contrasts. Therefore, it was our request, rather than "development," leading to an increased use of English, that was responsible for the change in quantity and quality of code switching (switching nouns and address terms earlier—but in Spanish texts—and articles and conjunctions later—but in English texts). With the added burden of English, punctuation was avoided in the first-grade journals written in April.

It was also likely that assigned topic and function (reporting about a school event involving popcorn, Cheerios, etc.) rather than some more overarching change was what prompted more code switching in fourth collection letters by first graders.

Several changes over the course of the year in the total collections from second grade can be attributed to the assignments the teacher gave. One was an increase in exploratory handwriting. Ms. C assigned more books and stories in the fourth than the first collection. Since these were the types treated to such graphic explorations, it might easily have been the case that designs and *cholo* writing would have also appeared in the first collection if only "hospitable" genres had been assigned. A decrease in the percentage of second graders' pieces accounting for the audience by means of headings or closing pronouns was a function of fewer letters being assigned later in the year. A higher frequency of chronologically based organization in the fourth collection was probably related to a greater number of assignments asking for a recounting of movie content or school activities.

Several differences between the first and last collections written by the third graders also seem to have been connected more with the teacher's assignments than with any developmental advance in literacy. However, the shift in assignments in this classroom most likely did not reflect the phenomenon of the teacher adjusting to the children's growth. Ms. S did not assign stories—usually considered more basic, easier, more concrete, more likely a genre for which children would have a schema—until mid-year. The more abstract, non-narrative genre (expository writing) made up the bulk of beginning-of-the-year assignments for third graders. Third graders' favored beginnings and endings from early and later writing were different because of the different genres. Later writing (but actually stories) used more classificatory organization, a more mature basis than associative. End of the year writing (again, because of so many stories) also received higher quality ratings than did other genres. When looking only at expository pieces, however, it is less reasonable to appeal to adult activities to explain the differences. And when examining any of the shifts made by Grade X, the same comment can be made: all seem to be due to "development."

Differences over Time Attributable to "Development." "Development" appears in quotation marks because I am not certain the term is adequate or correct for the phenomena we encountered. Some of the tallied changes seem to me to be "marks of development"; i.e., a change in abilities due to direct teaching (cursive script, for example, or more conventional segmentation stemming from direct teaching of "words"). Some seem to be "developmental"; i.e., a change in the hypotheses being made as a result of increased interaction with print coupled, perhaps, with other conceptual or linguistic changes (some of the fluctuation in segmentation might be an example here). But then a few tallied changes seem to be neither "marks of development" nor "developmental" in these senses. Nor can I tie them directly to teachers' or researchers' activities. In some cases, they even seem to be "marks of regression" (e.g., the lower quality of second-grade pieces at the end of the year). Most changes could not be viewed this way. Rather, the majority seem to have represented manifest improvements and likely reflections of underlying reorganizations regarding literacy. Nevertheless, because this section is based on data pooled from several children per grade and because there were no observations during the production of the pieces, which might have disambiguated the findings, I will keep the quotations around *development*.

Table 16 summarizes which features of children's writing, in which grades, benefited from "developmental" changes in one year's time. Increased length and the number of different lexical links between clauses (a probable reflection of vocabulary development) were characteristic changes over time for each grade, regardless of the type of piece considered. For most but not all grades, segmentation, type of link, and punctuation revealed "developmental" differences. When it could not be attributed to differential assignments and therefore a greater incidence of the "better" genres, quality of content also improved at each grade level.

First graders decreased their clustering together of two major constituents (entire clauses and noun phrases) and increased their use of syllabic segments and one "small" syntactic one (clustering together the conjunction and an adjacent word). First graders shifted from an absence of lexical links between clauses to clause-tying with *and* along with a sprinkling of other links. Invented punctuation patterns using designs or periods and focusing on lines or words decreased.

Second graders decreased their use of a major syntactic basis for segmentation (no space within a verb phrase) in favor of an increase in grouping together more minor syntactic units as well as in segmenting by syllables. There was also an increase in second graders' use of one of the "anti" bases—leaving single letters stranded. This last seems to constitute a regression in segmentation. (As has been mentioned already, it may be the case, however, that this sub-category was at first as much a reflection of two children's erratic handwriting as of peculiar segmenting.) Second graders also moved from fewer linked-together clauses to pieces where most clauses were linked by *and*. In punctuation, they switched from using only periods to mark the ends of entire pieces to sometimes enclosing the whole text with a set—a capital to start and a period to finish.

Third graders' unconventional segments shifted from a syllabic basis back to a syntactic one, but by the end of third grade, segments clustered together on a

Table 16. Summary of "Developmental" Changes for Each Grade

Type of Collection	Categories that Changed	Grade 1	Grade 2	Grade 3	Grade X
Total	Length of piece	X[a]	X	X	X
	Type of link	X	X		X
	Different links	X	X	X	X
	Segmentation	X	X	X	
	Punctuation	X	X		X
	Unsupplied tildes	X			
	Bases of Spanish spelling inventions	X			
	Quality of content	X			X
	Handwriting			X	X
	Stylistic syntax-tense				X
Letters only	Length of piece	X	X	N/A[b]	N/A
	Type of link	X	X	N/A	N/A
	Segmentation	X	X	N/A	N/A
	Punctuation	X		N/A	N/A
	Exophoric Reference	X		N/A	N/A
	Bases of Spanish spelling inventions	X	X	N/A	N/A
	Quality of content	X			
	Accounting for audience		X		
	Stylistic syntax-tense		X		
	Bases of English spelling inventions		X		
Expository only	Length of piece		X	X	
	Type of link		X		
	Segmentation	N/A	X	X	N/A
	Punctuation	N/A	X		N/A
	Quality of content	N/A	X	X	N/A
	Bases of Spanish spelling inventions	N/A	X		N/A
	Bases of English spelling inventions	N/A		X	N/A
	Stylistic syntax-tense	N/A	X		N/A
	Beginnings			X	
	Handwriting			X	
Journals only	Length of piece	X	N/A	N/A	N/A
	Type of link	X	N/A	N/A	N/A
	Segmentation	X			

[a]X means there was a "developmental" change for that grade on that category.

[b]Not applicable/NA means no pieces of that type were produced by that grade in both early and late collections; therefore, no comparison was possible.

syntactic basis only included minor units (conjunction and adjoining word (*en-then*) or prepositions plus indirect objects (*ami*/a mí)).

Grade X children shifted in their use of links between clauses. In fact, on this feature, they resembled first graders. These children began to punctuate in the fourth collection by putting a capital at the start of a page.

There were other features for which changes can be noted for only one grade. Failure to supply required tildes decreased in first grade. First graders also shifted their bases for inventing Spanish spellings from one less dependent on instruction (the use of phonetic features) to one more tied to instruction (the use of phonics generalizations). Third graders began to write mostly in cursive, and Grade X children switched from inconsistent tense usage to use of consistent past tenses.

Table 16 also shows which grades enjoyed "developmental" changes in which features for particular types of pieces. There were sufficient first-grade journals to compare over time, but this type was not available for comparison from other grades. The nature of the changes in journals (in length, type of link, segmentation) matched the changes described in relation to the total collections. This was not the case with letters, however.

Several changes in first-grade letters were secondary effects of a change in length. Longer letters at the end of the year permitted an invented punctuation pattern of using a capital to start each page of a multi-page letter as well as a higher incidence of exophoric reference.

Changes in length, links, and unconventional segments were similar for second-grade letters and for the total second-grade collection. April's second-grade letters, however, contained more of the conventional means for accounting for an audience (closing pronouns, politeness). Since it was first collection letters that were subject to more coaching, this increased conventionality was probably a sign that children were learning these forms. They also showed a move from consistency to inconsistency in tense usage, perhaps because first collection letters were written simply and in the simple present, while fourth collection letters were functionally, semantically, and syntactically more complex. While neither English nor Spanish spelling changed in the total collection, both did when considering only letters. Spanish spelling inventions in letters were increasingly based on Spanish phonic generalizations. Interestingly, with as yet no formal instruction in English phonics, by the end of the year, second graders were basing some inventions of English words on English phonics generalizations.

In second graders' expository pieces, the nature of the changes in length of piece, bases for Spanish (but not English) spelling inventions, and type of links were similar to that seen in letters. However, while shifts in segmentation in expository pieces (as in letters) were characterized by an increasing use of stranded letters, they differed from letters by including two other types of unconventional segments. Both of these were more typical of third-grade writing: a steady use of syllabic segments and an increased use of conjunction + adjacent word clusters.

Except for English spelling, third graders' expository pieces showed transformations similar to those of the total third-grade collection. Length increased, syllabic segmentation decreased while there was an increase in unconventional linking of minor syntactic units (conjunction plus adjacent words, prepositional phrases), ratings of quality of content went up, beginnings began to include titles, and handwriting shifted to cursive for both total collections and expository pieces. The one feature that differentiated changes in expository pieces from changes in the total collection was an increase in the number of English spelling inventions which were related to incomplete second language acquisition. Third graders were writing more in English by the end of the year (this was a function of curriculum goals and language acquisition, *not* of our request to have one English piece from each child, as it was for the first graders). This would have given them more chances to display a second language proficiency characterized in part by missing or overgeneralized verb affixes.

Cross Sectional Differences

Rather than repeating how each grade's total collection differed from the others in relation to the major aspects for which we coded (this has been discussed earlier under ''A Look at the Aspects''), I will present just one interesting comparison here—Grade 1 compared with Grade X.

Early in the year, the two Grade X children, relatively unschooled, recent immigrants from rural Mexico, were similar to first graders in the following:

> all writing was in Spanish
> there was no unassigned writing
> there was almost no mention of culturally specific topics
> the only audience was the teacher
> endings consisted mostly of comments on earlier parts
> most clauses were not lexically linked; the only lexical links fell in the *and* category (*y, también,* etc.)
> the major organizational principle was associative or time-based
> unconventional segments were often whole sentences
> there was a frequent absence of required tildes and accents
> tense usage was mixed
> only manuscript writing was employed
> raters judged the quality of content very low

Some of these characteristics (assigned writing, audience, no mention of certain topics) could easily have been a function of classroom assignments. It is possible to attribute others, however, to limited experience with writing—characteristics such as text construction (quality, endings, organizational principle, links between clauses, tense consistency), large syntactically based unconventional segments, and script.

To complicate matters, Grade X and first-grade writing were also different. Grade X:

> wrote longer pieces
> used no formulaic or first-part beginnings
> used no punctuation at all
> based most Spanish spelling inventions on phonic generalizations rather than phonetic features
> did no code switching at all
> used a mixed rather than a first person perspective
> segmented syllabically in addition to syntactically

Some of these differences may have been attributable to at least some prior schooling (e.g., using phonics generalizations in spelling), to Grade X's monolinguality early in the year (and therefore no code switching), or to the respective teachers' assignments. However, others may have been related to age and more advanced language acquisition rather than schooling.

CHANGES OVER TIME FOR INDIVIDUAL CHILDREN

After the four collections had been coded, members of the coding teams for each aspect submitted their recommendations for "interesting" children to look at individually. Two children per grade and one Grade X child were so designated. As it turned out, the two per grade each represented one "high" and one "medium" writer from the original subject selection.

We considered two other ways of dividing up the children, besides targeting a few to look at as individuals. The intent was to take one dividing characteristic, and see if that characteristic was "symptomatic" of a whole complex of other differences. That intent was never fulfilled, but the reasons we abandoned the idea are enlightening.

One division we tried was much versus little code switching. We tried grouping children by the number of words and phrases they switched, regardless of the length of the piece, and also by the number of switches where length of piece was controlled. In either case, children who code switched frequently in writing (as well as those who code switched infrequently) made such a diverse group that it seemed that any finding of other differences (perhaps in content quality, segmentation, number of different links, or whatever) between the two groups would be an arithmetical but not a substantive discovery.

The same can be said for our efforts to divide children according to "conventionality." We made a group out of the children whose writing contained five or more types of unconventional segments, with some types (i.e., the "anti"-syntactic and "anti"-phonological types) receiving more weight because of their extreme unconventionality. These constituted the highly unconventional group. Highly conventional children were those with two or fewer types of unconventional segments. We also tried to define conventionality on the basis of spelling, so that children with a ratio over .8 of spelling inventions to total words were considered extremely unconventional; those with fewer than .35 inventions to total words in first grade, .25 in second grade, and .10 in third grade were considered highly conventional.

As with code switching, whether we determined conventionality by segmentation or spelling, we obtained a grouping that included the children who wrote a lot and those who wrote a little, those who wrote coherently and those who did not, more and less original writers, more and less conventional spellers (if we grouped by segmentation), and more and less conventional segmenters (if we grouped by spelling). And although we did not try it, I suspect that the same could be said about any effort to group by high or low ratings of quality of content. In other words, although a few children were indeed "better" or "worse" on all features we coded, most others were idiosyncratically variable.

There are at least two morals to this story. First, the mechanics the general public (including politicians and policy makers) clings to as markers of educational achievement (e.g., spelling, punctuation) did not live up to their reputation. Too many good spellers wrote incoherent stories; too many pieces by bad spellers were spellbinding. It behooves us then to try to convince the public to put its faith in something more complex than single, often superficial signs of achievement in literacy. Second, for putting children in research or instructional categories, it would seem unwise to try to predict what kinds of hypotheses children would make about the various aspects of written language we chose to look at (and perhaps others as well) by looking at how they treat only one aspect.

We did, however, look at individual children. So that readers might come to know our "interesting kids" as writers rather than tally producers, an over-time sample of each child's writing is presented along with the tallied findings.

Child #3   (Examples 67 through 70).

Example (67). Collection 1

Hoy es miercoles.

ayer esimos una.

tepi con un cavoyo.

i todos estaban

presente i con

volitas rojas

Example (68). Collection 2

(68)   Hoy es miércoles. Ayer hicimos una teepee con un caballo y todos estaban presente
y con bolitas rojas.

(Today is Wednesday. Yesterday we made a teepee with a horse and everybody
was here and with little red marbles.)

Example (69). Collection 3

(69)   Había una vez que había cuatro niños solos en una casa muy vieja y tenían mucho
miedo porque había una bruja que se riaba como un brujo porque los cuatro niños
estaban muy chicos.

(Once upon a time that there were four children alone in a very old house and they
were very afraid because there was a witch that was laughing like a warlock (male
witch) because the four children were very little.)

Monstruo y Señorita Monstruo y el paseo en bicicleta la bicicleta empieza y bajar por la loma demasiado rápido. Los niños ven lo rápido que van pero Monstruo y la Señorita Monstra no se dan cuenta. Monstruo sigue mirando a la Señorita Monstruo y sigue hablando y hablando ¿De qué estarán hablando? Monstruo debería estar mirando por donde va la bicicleta empieza a irse más y más rápidamente.

Example (70). Collection 4

(70) Monstruo y Señorita Monstruo y El Paseo en Bicicleta
La bicicleta empieza a bajar por la loma demasiado rápido. Los niños ven lo rápido que van pero Monstruo y la Señorita Monstruo no se dan cuenta. Monstruo sigue mirando a la Señorita Monstruo y sigue hablando y hablando. ¿De qué estarán hablando? Monstruo debería estar mirando por donde va. La bicicleta empieza a irse más y más rapidamente.

(Monster and Miss Monster and the Bicycle Ride
The bicycle began to go down the hill too fast. The children see how fast it's going but Mr. and Miss Monster don't realize it. Monster keeps on looking at Miss Monster and keeps on talking and talking. What must they be talking about? Monster should be watching where he's going. The bike begins to go faster and faster.)

Christina, Child #3, started out as a more advanced writer. She had already passed the stage of no links, if there is such a stage, and had reached a high degree of text-tying with *and*. She used no segments that joined whole sentences, employed a clear invented punctuation pattern (periods at the end of every line), and relied on phonic generalizations for both Spanish and English spelling inventions. Over time her content became more complex (more semantically varied ties between clauses) yet less neatly conveyed (more inconsistent tense usage). She also tried out new forms later in the year—accents, question marks, tildes. As a whole, Christina's content and form improved together. The only exception was her increasingly erratic handwriting (shown by what we coded as punctuation—capitals for certain letters).

Child #6. The other first-grade target subject was José (examples 71 through 74 are his).

Example (71). Collection 1

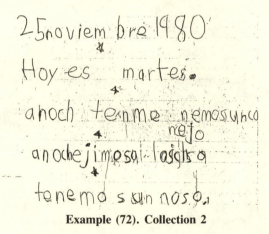

Example (72). Collection 2

(72)   Hoy es martes. Anoche teníamos un conejo. Anoche fuimos a la iglesia. Tenemos un oso.

(Today is Tuesday. Last night we had a rabbit. Last night we went to church. We have a bear.)

(73)   Hoy es jueves. Fuimos a comer. Fuimos a PE. Fuimos a la tienda. Fuimos a las vistas. Fuimos a la K Mart. Fuimos a la Circle K. Compraron sodas y cacaguates y Kool-Aid y plátanos y paletas y una piña colada, una soda.

(Today is Thursday. We went to eat. We went to PE. We went to the store. We went to the movies. We went to K Mart. We went to Circle K. We bought sodas and peanuts and Kool-Aid and bananas and popsicles and a pina colada, a soda.)

Hoy es juebes.

juimos acomer

jyimos a pi

juimos ala tenDa

juimos a los bistas

juimos alasceimar

juimos dla sincocei

comparon soDas

i ca cagyates iculei

iplatanos i paletas

i xx una piña acaDa

una soDa

Example (73). Collection 3

El Monstruo

y El-Niño

ysieRon una

piel de Monstruo

de galletas

y El Niño pienso

de Eso

de galletas

buenas.

y conpaRon

aRina y galletas

y leen un lybro
de cosinaR.

Example (74). Collection 4

(74)   El Monstruo y El Niño

Hicieron una piel de Monstruo de galletas y el niño piensa de eso, de galletas buenas. Y compraron harina y galletas y leen un libro de cocinar.

(The Monster and the Boy
They made a monster skin out of cookies and the boy thinks about that, about good cookies and they bought flour and cookies and they read a cookbook.)

José's progress was not quite as steady as was Christina's. He was one of the few who refused to comply with our request to write in English. Toward the middle of the year, his content dipped (it was rated lower; he continued to provide no closure for endings and reverted to many clauses with no links) as he jumped forward in form (he shifted from having no spaces within sentences to using a syllabic basis for segmentation; he started to use phonics generalizations as the basis for invented spelling, and stabilized his spelling inventions; and he stopped using his charming but childish invented punctuation designs). Then, in the fourth collection, both content and form surged ahead, length increased, beginnings sometimes had titles, content received higher ratings (but still not as high as at the start of the year), hyphens appeared, phonetic feature spelling decreased, and segmentation became more conventional. José's progress was thus uneven during part of the year, but a meld of advances in both content and form at the end.

Child #11.   One of the two second graders we followed was Manuel (examples 75 through 78).

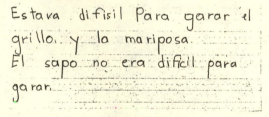

Example (75). Collection 1

(75)   Estaba difícil para agarrar el grillo y la mariposa. El sapo no era difícil para agarrar.

(It was hard to catch the cricket and the butterfly. The toad wasn't hard to catch.)

(76)   Es un Santo Clos y él se mete por la chimenea. Él me da presentes y él tiene bigotes y tiene un gorra y tiene un cinto negro grande y tiene un traje rojo y las botas son negras y tiene un trineo con venados.

(It's a Santa Claus and he goes through the chimney. He gives me presents and he has a mustache and he has a beard and he has a big black belt and he has a red suit and his boots are black and he has a sleigh with deer.)

(77)   Las kachinas son muy importantes porque tienen espíritus en todas las kachinas y todas las kachinas son echas de las raíces de los árboles. Y esas muñecas son bien importantes porque tienen un espíritu que las kachinas creen y todos los días ayudan y les dan buena suerte.

martes, 12-3-80

Es un santa dos y el se mete por la
chiminella el me da presentes y d
tiene bigotes y tiene una gorra y
tiene un sinto negro
grandre y tiene un
traje rojo y las botas son negras y
y tiene un trineo con benados.

Example (76). Collection 2

las Kachinas son muy inportontes
porque tiene espiritu en todos las
Kachinas y Todas las Kachinos son
echas de las rayzes de los ardoles

y esas muñecas son vien importante
porque tiene un espiritu que
los Kachinas grellan y todos los dia
les alludan y les da uenasuerte.

Example (77). Collection 3

(Kachinas are very important because they have spirits in all the kachinas and all the kachinas are made of the roots of trees. And these dolls are very important because they have a spirit that the kachinas believe and every day they help out and they give them good luck.)

A mi me gusta aser
libros y Yo los ago y
a-mi me gusta liellerlos
yo le ise uno a
mi mamá y le gusto
mucho y eya lo
tiene todavía.

Example (78). Collection 4

(78) A mí me gusta hacer libros y yo los hago y a mí me gusta leerlos. Yo le hice una a mi mamá y le gustó mucho y ella lo tiene todavía.

(I like to make books and I make them and I like to read them. I made one for my mom and she liked it a lot and she still has it.)

Until the fourth collection, Manuel made some advancement—a few pieces in mid-year were organized hierarchically, there was a switch from "no links" between clauses to *and* and other links, and punctuation began to be text-based. However, this child regressed from using English phonics generalizations in English spelling to relying on Spanish orthography, from having no unconventional segments at all at first to using syllable-based, major syntactic-unit-based, and even an "anti" phonological basis for segmentation. In the fourth collection, his content was rated lower than it had been previously. This confirms what his teacher reported about Manuel—that his beginning-of-the-year improvement was reversed, that by the end he seemed "not to care" about either content or form.

Child #15.   Arturo was the other second grader singled out for individual analysis (examples 79 through 82).

llamatoconejos dos con ejos semueren.

a,ialgunos seescondn

tambien se escondn

prosarboles

lesiro una perdo

isolen corlendo

llols mato imesalenmasconejos

Example (79). Collection 1

(79)   Yo mato conejos y los conejos se mueren y algunos se esconden. También se esconden por los árboles. Les tiro una piedra y salen corriendo. Yo los mato y me salen más conejos.

(I kill rabbits and the rabbits die and some hide. Also they hide by the trees. I throw a rock at them and they come out running. I kill them and more rabbits come out for me.)

(80)   Yo tengo un mono que sé quien es. Yo digo que es un hombre bueno que da paletas o regalos. A mí me gustaría una moto. Esos son mis favoritos. A mí me gustan también unos go cars.

(I have a doll that I know who it is. I say it's a good man who gives popsicles or presents. I would like to have a motorcycle. Those are my favorites. I also like go cars.)

martes, 12-3-80
llo tengo un meno ce se
cienes llodigo one es un
on bre gueno y ceda paletos
o regalo ami me gastaria
un am oto esas son mis
raboritos ami me gusta
tan bien unos gou cars

Example (80). Collection 2

una bos abian dos señores ce estaban siegos
ytamien abia un mapache yel mapache
les jugaba trecs alos siegos yun siego
le dijo a alotro siego ce el mapache
estaba aci yel ma pache los engañaba

y un dia el ma pa che ceria ggarar un
pescado pero bido a los dos siegosi los
bido dor midos yun siego le dijo cetenia
seyel otro siego jue a traile agua
yel ma pache lo ben gaño yle lle bo
la agua yel otro siego le dijo ce
lla tenia ambre yel ma pa che se
les puso mi engaño ni yel ma bache
yba a comer la carney los dos
siegos dijieron ceno mas ceda ban
nomas dos carnes y sepelia baron

Example (81). Collection 3

(81) Una vez habían dos señores que estaban ciegos y también había un mapache y el mapache les jugaba tricks a los ciegos. Y un ciego le dijo al otro ciego que el mapache estaba aquí. Y el mapache los engañaba. Y un día el mapache quería agarrar un pescado pero vió a los dos ciegos y les vió dormidos. Y un ciego le dijo que tenía sed y el otro ciego fue a traerle agua y el mapache lo engañó y le llevó el agua. Y el otro ciego le dijo que ya tenía hambre y el mapache se les puso engañó y el mapache iba a comer la carne y los dos ciegos dijeron que nomás quedaban nomás dos carnes y se pelearon.

(One time there were two men who were blind and also there was a raccoon and the raccoon would play tricks on the blind men. And one blind man said to the other blind man that the raccoon was here. And the raccoon was tricking them. And one day the raccoon wanted to catch a fish but he saw the two blind men and saw them sleeping. And one blind man said he was thirsty and the other blind man went to bring water and the raccoon tricked him and he took the water. And the other blind man said to him that he was hungry and the raccoon tricked them and the raccoon was going to eat the meat and the two blind men said only two pieces of meat were left and they fought.)

llo cu an do estoi en mi
casa miro cartunes y abeses
ago istorias de los cartu
nes i a beses me apagan
la telebisien y
me enojoy les pego
alos ce mela apagen q̵

Example (82). Collection 4

(82) Yo cuando estoy en mi casa miro cartunes y a veces hago historias de las cartunes y a veces me apagan la television y me enojo y les pego a los que me la apaguen.

(When I'm at home I watch cartoons and sometimes I make stories out of the cartoons and sometimes they turn off the television on me and I get angry and I fight the ones who might turn it off on me.)

One way to describe Arturo's writing over the year is "erratic." This child seemed to relate genuinely to an addressee—by complimenting, switching languages, and explicitly empathizing. He also had some idiosyncrasies of style; e.g., ending many pieces with "something nice." His content plateaued (in length and beginnings), improved and then worsened (links), and also steadily deteriorated (quality rating). On form, Arturo at first relinquished his most unconventional syntactically based segments (joining words from different constituents), but then he adopted the most unconventional of phonological segments (allowing single letters or non-syllabic clusters to stand alone). His Spanish spelling inventions became more literate while his English inventions became less mature. In sum, Arturo's writing became both "better" and "worse" on content, "better" and "worse" on form between any two collections.

Child #20.   Ray, the child whose first written language was English, was one of the third graders chosen as an "interesting child" (examples 83 through 86).

(83) If we win the trophy again it's going to us and I hope it keeps going to us. Nobody is going to take it from us. It'll stay with us forevermore because we're coming every day, every day.

IF we win the Trophey
agen its gowen to us and
i hop it Keps gowin to us
nobude is gowin to take it fron
us ittle stay with us for
ever more becaause wer cumen
evore day avre day

Example (83). Collection 1

i still remembr obout yester day nite

ue had to do the play obout

the thanx giveng sosey erre bude

ue emberast but it uus were fin

Example (84). Collection 2

(84)   I still remember about yesterday night. We had to do the play about the thanksgiving sausage. Everybody was embarrassed, but it was very fun.

a day in the woods
one day   I wus camping
and I found sum cubs
and wuen I got one
in my hands a big
nois I wunderd whut
it wus enthen I
cood see a site but I
thot for a secent how
cood I see a site
in the nite it wus
sow big and mad

it mad me run
as faster a jack rabit
enthen I lost it
and I stopt and
from that daye I
never pict ips a little
cub the end

Example (85). Collection 3

(85) A Day in the Woods
One day I was camping and I found some cubs and when I got one in my hands a big noise. I wondered what it was and then I could see a sight but I thought for a second, how could I see a sight in the night?! It was so big and mad. It made me run as fast as a jack rabbit. And then I lost it and I stopped. And from that day I never picked up a little cub. The End.

Example (86). Collection 4

(86) Today we went to D High School to see girls and boys dance and we also saw a band and it was very very fun. And it was in a gym and there was a boy and a girl singing and there was a little volcano that would shoot out smoke that would stink. And they were dressed very nice and they would have strings with colorful stripes and they shined strobe lights at them and then we came back. And that's all what happened.

Ray's writing presents both a tandem and a teeter-totter progression. In the second collection, this youngster showed signs of more mature writing in both content (his endings summarized the texts, ratings of quality improved) and form (punctuation, cursive handwriting). This was the tandem pattern. A see-saw occurred between the second and third collection (down in content—endings, quality ratings; up in content—links—and also in form—handwriting). Between the third and fourth collection, his writing see-sawed again; this time, up in content (rating of quality, links) and down in form (leaving out text-based punctuation and tying capitalization to letters or words rather than to text beginnings, titles, or other units of written discourse).

Special note should be made of the ratio of Ray's vowel to consonant spelling inventions in both English and Spanish. Ray was the only child for whom Spanish was the second *written* language. (Although, according to family sources, Spanish was his first oral language, he insisted on writing in English despite being in the Bilingual Program in first, second, and third grades.) And he was the only one who invented more spellings for *both* Spanish and English vowels than he did for consonants. That is, Ray's spelling showed that Spanish vowels were not inherently easy for every learner.

Child #22. The other third grader looked at individually was Martín (examples 87 through 90).

Example (87). Collection 1

(87) Yo pienso que cuando estaba chiquito no me hacía un penny. Por eso no me hago penny.

(I think when I was little they didn't make me into a penny. Therefore, I don't become a penny.)

(88) Yo fui a la cebolla 3 días porque el domingo no hay cebolla y el domingo de lo que saqué en la cebolla me compré en los perros una bicicleta de 15 dólares. Me gané en tres días 15 pesos y luego andaba yo arriando la bicicleta y luego estaba una bicicleta muy bonita y me la quiero comprar y tenía las llantas gruesas.

(I went to the onion field 3 days because Sunday there's no onion field (work) and

Yo fui a la sebolla 3 dias
porque el domingo no
all sebolla y el domingo
de lo que me saque en
la sebolla me compre
en los perros una
biciclefa de 15 dolares
me gane en tres dias
15 pesos y Luego
andaba yo arriando la
bicicleta y Luego esta
ba una bicicleta
muy bonita y me
la quiero comprar
y tenia las dianta
gruesas

Example (88). Collection 2

Sunday, with what I got from the onion field I bought at the dogtrack a bicycle for
15 dollars. I earned, in 3 days, 15 dollars and later I went riding the bike and then it
was a very nice bike and I want to buy it and it had thick tires.)

La nuez podrida
Un dia estaba en mi casa
comiendo nueces i yo pelé
una y adentro no estaba una nuez
salio Abraham Lincoln y estaba
recien nasido y pararon años y años
y Luego el tenia 20 años y Luego se
caso y a el le gustaba leer la
Biblia y Luego sus besinos le
traan Libros para que los
leera y se pasaba toda la
noche en la chiminea leeyendo
los libro y Luego era precidente
lo Precidente y el se paresia
a la nuez porque el nacio
en la nuez el fin

Example (89). Collection 3

(89)   La Nuez Podrida
Un día estaba en mi casa comiendo nueces. Yo pelé una y adentro no estaba una
nuez. Salió Abraham Lincoln y estaba recien nacido y pasaron años y años y luego
él tenía 20 años y luego se casó y a él le gustaba leer la Biblia y luego sus vecinos le
traían libros para que los leyerá y se pasaba toda la noche en la chiminea leyendo
los libros y luego era presidente, 16 presidente, y él se parecía a la nuez porque él
nació en la nuez. El fin.

(The Rotten Nut
One day I was in my house eating nuts. I peeled one and inside there wasn't a nut.
Out came Abraham Lincoln and he was just born and years and years passed and
then he was 20 years old. And then he got married. And he liked to read the bible
and then his neighbors brought him books so he would read them and he would
spend all night on the hearth reading the books. And then he was president, 16th
president, and he resembled a nut because he was born in the nut. The end.)

Example (90). Collection 4

(90)   El Mágico Huevo
Un día un niño pasó junto de un huevo y se paró a mirar que tenía ese huevo. Y
luego el huevo se desapareció en ese instante. Y el niño se sorprendió y luego el
huevo había aparecido y el niño agarró el huevo y se lo llevó y lo puso en la mesa y
luego el niño lo quebró el huevo.

(The Magic Egg
One day a boy passed by an egg and he stopped to look at what the egg had. And
then the egg disappeared instantaneously. And the boy was surprised and then the

egg had appeared and the boy grabbed the egg and took it and put it on the table and then the boy broke the egg.)

Martín's progression was similar to Arturo's—better and worse on both content and form. Like José, Martín was a "resister." He resisted carrying out the teacher's requests for an English piece. He resisted the teacher's topics (see Collection 1, example (87), which was supposed to be on the topic "If I Were a Penny"), and he did not censor out culturally specific topics. His experiments with punctuation in the second collection never reappeared. Overall, Martín's quality ratings deteriorated, as did the variety of links he used. However, other content features (beginnings, tense and person perspective) improved. Form too moved bi-directionally, switching to conventional segments and cursive script and at the same time increasingly leaving out punctuation and tildes.

Child #25.   If Martín's over-time picture was bi-directional, Davíd's was not. Davíd was the Grade X child chosen for an individual look (examples 91 through 94).

yo Jue Jo con mis er manitos
con uno visicletos

Cuando andaranos Juj andsasalia
Vha viroraLe arcoron amierrmano
Lamato Yobi bastanvna casa
llotenaJaun Perito Cesellama
Lucas iJueJo con osotros,

Example (91). Collection 1

(91)   Yo juego con mis hermanitos con unas bicicletas. Cuando andábamos jugando salía una víbora. Le hablaron a mi hermano. La mató. Yo vivo en una casa. Yo tengo un perrito que se llama Lucas y juego con nosotros.

(I play with my little brothers with some bikes. When we were playing a snake came out. They spoke to my brother. He killed it. I live in a house. I have a puppy named Lucas and he plays with us.)

(92)   Ayer jugué en la bicicleta. Jugué carritos. Ayer se me pasó el bus. Ayer anduve brincando en las bajadas. Ayer estuve en la casa. Ayer comí. Ayer vi un avión volando.

(Yesterday I played on the bike. I played little cars. Yesterday a bus passed me. Yesterday I went jumping on the slopes. Yesterday I was in the house. Yesterday I ate. Yesterday I saw an airplane flying.)

(93)   Abraham Lincoln
El 12 de febrero es el día de su cumpleaños y fue muy bueno y los negritos sufrieron mucho.

aller Juge en la visicleta
Juge carritas, aller
se me pasa el Las
aller andube vrincanda
en las vaJota
aller estube en
La casa aller comi
aller vide uarian valad

Example (92). Collection 2

el 12 ervogenLicoh
Defevrero
es el dia de
su cumplianos
i Gue mUi
gueno i Los negritos
su frerion mUcho

Example (93). Collection 3

(Abraham Lincoln
The 12th of February is his birthday and he is very good and the negroes suffered a lot.)

(94)   A mí no me gustó nada de ellas (riegos?). A mí me gustó las canciónes con la támbora y el cohete. También me gustó porque hechaba humo y cuando hechaba papelitos y es todo lo que me gustó. Todaviá no les cuento todo. Y a mí también me gustó cuando le pegaron al platillo. También me gustó las támboras porque se oía bien recio. Luego nos venimos y fuimos y la (carer?).

(I didn't like anything about those (?). I liked the songs with the drum and the firecrackers. Also I liked it because it sent out smoke and when it sent out little papers and that's all I liked. Still I am not telling it all. And I also liked when they hit the cymbal. Also I like the drums because they sounded really loud. Then we came back and went to the (?).

Except for gaining ground and then losing it regarding punctuation, Davíd's writing became generally more mature over the year. His content rating improved more than any other child's. (It also started off lower.) He grew in fluency (length), variety and number of links between clauses, handwriting, bases for inventing spellings, and bases for segmenting. In fact, features of his writing that resembled those of first graders' (segmentation and spelling) shifted to being third-grade-like by year's end.

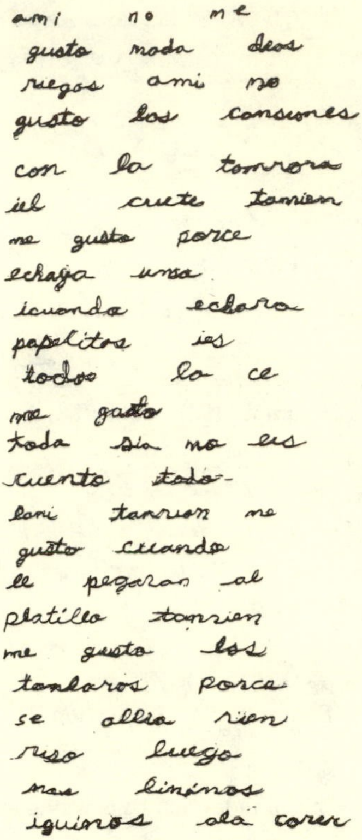

[handwritten Spanish text]

ami   no   me
gusto noda deos
ruegos ami no
gusto los consiones
con   la   tomrora
iel   cruete tomien
me gusto porce
echaja unsa
icuando   echara
papelitos   ies
todos   la   ce
me gusto
toda sia no es
cuento todo
lomi tanzion me
gusto cuando
le pegaras al
platillo tanzien
me gusto los
tanlaros porce
se allia rien
riso luego
mas limimos
iguimos ola corer

Example (94). Collection 4

One very important lesson can be learned from looking at these most individual of progressions in the writing of these interesting individuals. That is, though data pooling can and did provide us with some overall patterns on each aspect we analyzed, there was no common progression for the fine details of any category for any of these individuals. It was not even possible to find a shared pattern in the relationship between progress in form and progress in content. One child advanced in some content categories while regressing in form categories (or vice versa); another became more mature in both; still another both advanced and retreated, and on and on.

SUMMARY OF FINDINGS

With so many findings, it might help to summarize the major ones—and, along with the summary, to relate the findings of some recent research on young children's writing to ours. I will refer especially (though not exclusively) to work by Dyson (1982, 1983), Calkins (1983), Harste et al. (1983), and Ferreiro and

Teberosky (1982). Dyson's was a participant-observation study in a kindergarten classroom in the Southwest. She analyzed her five targeted case study children's writing, drawing, and talking (to themselves, to other children, and to her), as well as many aspects of the classroom environment, for the purpose of investigating how the children structured their own engagement with and learning of written language. Her interest was to describe an activity as it occurred (i.e., early writing), with all its supports (drawing, talking, and graphic marking), from the point of view of the child writer.

Calkins was a researcher in Donald Graves' (1983) longitudinal study of 16 children moving from first to second and from third to fourth grade in a school in the Northeast. Calkins too was a participant-observer, but she was looking at children's growth as writers not before formal instruction began, but in interaction with adults' activities as teachers of writing. Calkins focused in particular on children's changing perceptions of revision, changes growing out of their participation in activities established by their teachers (e.g., conferences, writers' workshops) but shaped by all who participated.

Harste et al. (1983) videotaped 48 3- through 6-year-olds with lower and middle class backgrounds in Indiana engaging in a variety of writing and reading tasks with a researcher (e.g., uninterrupted writing, writing a story, writing a letter, reading environmental print). Their intent was to come to better understand psycholinguistic and sociolinguistic processes in the evolution of literacy from the point of view of the learner. Ferreiro and Teberosky (1982) interviewed 108 4- through 6-year-olds from lower and middle class sectors of Buenos Aires, Argentina. Working from a Piagetian stance (that written language is a cultural object whose workings pose logical problems for learners), and relying on Piaget's clinical open-ended interview as method, Ferreiro and Teberosky devised a series of ingenious tasks to allow children to reveal their own interpretations of the nature and function of the written system.

These studies are obviously different from each other and from the one I am reporting on here. With the exception of Calkins' (and Graves') subjects, the children were younger than ours. Though methods certainly varied (both participant-observation of natural, ongoing activity and researcher-elicited responses were employed), researchers in these four investigations were all present as the children wrote, revised, talked, explained, reasoned. As I have discussed at length, for good reasons we were not. Thus, while all five studies aimed at inferring the learners' point of view, there were considerable differences in just exactly what the child was viewing. The child's perspective on reading and writing tasks set by the researcher was what Harste et al. and Ferreiro and Teberosky were able to infer. The child's view of how the adult system *qua* system works is what both Ferreiro and Teberosky and our research team studied. However, in Ferreiro and Teberosky's research design, children had much more latitude than in ours to define that system themselves, to reveal what they counted as part of the system of written language. The learner's view of an activity (rather than a system), defined by the participants is what Dyson, Calkins, and Harste et al. were able to infer. Additionally, Calkins was interested in the child's perspective on writing as a craft. We too were interested in understanding writing from the learner's perspective, but our design constrained us to look only at children's perspectives on parts of an activity, defined not by the children but by us, the researchers. By documenting their perspective on many parts of that activity and system, we hoped to provide baseline data for a population of children whose writing had previously been ignored.

Despite these major differences, I will try to relate findings and viewpoints from these other studies to our own where possible in this summary of major findings. First, there was no common developmental pattern that each child experienced in detail. Dyson (1982), Calkins, and Harste et al. made the same point. Despite the idiosyncratic details concerning progressions, however, we did find many overarching generalities. Only the most general of these will be listed here.

(1) There was little written code switching. Switches in English texts seemed like "slips of the pen" while in Spanish they were more substantive. What little code switching there was decreased in the higher grades.

(2) Spelling was not merely right or wrong, invented or conventional. There were both more and less literate inventions. Temple, Nathan, and Burris (1982) and Ferreiro and Teberosky also found a progression of invented spellings. Our youngest children were already beyond the earliest kinds of inventions described by Temple et al., and at least at the level of moving from the syllabic hypothesis (that every syllable should be encoded with one letter) to the alphabetic principle described by Ferreiro and Teberosky. For our children, more literate Spanish invented spellings were those based on phonics generalization; less literate ones were based on phonetic features. Beginning English inventions were based on Spanish orthography. As children became more aware of the system of English spelling, they began to invent based on English phonics generalizations. All along, the systems were kept separate to some extent (e.g., saving the letter *k* for English, tildes and accents for Spanish).

(3) There were four bases for unconventional segments: syntactic, syllabic, "anti"-syntactic, and "anti"-phonological/morphological. The last two were used by just a few children. Over time, larger and more central syntactic units became conventionally segmented before smaller and more minor ones. This is similar to Ferreiro and Teberosky's discovery that an early approach to segmentation was to attribute a whole sentence to a single segment; a later hypothesis included the encodability of major parts of a sentence (nouns, verb phrases) in separate segments, but not articles; finally, articles were considered encodable.

In our data, syllabic segments gained then lost popularity. This finding, that syllables were important units to be reckoned with at different ages, has backing from Clay (1977), whose 4- to 6-year-olds preferred the syllable to the phoneme in metalinguistic analyses, and from Ferreiro and Teberosky. The Argentine children too held a stage-specific hypothesis focused on the syllable. Syllables also appeared in Harste et al.'s data. The Indiana researchers classified segmentation as spelling (spelling the way it looks) and called children's early segments reflections of "writing systems." They found, as we did, that the same child often tried out several systems in one piece—chunking according to meaning (what we called no space within a formula—e.g., *habíaunavez*/onceuponatime), chunking by syllables, and chunking by words. However, with theoretical justification, Harste et al. refrained from comparing which of these "systems" were favored by different aged children. In our study, by the end of the third grade, most children were segmenting conventionally most of the time.

(4) Early invented punctuation patterns focused on local units—the word, the line, the page—and often concerned separation. Later invented patterns focused on text-ness. Others have reported on punctuation, but on its psychogenesis or on its correlation with classroom practice. Ferreiro and Teberosky's children at first made no separation between letters and punctuation marks. Their most mature hypothesis not only made this differentiation but began to assign different functions to the two. Calkins found that greater knowledge of punctuation marks (more varied types and greater understanding of their uses) was attributable to more classroom experience with genuine writing, writers' conferences, and editing for a purpose as contrasted with more classroom time spent on punctuation exercises.

(5) Tildes were used frequently and usually correctly; accents were not. Not surprisingly, cursive handwriting predominated by mid-third grade. However, even first graders made some use of cursive writing.

(6) Content of upper graders' writing was rated higher on various dimensions. That English pieces were rated higher was due to the fact that most English pieces had been written by third graders. Likewise, the quality of the content of unassigned writing was rated lower because first graders had written most of the unassigned pieces.

(7) Links between clauses moved through the following progression: "no links," then tying nearly all clauses with *and,* then using an increasing variety of lexical links including a return to the "no links." Such a pattern may have reflected a more general and changing conception of what constitutes a text: unrelated clauses on a single sheet of paper; clauses tied only by virtue of the glue of *and;* clauses tied through various semantic relationships. Unassigned writing, even though written mostly by first graders, contained a greater variety of lexical links.

(8) There were few culturally specific and "bootlegged" topics altogether; of this low number, most appeared in Spanish pieces.

(9) The most common principle used in organizing pieces was the logic of association, followed by the logic of time. If the piece was instigated by the child rather than the teacher, it was more likely to be organized according to time.

(10) Beginnings were often formulaic and genre-specific. Titles became common in third grade. Some genres (e.g., stories) elicited more closure than others.

(11) Explicit acknowledgement of a reader appeared more often in certain

types of pieces and those written under certain conditions. Letters and books contained more marks (e.g., arrows, notes) directed to a reader than other types of writing. However, the more child-involved pieces (coinciding with the unassigned) usually contained no acknowledgement of a reader.

While we found contextual variation but no "developmental" differences in accounting for the reader in the products created by children in different grades, Calkins found significant changes in the ways her young writers accounted for readers as they were actually engaged in the process of planning and revising their work.

(12) Almost all books displayed essential features of "book lay-out." Journals frequently had no comment about what was important in the event mentioned—just bald statements that an event had occurred. Letters contained fewer adult features of structure and layout. Most stories were multi-episodic yet incomplete.

(13) Language of the piece affected many of the aspects we examined. English pieces were rated as having higher quality content, were more often organized on the basis of time, were more conventionally segmented—all artifacts of the demography of the sample. A more genuine influence from "language" was that code switching was almost non-existent and inadvertent in English pieces, more frequent and referential in Spanish pieces. Punctuation in English pieces was more related to handwriting than to text-ness; the reverse was true for Spanish pieces.

Some children "did the same thing" in both Spanish and English pieces (i.e., used similar segmentation bases, similar solutions for how to end a text, and so on). Others did things differently depending on the language. Regardless of whether surface features for a given child were "the same" or "different" they reflected one underlying process: application of knowledge of first language writing to writing in the second language.

(14) When children wrote out their own intentionality, they used more marked and elaborate endings and less punctuation. More importantly, they wrote different types (stories, jokes, songs, invitations) and struggled with hypotheses that never seemed to surface in pieces spurred by the teacher's intentions. When, in addition, they wrote as part of a genuine relationship between writer and reader, the purposes of the pieces were obvious and seemingly more sincerely "owned" by the writers.

Calkins's meaning of intentionality was similar to ours. She treated the issue of intent in relation to ownership, as we did. It was a major theme as she discussed optimum conditions for growth in writing. Borrowing a metaphor from Graves, she claimed that if writers "rented" rather than "owned" their pieces, if they wrote someone else's topics for someone else's purposes, they did not take as good care of them, hardly cared for or about them.

Dyson (1983) and Harste et al. also discussed intentionality, but with somewhat different meanings. Dyson explained that if researchers and teachers do not allow very young children to show them how they structure an activity at least in part designatable as "writing," they miss capturing the child's meanings and intentions and only discover the child's view of researcher-defined tasks and intents. She incorporated her argument into her research design and found that young kindergarteners wrote as an alternative to other means of expression, to create objects where drawing and talking elaborated and specified the meanings of the graphics.

Harste et al. approached intentionality as something attributed to written language by readers. In their framework, intentionality meant something akin to deliberateness. Even very young children in their study saw marks on a paper as being put there intentionally to convey some meaning. Harste et al. argued that it is the pervasiveness of literate people's (even extremely young literate people's) tendency to attribute intentionality to instances of writing that drives them to invent strategies to create and impute meanings and intentions for texts (i.e., to read).

(15) Teachers' activities and beliefs affected children's writing at all levels. Teachers affected writing *directly* through the assignments they gave (these were primarily responsible for the genres written); through the centers and materials they provided (pieces with poetic phrasing came out of writing centers and were written on large paper with markers rather than being assigned and written on regular paper); through the values and beliefs they held (encouraging great length and sound-based spelling strategies); and through the modeling and coaching they did (eliciting added-on revisions in response to requests to "tell me more"). Teachers affected writing *indirectly* through the print environments they created (which likely discouraged code switching, especially in English texts); through the materials they provided (colored markers elicited color topics, unlined paper pushed children to draw numbered lines we categorized as punctuation); and through various beliefs (defining pieces assigned for non-existent audiences as functional writing; assigning "motley genres" resulted in pieces organized with big shifts; believing that writing development came from correct spelling taught through intense and exclusive use of workbooks probably caused children to conceive of a text as an unrelated collection of workbook-like phrases; thinking written language was best used for relating to another person engendered pieces children were highly involved in; feeling children were best left alone to write allowed children to repeatedly wrestle with problems they invented for themselves).

Each study, including this one, gave many indications of the powerful role of instruction and teachers' beliefs on what and how children wrote and thought about written language. Ferreiro and Teberosky did not incorporate the teacher's influence or the effect of classroom instruction into their research design, but they inferred teachers' effects on children's knowledge of written language. By offering a traditional curriculum, Ferreiro and Teberosky asserted that teachers ensure success only for those with quite advanced concepts of written language, unwittingly contributing to the illiteracy of those without such concepts.

Dyson (1982) documented the ways teachers' ideas of how to teach writing limited rather than expanded the children's own strategies for controlling written language. Calkins (and Graves, 1983) described the ways children incorporated predictable and recurring teacher strategies for questioning and planning into their conferences with peers and eventually into their "conferences" with themselves. Harste et al. presented evidence of how a teacher's tactics and directions regarding format appeared in a child's layout of letters on a page.

(16) A piece's type affected what appeared in that piece. Different genres usually looked like what they were. Some genres were written under different conditions (e.g., first-grade letters were coached by the teacher) so conditions and genre differences were sometimes interrelated. Writers were more involved with stories and books, which were also rated as having better content than expository pieces or journals. These were also the types that had some of the most advanced features.

(17) Differences over time were artifacts of teacher or researcher requests as well as "development." Still, there were "developmental" changes over the year for all grades. These included increasing length, increasing variety of lexical links, and higher ratings of quality of content.

(18) Additional "developmental" differences for first graders included: a shift from unconventional segments based on major syntactic units to segments based on syllables and smaller syntactic units; a shift from the use of phonetic features to phonics generalizations as the basis for inventing Spanish spellings; a decrease in invented punctuation patterns focusing on lines or words.

(19) Additional "developmental" differences for second graders included: decreased reliance on chunking together major syntactic units as unconventional segments and an increased use of syllabic segments; a move from fewer to more links that were variants of *and;* and an increasing use of punctuation based on units of text rather than units of paper.

(20) Additional "developmental" differences for third graders included: a shift from syllabic to syntactically based unconventional segments with the latter being small, minor syntactic units, and increasing conventionality in segmentation and spelling.

(21) "Developmental" differences in links for Grade X children resembled first graders' progression. Beginning of the year writing by these two sets of children was alike in certain other respects too (endings, organizational principle, syntactically based segmentation, tense usage). These features might therefore be related to experience with literacy. Harste et al. saw their subjects' responses as bearing essential similarities regardless of age. In fact, they claim adults' and pre-schoolers' literacy decisions should be separated only on the basis of experience with print, not according to any (non-existent, they argue) difference in stages or levels. Thus, our Grade 1 and Grade X similarities support their argument. However, the two sets of writing also differed in other respects. Grade X pieces were longer, contained no code switches and no formulaic beginnings or invented punctuation, relied more heavily on phonics as the basis

for spelling inventions, and from the start of the year made use of the syllable as a basis for segmenting. These features might therefore be more related to age and language development than to schooling or experience with print. (However, although Grade X children, like first graders, had less experience with print in school than the other children did, their advanced age may well have allowed them to have more and different kinds of print experience. Thus experience might still not be able to be ruled out as an explanation for the contrasts between Grade X and Grade 1 writing.)

SUMMARY OF THE SUMMARY

I have presented some of the specifics of change, if not "development," in the writing of these children attending a bilingual program. Even with the disclaimers about the difficulty of making strong claims for "development," I have certainly presented implicit or explicit notions about that topic. So did other investigators of children's writing. Calkins saw growth as a change in children's general, overall theories about "good writing" and an increase in number, sophistication, and density of their concepts of writing. Dyson (1983) interpreted change as following an orthogenetic principle—an undifferentiated fusion evolving into distinct concepts gradually becoming integrated so that concepts maintained their new distinctiveness at the same time as they became linked with each other. Ferreiro and Teberosky defined growth as the acquisition of more adult-like concepts about a cultural object of knowledge, as the recurrent resolution of cognitive conflicts in relation to that object until no further conflicts were engendered. Later resolutions depended for their existence on earlier ones interacting with the object of knowledge itself. Harste et al. presented growth as a change in the content, but not the process, of making literacy decisions. They found the *process,* regardless of the age or experience of the decider, to include the following features: organization, intentionality, generativeness, risk, social action, context, text, and demonstration. The changeable *content* did not consist of isomorphic aspects. Instead, content took shape as a result of a single decision on the question: what text is right for this context? Greater experience answering that question was what accounted for change in the content of the decision.

Each of these researchers presented somewhat different perspectives on growth. Yet they share with us at least one essential point: growth consisted of reorganization rather than accretion. Both the tallied findings in this chapter and the evidence countering various myths in the preceding chapter substantiate the following position. Change over time in writing should be seen as changes in purposes and their means of accomplishment, as changes in the repertoires of internally generated, externally influenced hypotheses. These concerned amount of information, length, punctuation, links between clauses, handwriting, accommodating to an audience, and more. The hypotheses were formulated, modified, and abandoned through interaction with various contexts. These contexts varied from classroom to classroom, print environment to print environment, piece to piece. They included teachers' activities and beliefs, motivation for the writing, type and language of the piece, administrative mandates for classroom practice, expectations for children's success with literacy, and community perceptions of literacy and its functions. It was not merely *in* each of these overlapping contexts that children generated hypotheses about the various sub-systems of written language, but *through* them. Some constellations of contexts encouraged hypotheses with certain systems of written language while discouraging attention to others. Other constellations seemed more neutral, as if they were "granting permission" for writers to focus on any part of the systems at any given moment. But it was only *through* contexts that growth in writing occurred.

This has many important messages for both practitioners and researchers. It means that teachers and administrators must examine the contexts they are providing for children, knowing that children's repertoires of hypotheses about written language (i.e., what they acquire) will be constrained or liberated by external factors. It means that evaluators and researchers must understand that any one piece of writing cannot show what a child can do. At the very least, it requires acknowledging the interdependence of internal processes and external factors in writing.

Chapter 6

SOME INDIRECT IMPLICATIONS AND A FEW MORE QUESTIONS

In most chapters so far, I have either implicitly presented and tentatively suggested or explicitly and strongly urged certain future directions based on our data analyses. These direct implications are scattered throughout, but are especially concentrated at the end of Chapter 4, in the discussions of certain tables in Chapter 5, and in regard to certain issues summarized in Chapter 5 (particularly language of the text, instigator of the piece, teachers' beliefs and activities). However, our findings also suggest some implications that are less directly tied to particular data. These concern the value of studies on bilingual populations, the effect of children's writing on teachers, unmet needs regarding bilingual print environments, and new views of classroom management.

INDIRECT IMPLICATIONS

A Study of a Bilingual Population

In some places there are a great many Spanish speaking or Spanish/English bilingual children becoming literate and also acquiring greater proficiency with English. This study is obviously pertinent to the concerns of educators who teach, plan for, and do research with these children. But there are even more places in the world where minority language children are not Spanish speakers, where the second language to be learned is not English, or where the children are native speakers of either the majority or the school language. When monolingual children are native speakers of the single school language variety (albeit comprising multiple style levels and registers), their "only" language task is mother tongue development, including acquisition of written language. Does a study of Spanish/English bilingual children learning to write have anything to say to people concerned with populations with different patterns of multilinguality?

Does it imply anthing for those connected with "plain ol' regular" monolingual education?

It was only by examining the relation of first and second language writing by beginning biliterates that it was possible to uncover certain strategies and knowledge the writers used in their writing. Because we were privy to seeing children write a language before they could (or at least would) speak it, we were able to understand more completely the error in some current ideas about sequencing in Language Arts programs (e.g., oral before written). Bilingual programs are one of the few contexts that enable anyone to investigate such sequences, since children who acquire literacy only in the mother tongue already have oral proficiency on entrance to school. (Another is programs for non-oral physically handicapped youngsters.) People involved primarily with monolingual education, then, would do well to find out more about the work of researchers and practitioners committed to bilingual education. Other populations, other contexts, always have the potential for providing a new perspective on issues of import on the home front.

Surely, bilingual education personnel benefit from obtaining information on linguistic, cognitive, and social processes derived from research with subjects who do not have the exact language and cultural backgrounds as a particular student population. Not so obviously recognized are the advantages to monolingual education personnel of learning how these processes are revealed in bilingual classrooms. Yet this study alone (not to mention the many others concerned with bilingual populations that are rarely cited in research reports on mainstream populations, and are rarely referred to in policy decisions) has many implications for "regular" education. Research on bilingual populations or on bilingual education could enrich the understandings of all educators; continued parochialism, on the other hand, has little to recommend it.

Effects of Writing on Teachers

When interviewed, the three study teachers and three aides said that seeing their students' ideas expressed in writing made them realize that their students had good ideas, were smart, capable, and so on. Moreover, they said the children's writing had made teaching a "more interesting job." Additionally, Bergionni, the Bilingual Program Director, reported that it was a rare day that some classroom adult from one of the other bilingual classes did not come to her office waving a child's writing, exclaiming she or he had never before realized so-and-so was so smart, but "look at this!" An emphasis on writing, it seems, enhanced these children in the eyes of teachers and aides. And it was writing in the language of their choice in a Program designed to develop both their first and second languages that permitted them to reveal previously unnoticed abilities. I have no proof to offer, other than alluding to teacher expectation literature, but it is reasonable to suggest that such enhanced perceived status would increase the children's chances of actual success in school.

Before attributing such an effect to writing *per se,* however, it is necessary to understand something else about contexts to appreciate how children's writing could brighten their star in the eyes of classroom adults. At the time of this study, school writing was not commercially packaged like school reading was. There were no writing process kits, no writing process workbooks, no writing process computer software, no canned scripts to be used for conferences, no uniform commercial-program or standardized writing-test-inspired criteria for evaluating and instructing. Instead, teachers could look at children's writing *almost* directly; they could view it through only one filter—their own biases. Their view was not also clouded with the biases of some commercial instruction and evaluation scheme. Without the constraints imposed by packaged writing materials, it was probably easier for the teachers in our study to avoid confusing progress in some ''instructional'' scheme for progress with a process; it was more likely that they could catch glimpses of and come to appreciate the process itself. The teachers could then act as professionals, allowing themselves to be more insightful, to make more qualified and subtle judgments (as opposed to checking off answers on a ditto sheet or itemizing skills mastered in a ''levels'' program). No wonder that teaching was ''more interesting'' when children did a great deal of writing!

All of this strongly implies that efforts must be made to prevent writing from becoming packaged (and profitable for someone other than children and teachers). School boards and administrators must be convinced that there is no need to invest money in packaged writing programs in order for children and teachers to reap benefits. Indeed, they should be shown how such packages might prevent full realization of these benefits. Teachers must be persuaded that they do not need such ''help.'' The teachers in this study were not only imperfect teachers of writing; their imperfections were also individual. I have indicated several times that what the teacher believed, what the teacher did or did not do, was reflected in children's writing. Still, the answer to varying imperfections is not to package writing as so much else has been packaged in education, relegating teachers to the role of materials dispensers and test scorers. Rather, the answer is to help teachers understand the nature of the writing process and language acquisition processes generally, to support them as professionals.

Print Environment

From observations of the actual print environments (what print materials were available and which were used) in a half dozen Bilingual Program classrooms, from observations of children interacting with those print environments, and from reflections of the print environments in children's writing, it seems that both Spanish and English print environments were inadequate. Children were not read to frequently from good children's literature, and they spent little time reading themselves.

The Spanish print environment was especially insufficient. Since it barely existed outside of school, what existed in school was almost all there was. This included little except stories (almost no science, social studies, health, music, or reference materials, very scanty "environmental print" in Spanish). It was largely of poorer quality (stories were often cut out of primers, materials were dittoed). It is possible that some aspects of the older children's writing at least (e.g., persistent unconventional segmentation, absence of any punctuation in many pieces) might have reflected, in part, minimal interaction with a meager print environment. (Of course, there were also other explanations.) It is urgent, then, that both practitioners and researchers examine print environments if they are concerned about literacy. I have no easy solutions to offer for the problems of limited funds in bilingual programs and limited supplies of other-than-English print. However, settling too quckly for meager environments or ignoring the issue entirely do not seem like the most appropriate responses. Short of a complete change in the language situations of both local and wider communities, only focused attention and a great deal of ingenuity can remedy the problem.

Classroom Management

It is hard to believe that the purposeful, orderly, polite, and cooperative activity we saw in some of these classrooms was due simply to teachers' skills in planning, organizing, and managing their classrooms. These were classes where discipline was rarely an issue, where children and teachers saw each other as sensible beings, where children took out their own materials and cleaned up after themselves without direction, where teachers seemed to be "playing themselves" rather than "playing teacher," where subject matter areas were not tightly bounded, where children and teacher collaborated on some of the planning, where curriculum was experienced in relatively large time blocks. From an outsider's perspective, what seemed to undergird the pleasant and productive atmosphere was not "management" but curriculum and a particular quality to the interpersonal relationships in those classes. Unfortunately, I have no information on how the teachers established that crucial classroom climate at the beginning of the year, but my strong hunch is that it was built with three basic ingredients: (1) certain kinds of verbal interaction between adults and children, demonstrating and demanding mutual respect and caring; (2) deliberate efforts to turn some legitimate power over to the children; and (3) a curriculum that includes children having control over at least some of their reading and writing.

Even without information on how the climate was established, however, it is still important to note that these children, who have been considered as requiring close supervision and a highly structured curriculum so that they stay "on task," in fact displayed extraordinary self-direction with loosely structured curricula. It seems obvious from these data and others (see Edelsky et al., 1983a) that the "truisms" about classroom management and effective teaching (e.g., keep objectives clear and short-term, do much whole-class instruction, keep transitions short, maintain a quick and lively pace, break tasks down into small parts, etc.) do not hold for classroom practice based on alternative literacy practices.

If my hunch about these three basic ingredients seems wildly speculative, the descriptions of these classrooms should prompt even the most suspicious to at least consider this proposition: *what* one manages has great influence over the management that is required. In the few classrooms in this Program where a different conception of literacy seemed to undergird at least some activities (child-controlled writing, projects for science and social studies), the usual management techniques that correlate with "good discipline" were nowhere in evidence. Yet children in these classrooms were clearly calm, pleased with school, and productive. Something is clearly missing from the usual content-free conceptions of "classroom management." My candidate for missing link has a surface name: curriculum. But much more profoundly missing is a full acknowledgement of the impact of the teacher's theoretical orientation to literacy (Harste & Burke, 1977; Edelsky & Draper, in press) on the intertwining of curriculum, instruction, and "management."

AND A FEW MORE QUESTIONS

Although we had anticipated it with our stance on the importance of contexts, until we were well into the coding we did not appreciate how extensive the teacher's influence was on children's writing. Donald Graves conducted a marvelously useful study at a site where practice differed from what we saw (Graves, 1983; Calkins, 1983). For instance, teachers in the New Hampshire setting gave few assigned topics but expected writing; they used revision as a tool for rethinking and differentiated it from editing; teacher–child and child–child conferences focused on the writer's information; selected writing was published. The examples Graves and Calkins provide in their reports of children's native English language writing at that site are considerably different from the writing of our children—more carefully crafted, more stylistically powerful, more focused, more writer-involved, more coherent, more conventional. Still, the two studies were conducted so differently that even the gross contrasts just cited may be partly attributable to features of research design and reporting as well as to differences in practice. It would be revealing, then, to look again in a more Gravesian way (daily on-site participant-observation) at writing in a bilingual program where teaching practice was examined as carefully as the writing and in classrooms where practices varied fundamentally. It would also be important to look closely at the writing of children in bilingual programs where the teachers have other characteristics (e.g., preparation in the teaching of writing, informed theories on the writing process, knowledge of children's literature in both languages, proven interest in writing themselves), and where the print environments have other characteristics (e.g., where the Spanish print environment rivals the English one in quantity, quality, and use). We know now that the children's writing would be unlike what we saw. The question is: how? Would it be possible to make any direct connections between specific features of writing and any of these contextual factors? Even more interesting would be to look for the processes and mechanisms whereby any of these contextual factors interact with children's hypotheses about written language.

Similarities and differences between the writing of the older, relatively unschooled Grade X children and that of first graders raised an old issue once again. Which kinds of literacy hypotheses are attributable to type and amount of experience with print and which owe more to social, cognitive, or linguistic maturity? Asking questions about writing development by asking about age hides the effects of experience with print as contrasted with various kinds of development. Teasing out the influence of often confounded factors is certainly not a new venture. Ferreiro and Teberosky (1982) looked at their data to see which aspects of growth in understanding of how the writing system works could be traced to socio-economic class-based experience and which could not. Scribner and Cole (1981) worked to sort out the effects of schooling from the effects of literacy on cognitive processing. But just which hypotheses in which realms of written language are more influenced and which are less influenced by experience with print remains an open question.

From our perspective (and from most of the work of the last two decades on child language), the children's "errors"/inventions in our data provided wonderful windows onto otherwise hidden processes. Surely there would be benefits from changing the traditional school attitudes toward "errors" (e.g., instruction directed mainly toward eradicating them). "Errors" could be more productively viewed as signs of healthy active hypothesis construction; instruction could then be geared more toward helping children deepen and extend their information and their ways of knowing. But aside from the implication of a change in attitude toward "errors" in writing, what are optimal educational strategies in this regard? And what should count as an "error" (e.g., if early writing makes use of drawing for conveying part of the text, should drawing that shows poorly proportioned people be corrected? Should the spelling PEPL be corrected?)

It is obvious to us that this study did not extend over a long enough time to look at the development of individuals. For instance, the two second graders who segmented most unconventionally (e.g., *pous T r*/poster; *ra cks*/rocks) used more of this kind of segmentation at the end of the year than at the beginning. One year was not long enough to take a systematic look at when they abandoned this hypothesis, or to find out what led to its modification. (The answer to part of this question appears in Chapter 7.) Another example: in order to get more than a glimpse of the connection between changes in the use of links between clauses and changes in conceptions of what constitutes a text, it would have been necessary to have writing samples from the same child, beginning before first grade and extending at least into third grade. In other words, the condition for answering these questions is another implication: a *long*-itudinal study (three or more years) of the writing of a few children in a biliteracy program would provide information that cannot be gained in one-year "longitudinal" efforts.

And a related question: if some Program effects could be seen in one year, but if one year were too short a time for seeing an adequate picture of the writing development of individuals, then one year was also insufficient for assessing many other effects of the bilingual program. What were those effects that did not appear immediately? What was the more lasting impact of having begun to read and write in Spanish, for instance?

Smith (1980, 1982) has theorized at length on the effect of writing on the writer, praising its potential for instilling feelings of competence, control, understanding. Perl's (1983) study explored children's struggles and insights about themselves as writers in a monolingual English-speaking public school. We did not observe children in the act of writing over the entire year, nor did we interview them. We are limited to teachers' and aides' reports on the topic for our information on how writing affected these writers. We still do not know, therefore, how a particular writing curriculum affected writers' views of themselves in this particular bilingual program.

This brings us to the end of an out-of-balance trilogy—a short history of the theory, prior to the data analyses, underlying the proddings and cajolings of the Bilingual Program Director in Duncan District and her consultants; a brief description of different parts of that Program, its role in the community, and other aspects of different contexts; and a very long tale of many features and changes in the writing of children in Duncan's Bilingual Program and the implications and questions these raised. But wait; each story in the overall account—theory, Program, children's writing—has yet one more turn on center stage.

Chapter 7

AFTER THE STUDY: THREE EPILOGUES

These three "tale-ends" will not be so out of balance. There is as much to tell in the story of the theory that drove the study and about what was going on in Duncan District after the Spring of 1981 as about the children's writing in the year following the study. Unfortunately, the stories of writing and of Program do not have very happy endings; at least a partial explanation can be found in the stories of theory and Program.

THE THEORY FIRST

By the time we began collecting data, I was committed to viewing writing and reading from my conception of a "whole language" theoretical orientation. As I indicated in Chapter 1, that meant thinking about written language as a super system consisting of sub-systems. More critically, it also meant that any instance of written language use simultaneously offers cues to meaning from interdependent and interactive sub-systems. In 1980, we considered the sub-systems to be the graphophonic, the syntactic, and the semantic. These, we thought, operated together and were influenced by a particular context—but the context was separate from the instantiation of written language. And though we put both readers and writers in an active posture, interpreting or creating meanings, we had not yet come to understand Rosenblatt's (1978) or Harste and Carey's (1979) ideas of people *transacting* meanings *with* "text potentials" to create *text*.

We thought then that some activities designated as reading and writing in school lacked the potential for contributing to a child's written language development. Filling in blanks, reading flashcards, writing word lists, completing sentences in a workbook, participating in round robin reading of paragraphs in controlled-vocabulary readers—we considered all these ordinary classroom literacy activities to be impoverished uses of written language. We took seriously the theoretical proposals and research findings (Hymes, 1970; Ervin-Tripp & Mitchell-Kernan, 1977; Halliday, 1978) that indicate that people *use* language (1) for a variety of their own (even if culturally delineated) purposes, and (2) to convey multiple meanings. The trouble with spelling exercises, round robin reading, finishing some workbook-writer's sentences, and the like was that these seemed to be examples of reading and writing with little purpose other than to comply with an assignment and provided little opportunity for children to create their own meanings. We naively thought that if children wrote invitations to real parties, birthday greetings on people's birthdays, letters requesting information they would use in class, and so on, *their* purpose for writing would really be to invite, to greet, to request. We overlooked the fact that there is more to having a purpose than producing invitations, greetings, letters of request, and other genres whose names imply such purposes.

As we began to collect the data and develop coding categories, the perfunctory quality of much of the children's writing became apparent. Children were in fact producing messages in whole texts (not just sentence completion exercises), pieces with a surface, "real world" purpose at least (not just an "instructional" purpose like learning to spell the weekly spelling list). Yet the superficiality and the writer's lack of involvement with the text hardly seemed conducive to great developmental leaps in the acquisition of written language. Perfunctory though "purposeful" writing (e.g., assigned invitations to the principal to come to a class party) contrasted on many dimensions with involved, seemingly purposeless but unassigned writing (e.g., descriptions of multi-colored clothing written spontaneously at a writing center). And the contrast was usually to the detriment of the former. I began to suspect that if even these whole assigned texts could be found so wanting, maybe our disregard for "meaningless purposeless" writing exercises was really a disregard for assigned writing. I began to argue that the distinction we had been making between purposeless, unproductive-for-development and purposeful, productive-for-development writing was more accurately a distinction between assigned and unassigned writing. And that is where the analysis ended in 1981.

Fortunately, new information continues to confront old analyses. Lee Odell (1982) described the distortions and peculiarities in law students' *assigned* reports for their professors as contrasted with the accurate meshing of information with audience needs in *assigned* reports on bills written for legislative committees they worked for. Thus the feature of assignment or spontaneity could not be the whole issue either.

Then in 1982, I was a participant-observer in a truly "whole language" inner city sixth-grade classroom (Edelsky et al., 1983a). What I saw there contributed greatly to my notions on how to separate writing wheat from chaff. Children in that class wrote for their peers, revising to make their writing believable, appealing, and comprehensible. They took part in conferences focusing on composition issues as well as editing points (punctuation and spelling). They read whole books in as many sittings as necessary either for "sheer enjoyment" or for literature study discussions. They kept journals on certain books they were reading, guessing what would happen next and justifying their guesses. They planned, rehearsed, and carried out plays and elaborate presentations for peer and adult audiences. They ferreted out the interests of their own "assigned" first grader in order to pick out appropriate books to read aloud to that child, practiced the reading-aloud so the performance would be entertaining, and figured out ways to attract that first grader to written language use. They devised their own science experiments, kept written records of manipulations and changes in variables, and wrote up the results for replication by others. *And all of these literacy tasks were assigned by the teacher.*

In September, these sixth graders treated the assignment to write dialogue journal entries to the teacher as if it were a task *for* the teacher. They complied, but seemed not to care much about what they wrote. They allowed me to look over their shoulders as they wrote "nice" entries to a "nice" teacher from "nice" children. A month later, producing journal entries had become a changed activity. Now, instead of open-to-the-public, superficial niceness, the entries were written with shoulders hunched over, arms shielding the content from others' eyes, about sometimes troubled but always private topics. What had happened? The journals were still assigned but the children had come to share with the teacher ownership of the assignment, of the intent to write.

Just about that time, I read a review of writing research by Newkirk (1982) which pointed out critically that the problem with writing assignments was not imposition, but inauthenticity. Asking people to write essays on assigned topics, Newkirk argued, distorts the essence of essay writing, which is struggling to discover precise meanings that match more general topical intentions.

It had been slow in coming, but at last the light flashed on! The problem with most school literacy activity was not just purposelessness. (In fact, it was produced with purposes of compliance and evaluation.) It was not assignment vs. spontaneity or in-school vs. out-of-school. It was that most of what is called reading and writing in school is inauthentic, only a facsimile, not the real thing. Some of the activities masquerading as reading and writing are inauthentic because meaning-creation is not a central goal. Some are inauthentic because they don't require that children wrestle with all the cuing systems. Some are inauthentic because one set of pragmatic constraints prevents the operation of another set. But regardless of the reason, the overarching characteristic that applies to both exercises we had argued against as well as much of the assigned writing we had as data that seemed so lacking in—well—authenticity—was in fact inauthenticity. Like other research operationalizations or laboratory tasks that are supposed to represent some phenomenon in the real world but in fact do not, much of the writing from our study and others and most of the reading and writing in schools was actually one phenomenon (pseudo-reading/pseudo-writing) sub-stituted for that which people were originally interested in (reading and writing).[1]

Now surely, this must seem like an extreme, even outrageous position to some. Let me place the concept in relation to a body of literature, define it as I now understand it or at least present the features of authentic reading and writing, and then provide examples with explanations of why they are or are not cases of authentic reading or writing.

This idea of something that looks like, but isn't, actually reading (I am extending it to writing) is closely related to discussions by Harste et al. (1981) to the effect that, since print is predictable and functional, to make it unpredictable and non-functional and then to investigate people's responses to such a graphic display is to study something which is not reading. The idea has also been clearly influenced by the Goodmans' and Frank Smith's evolving theories of the reading process, especially their statements on readers' strategies of predicting and con-firming while making meaning (see Goodman, 1969; Goodman & Goodman, 1978; Smith, 1975, 1978). Rosenblatt's theory (1978) of a reader transacting a poem in concert with a text, Shanklin's (1981) psycho-socio-linguistic concep-tion of the relation of reading and writing—these too were part of the thinking on which the present idea is based. A few other researchers have also begun to refer to distinctions between "the real thing" and artificial simulations of talking and writing. In an article in which she disputes a popular claim that there has been a significant change in ways of teaching English as a second language, Raimes (1983) points out that despite appearances, students in English as a Second Language classes are still usually engaged in "language practice and not real discourse" (p. 544). And Staton, Shuy, Kreeft, and Reed (in press) distinguish certain entries in dialogue journals (those that were self-generated and propelled by the writer's intentions) from others which did not seem marked by "mutual participation." The idea I am proposing here, authentic versus simulated reading and writing, differs from its predecessors and from Raimes' and Staton et al.'s formulations in that it is more extreme and more explicit in definition and implications for research and instruction.

---

[1] A longer, more detailed theoretical proposal concerning authenticity in reading and writing appears in Edelsky and Draper (in press). The purpose in that paper was to argue the need to recognize the distinction between reading/writing and "reading"/"writing." In the present discus-sion, on the other hand, my purpose is to explain what is behind my dissatisfaction with various aspects of the study, the in-service I conducted, and the curriculum-as-offered rather than the curriculum-as-proclaimed in Duncan's Bilingual Program. But it must be kept in mind that the Bilingual Program, with its emphasis on what turned out not to be writing but more life-like simulations of writing, offered a less *in*authentic literacy program than did the regular program and than did any bilingual program we had seen up to that time. That is, while saying that Duncan's Bilingual program offered "writing" instead of writing is a criticism according to the theoretical stance I am presenting here, it is much more a criticism of those programs that do not even begin to approach this Bilingual Program in terms of aiming toward wholeness of written language use.

To be authentically reading and writing, I now believe, a person has to be trying to create an authentic written language text—not necessarily an elegant text, not necessarily a socially approved text, but an authentic text. Such a text is a transaction between a person aiming for meaning-making and a graphic display with one crucial feature. That feature is the predictability which derives from cues offered by four interactive, interdependent systems (graphic, syntactic, semantic, pragmatic) for predicting and confirming meanings. The direct implications of this idea are that: (1) every literacy event (every event involving print) does not include an act of reading or writing; (2) every graphic display (everything with print on it) does not have the potential to be part of an authentic text; (3) it is important to distinguish reading/writing from their imitators; and (4) for studying, instructing, or evaluating reading or writing, one should look at, teach, or assess reading and writing.

Reading and writing are universal processes of predicting and confirming to make meaning with print providing pragmatic, linguistic, and conceptual cues in particular social situations. Features of authentic reading and writing then are: meaning-making; transaction of an authentic text; use of print with interacting graphic, syntactic, semantic, and pragmatic cues providing different kinds of meanings; use of predicting and confirming strategies. These features are at the same time cognitive, social, and linguistic. (Everything that happens cognitively—every single strategy, every last hypothesis—is not socially derived. And even the most cognitive aspects of reading and writing are not devoid of social organization or linguistic influence.) The features are universal and essential; they are present in genuine reading/writing in traditional and open classrooms (I am not simply renaming educational philosophies). They are present in essayist as well as non-essayist writing, reading of both alphabetic and non-alphabetic orthographies, mundane reading and writing (making grocery lists, looking up a TV show schedule, passing "illegal" notes in school, reading sewing patterns, writing recipes), and more elegant text creations (preparing court briefs, reading novels, writing poetry). If the essential features are not present, it isn't reading or writing.

Every time someone reads or writes, that is a literacy event; but every literacy event does not include reading or writing. Literacy events vary enormously in different speech communities. Who has access to print, how it is used, for what purposes, whether or not the literacy event includes the creation of a comprehended, comprehensible written language text—none of this can be presupposed for any given literate speech community. However, there are still literacy event universals—the main one being the use of a graphic display as a graphic display (rather than as material for wrapping fish or insulating walls) so that it functions in social life. Similarly, there are both universals and variations in oral language acquisition. Regardless of extreme differences across speech communities in the norms of speaking that are acquired, it is not the case that in one speech community babies acquire language by forming habits and in another by generating hypotheses. And despite often documented cultural differences in child rearing and language socialization practices, there are also universals in early language "teaching" too (e.g., more mature users present all sub-systems of the language at once rather than offering sound one day and grammar the next; they use the language with the learner; etc.). Likewise, norms for authentic reading and writing can vary across speech communities. Print can be treated as sacred and uneditable, as less trustworthy than talk, or as more true than talk; texts can have their own value or be mere reminders for other non-written language texts. But regardless of the surface variation, as long as a written language text is being created by a person (or persons) predicting and confirming with cues from all interdependent written language systems to make textual meaning, it is reading or writing. If a written language text is not being created, if the activity is not predicting and confirming to make meaning with cues from all sub-systems, if the graphic display or the situation does not permit the interaction of all written language systems, it may be a literacy event but it is not reading or writing.

Unfortunately, most of the literacy activity in most classrooms (including those in Duncan's Bilingual Program) and in most research (including much of what I have presented in this volume) does not consist of instances of reading and writing. Instead, it consists of instances of frequently substituted facsimiles, of "reading" and "writing." Just because the substitution is widespread and deeply taken-for-granted, just because the inauthentic is so typical in instructional practice and research operationalizations, does not turn the substitute into the real thing. What happens typically is certainly a phenomenon of interest in its own right, but it must be distinguished from other phenomena with which it shares only certain (sometimes surface) features.

To reiterate, for creating an authentic text, two things are needed: (1) reading or writing; and (2) print with all sub-systems intact. As I explain the different sources of inauthenticity in the following examples, I will be trying to clarify the concept of authenticity in relation to both the activity and the graphic display.

When my monolingual English-speaking twin nephews pronounced the Hebrew printed in the Torah at their bar mitzvah, they were "reading," not reading. True, they were creating a cultural event with meaning to all present, but for them the print was a prop. They were not, could not be, predicting based on the semantic, syntactic, and pragmatic cues offered by the print. They may have recited a text that had meaning to some of the congregants. They may even have known that the sound of certain sections belonged with one part of the service rather than another so that just any Hebrew print could not have been used as a prop. Still, they were not using all the systems to create a meaningful *text* (as opposed to a meaningful *event*) for themselves. Even though their grandparents proudly exclaimed about "the fine reading," in fact they had been reciting.

A counterpart is copying and calling that writing. Children copying the teacher's model of a letter to parents, adults copying an address in a foreign orthography—these are instances of "writing." Someone is creating an object with overall pragmatic meaning for him or herself, but is detouring around the syntactic, semantic, and even the graphophonic systems, relying instead on recreating the graphic display. Now recreating is certainly not a mechanical process and recreations can be *read* by others. But for the copier it is copying, not writing.

Those familiar with recent anthropological and historical research on literacy will recognize that excluding my nephews' performance from the category called reading implies that the Vai (Scribner & Cole, 1981) and other "famous cases" who "decode" languages they do not understand are also not reading. In fact, I *am* arguing that every activity using print is not reading or writing, that every graphic display does not have the potential to be used for reading and writing. Many anthropologically oriented literacy researchers—not to mention, of course, experimentalist educational psychology researchers and others who look at supposed parts of reading or writing—do not agree. Moreover, they do not acknowledge the basis I am using for making this distinction (that only meaning-making, written-language-text-creating activity is reading or writing). Thus Szwed (1981) appears to urge researchers to count all uses of print as reading or writing. Scribner and Cole (1981) certainly counted the Vai's pronouncing of Qur'anic script as reading. (And the countless positivist researchers who publish in predominantly positivist research journals and who provide the bulk of the studies on inference, word recognition, etc., equate the experimental responses with reading or writing.) But do many qualitative researchers who use literacy as a lens for viewing some other social phenomena in fact maintain such a stance on the basis of a well-articulated theory of the nature of reading and writing? It seems to me that, instead, they invoke an epistemological argument, take a relativist stance on surface variation, and then apply their own unacknowledged and deeply underlying assumptions regarding reading and writing without recognizing them as "cultural" assumptions. If the predominant view of reading and writing in the Western world in modern times is that these processes consist essentially of inherently separable, even hierarchically organized skills—decoding, pronouncing, inscribing, recognizing words, analyzing affixes, comprehending, etc.—then if they do not deliberately set out to examine such assumptions, anthropologically oriented researchers (as well as the more experimentally minded who are often criticized for their cultural biases) would be likely to share them. And sharing in separate-skills notions would permit them to see reading and writing as activities which could potentially include *anything* one might do with print.

I think the anthropologically/historically oriented researchers of literacy do in fact put limits on how much of the perspective of those they study will be considered and sought out, though those limits may not be acknowledged. Just as one example, if a social group believes deciphering the meaning of cloud formations is reading and drumming messages is writing, it is not likely that such a group would be chosen by a cognitive anthropologist for a study on the effects of reading and writing on cognition. Most likely, for such a purpose, anthropologists would choose their own over the Others' perspective when they selected the site for researching that particular problem; most likely they would include a demand that a graphic display (not just clouds or drumbeats) should be part of a study of the relationship of literacy and cognitive processes. Now for many purposes (e.g., discovering a society's own definitions and distributions of literacy events), societies which count interpretations of non-graphic phenomena as reading and writing as well as those which insist on a graphic display would certainly be considered as appropriate data sources. For other purposes, however (e.g., investigating the impact of literacy on memory), the researchers' definition would supercede initially in order to identify possible research sites and subjects. If the researchers' perspective is that reading and writing consist of composites of separate skills related to a graphic display, that would not only set outer limits; it would also allow tremendous leeway. It would allow them to designate as *reading* and *writing* word calling, handwriting practice, recitations of foreign language texts, signing one's name with an X, pronouncing printed nonsense syllables off wall charts, and so on. With an assumption that reading and writing consist of separate skills, it is a short jump to the idea that the exercise of any one of the skills in seeming isolation also counts as reading or writing.

My claim, on the other hand, is that separate reading/writing skills do not add up to reading or writing, that the use of some sub-part of the whole activity *outside* of the whole activity may have no relationship to doing that sub-activity *within* the whole activity. When my nephews and the Qur'anic "reading" Vai fail to use all the cuing systems, fail to transact a meaningful text with print, they are not reading, although they are certainly taking part in a literacy event.

Authentic reading and writing requires not only a person who uses all cuing systems but print that offers these systems working interdependently. For example, audience, conditions for viewing (speed on a superhighway), genre (product label on a billboard), and intention (to generate quick recognition, to mark the product for cost, prestige, rough-and-readiness)—all pragmatic features—produce the spelling of *lite* for *light*. Slot (e.g., title, beginning, middle, end) and genre (e.g., recipe vs. folk tale—pragmatic features) affect syntax (*take one stewing hen* rather than *once upon a time there was a hen*). Some cues appear *in* the print. Orthographic and syntactic cues are usually visible through arrangements of letters, spaces, punctuation marks, order of words. Semantic cues can be present in lexical items and word placement. Some pragmatic cues, tying aspects of the context to features of language usage, are also in the print. For example, slot and genre are "in" the print and affect syntax, lexical choice, and graphic display. Cues can also be beyond the print (Pratt, 1977). Size and quality of the paper, illustration, whether or not the print was published, location of the print (bathroom, classroom, subway wall), identity of writer and reader—all these are pragmatic cues lying outside the print.

Print that fails to provide cues from all the written language systems cannot take part in a transaction creating an authentic text. Thus a person who is capable of reading other print (i.e., who can create a text with text-able print), when faced with print with missing or distorted cuing systems, cannot read it because that print *no sirve para leer* (it doesn't work for reading, to extend Ferreiro and Teberosky's 1982 research phrase). Examples abound of intact print—recipes, football scoreboards, TV guides, fortunes in fortune cookies, classic literature, junk novels, holdup notes, dictionaries, grocery lists—each used in appropriate contexts. Unfortunately, there are also plenty of examples in classrooms of flawed print—print with missing or distorted cues.

It is obvious when cuing systems are absent, rendering print less predictable. Take the difference between bumper stickers and flashcards. A one word bumper sticker might offer *God, Jesus, America, Peace, Tennis,* and so on. It will not, however, present *through, under, the, with.* The genre "bumper sticker," a pragmatic cue, limits the semantic and syntactic choices. A one word flashcard, however, could be any word; i.e., the pragmatic genre cue "this is a flashcard" does not limit the range. Further, there are no syntactic cues (and usually no semantic ones unless the set of flashcards all pertain to some classroom theme).

It is not so obvious when cues are distorted. Sometimes distortion is due to an "impossible" situation. That is, right from the start, the supposed purpose of the piece (pragmatic cue) cannot be accomplished because the prerequisite conditions have not been met. This is the case when a person uses print—ostensibly to inform—and only simulates an informing performance, since the intended audience is in fact better informed than the "writer"; the prerequisite condition (a less informed audience) is not met. Another example of the use of print with artificially induced, conflicting pragmatic cues that result in an inauthentic activity occurs when 30 children in a second-grade classroom are assigned to invite the principal to come to a party. The situation of 30 invitations to the same person to attend the same event violates some assumptions about invitations (e.g., that the inviter is the source of information about time, place, and the like). When each child knows that every other is also doing the inviting, there is little need to include all information, less reason to think one is inviting the principal, more reason to think one is complying with an assignment. The whole enterprise is thus "writing" rather than writing.

There are many variations on this theme of distortions and contradictions in cues. For instance, when a teacher or researcher wants "creative writing," "mood pieces," or even "well formed stories" and the student or subject merely wants to produce something that will count as compliance, the global intentions (Smith, 1982) are mixed in type and ownership. The student owns and juggles the more focal intentions (what idea should come next, what word is best here) in relation to the global ones, but these are owned by different people. When people write out another person's intentions *without adopting them as their own,* the purpose of compliance interferes with the accomplishment of those other purposes owned by the person who gave the assignment.

It is not that print can have only one purpose. People can intentionally complain, inform, and display status in the same piece of writing. (Theatre critics are experts here.) Nor is it the case that to be authentic, language use has to be transparent and straightforward. Certainly writers (and speakers) can be devious, deliberately or unwittingly misleading, or indirect. The examples of pragmatic distortions I have presented are not related to honor or awareness, but to a "set up" that prevents the accomplishment of ostensible purposes.

Distortions can also arise through the severing of one system from the others, prohibiting the interaction of all four systems of cues. Test paragraphs are significant examples here. While their genre (test paragraph) provides length and format cues (paragraphs followed by questions, or paragraphs with words deleted), that genre does not interact with syntactic or semantic systems. The pragmatic genre cue ("this is a test paragraph") does not help a person predict topic or style. All it signals is that any cue the paragraph provides as to content or style cannot be taken as such but must be seen as a possible spot for evaluation. The four cuing systems, once they are embedded in the overriding genre cue ("test paragraph"), no longer signal the same meanings. They are also now arbitrary in relation to genre rather than all being interrelated. Unless it is obscene, blasphemous, or unpatriotic, any topic may follow any other on a test. Some "reading" tests now try to make use of real-world material like jokes, recipes, letters, or newspaper articles. Even tests constructed with such material are still open to the charge of consisting of print that is profoundly "untextable"; the larger genre (test) overpowers and detracts from the cuing potential of these embedded genres and their interacting systems. Though the jokes, recipes, and the like were originally text-able, once they become part of a test or an experiment the graphic, syntactic, and semantic cues are severed from a major pragmatic cue. What were once cues to content and style must now be taken as potential spots for evaluation, as possible tricks. Thus, what purports to be a test of reading is not only *not* a test of reading; it *is* a test of how well one performs a simulation of reading and also a test of how well one responds to a special kind of artifice.

Stories written by authors whose prime purpose is instruction-of-separate-systems rather than "story-ing"—stories written according to readability formulae or for teaching spelling patterns—these too are untext-able. *Dan has a pan and the man has a fan* violates conventions that story elements are not arbitrary. Distortions in the syntax of graded readers and series (e.g., elimination of normal cohesive devices and embeddings for foregrounding and backgrounding) in fact make such print less "readable" (Davison & Kantor, 1982) let alone unavailable for the production of an authentic text. Similarly, flawed or absent cuing systems in the print used in many studies of reading render these studies of "reading" instead.

To have all cuing systems intact, to thus be available for creation of an authentic text, is not necessarily to be elegant or even legitimate. Graffiti has such availability. So does a grocery list for the one who wrote it but not necessarily for someone who finds a lost one. Nor does it have to be unassigned. As long as the assigned print and the assigned activity is invested with a purpose which comes to be "owned" or accepted by the reader/writer, it is available for authentic reading/writing, for creation of an authentic text.

I am not proposing a continuum from inauthentic to authentic, though there is a continuum from less to more authentic *simulations*. Responding to the assigned topic "If I Were A Penny" is certainly more *like* writing than putting a word in a blank in a workbook sentence. *But the most authentic simulation is still a simulation.* It is not the real thing. What I believe can now be theoretically justified are two separate categories, not two ends of one continuum—a category of authentic use of written language (including print that is predictable), and a category of activity that may look like reading and writing but isn't (including print that pretends to be text-worthy but isn't). This category may consist of a great variety of reading and writing substitutes. But no matter how life-*like,* they remain simulations.

Much of the data in our study in Duncan's Bilingual Program were more like writing than like doing workbook exercises. Moreover, they were more like writing than the work produced in other bilingual programs we were familiar with in various parts of the country. Unfortunately, however, many pieces were still inauthentic "writing" rather than authentic writing.[2]

Surely there is value in looking at every part of school life, including activities that only pretend to be reading and writing. Still, it is important to distinguish authentic reading and writing from their imitators, if for no other reason than to come to see the relations between them. For example, probably, being able to *read* and *write* enables one more easily to do phonics exercises, pronounce words on flashcards, produce perfunctory descriptive paragraphs of "my desk top"— i.e., to simulate reading and writing. It may not be the case, however, that the reverse is true, that the widespread instructional and assessment assumption is valid. That is, despite the premises built into almost all literacy curricula that learning to do simulations of reading and writing leads to authentic reading and writing, this may not be the case at all. And despite the firm, widespread belief that testing people's simulated reading and writing is the same as (correlates with, predicts) their genuine reading and writing, there is no evidence to that effect. Instead, we have evidence that scores on simulations predict and correlate with judgments of performance in educational programs requiring simulations (including the advanced and sophisticated simulations found in much college coursework). The relation between simulations and the real thing is simply assumed, a taken-for-granted given. What I am arguing is not that that assumption is totally wrong but that it certainly cries out for questioning. However,

---

[2] Lest this study be seen, therefore, as less valuable than other studies of writing, I invite readers to ask themselves how many of the studies that claim to be about writing are indeed about writing according to the distinction I am developing here.

before any investigation can even be begun, there must first be an acknowledgment that there is a distinction between reading/writing and ''reading''/''writing.''

Such an acknowledgment is also needed in order to decide what classrooms should be used as models or as research sites for examining practices in Whole Language classrooms. To me, those that are rightly considered Whole Language classrooms (1) offer print with all systems intact and operating interactively, and (2) assign children to engage in literacy activity that uses all the sub-systems to create meaningful texts. That means they are classrooms where the main literacy activity is authentic reading and writing, where both print and assignment have the potential to lead to the creation of authentic texts. It implies a constant vigilance regarding the pragmatics of the reading and writing events (since that is the cuing system most likely to be centrally implicated in distortions). Moreover, it means constant effort (through understanding the issues and structuring the curriculum) to get students to respond to assignments not by complying but by accepting the ostensible purpose as their own.

As we found out in Duncan District, story or letter writing *per se* does not make a Whole Language classroom. And mislabeling can be dangerous on at least two counts. First, it allows an unfair charge of ineffectiveness. Providing only surface modification (in materials, techniques, scheduling) without a change in underlying theoretical orientation (without a shift from a reading-equals-separate-skills theory to a theory that says reading equals the creation of an authentic text by predicting and confirming with four interdependent sub-systems of print) results in adapting the new materials or techniques to the old theory. (Eclecticism at the level of theoretical orientation is a myth, as Harste & Burke, 1977, 1980, argue.) Without fundamental changes at the level of theory it is unreasonable to expect to see fundamental changes in literacy-life-in-classrooms and therefore unreasonable to expect any fundamental changes in children's approach to reading and writing. That means the innovation(which was proclaimed through labeling) can be denounced (*see, it didn't work*) although change in beliefs and ensuing practice actually never occurred. Second, mislabeling does nothing to prevent inappropriate conceptions of what to count as ''it works.'' If there is no principled basis for designating classrooms as Whole Language then it is frighteningly likely that those connected with the in-name-only variety may not understand why reading achievement tests are inappropriate means of eliciting authentic reading or writing for assessment. They could well believe that it is legitimate to prove that ''Whole Language works'' by comparing test scores—reflections of inherently *non*-Whole Language literacy activity. They would be unlikely to push hard and knowledgably for the development and use of alternate Whole Language ways to show that Whole Language works.

In the few years since this study ended, the theoretical notions that guided at least some parts of Duncan's Bilingual Program have changed considerably (and I expect they will continue to change). At the inception of the study, we mistook "writing" for writing. Although we did separate and compare unassigned and assigned pieces, that division was not exactly identical to a division between writing and "writing." Moreover, we did not design the study so we would ever be able to sort according to authenticity to compare the relation of changes over time in *writing* to changes in "writing."

How would this study have been different if we had understood with precision, several years earlier, many of the ramifications of the idea of authenticity in reading and writing? First, in our in-service activity with teachers we would have focused on this issue, trying hard to get across the idea of the *child's* purpose in reading or writing, trying to untangle the frequent confusion of instructional purpose with purpose implied by a certain form with child's purpose. (Just because a teacher's purpose is to teach children to include certain information in invitations, and just because the genre of written invitations implies that the writer's purpose is to invite, does not mean that the child producing an invitation has such a purpose or that an assignment to write an invitation provides an opportunity for learning how to write invitations through the context of an authentic invitation-writing event.) We also would have designed the study differently. I still believe it would have been important to look at all the pieces children produced, whether authentic writing or not, but we would have sought ways to identify them as either writing or "writing" in order to try to find relationships between them.

Now that it seems obvious that much of what we analyzed was "writing," a reasonable question is whether the findings have any value. The answer is yes on several counts. First, since most school-writing still falls into the category of simulations, our findings, unfortunately, are about the typical in-school phenomenon. Moreover, since most of the research on writing has not only been about "writing" but often about much less authentic substitutes than we found at Duncan, these findings add substantially to what is known about that which is usually *called* writing. Certainly, the information on when and to what extent our subjects code switched, the syntactic and phonological bases for their unconventional segments, the shifts in bases for their invented spellings, the differences between their assigned and unassigned pieces, and above all, the dramatic competence they showed during one year with a non-workbook approach to written language should fill some gaps and right some misconceptions in what is known about "writing." In addition, accompanied by this theoretical distinction, all of the findings here are now available for comparison with findings on authentic writing. Perhaps some of our findings on substitutes for writing are also pertinent to writing. Perhaps not. It is not that I am saying that everything we and other researchers have discovered is useless. Rather, I am trying to persuade people to recognize that there are two phenomena here, to stop blindly equating them, to begin to deliberately investigate the relations between them, and also to make informed and theoretical choices between them.

At times, it seems like educational policy makers, teachers, researchers, and the public alike not only equate tests of "reading" and "writing" with authentic reading and writing, not only believe instruction in "reading" and "writing" leads to reading and writing, but that they actually prefer the inauthentic to the authentic ("Don't ask me to listen to her discuss a book she has just read; what about the test scores?" "Never mind the novels she can write; can she write a paragraph for the SAT?"). It seems important to me that all people concerned with education (parents, teachers, students, administrators, gatekeepers of various kinds) begin to examine what in fact they do prefer. If it is authentic reading and writing, then the inauthentic must be greatly de-emphasized if not eliminated and a new theory and practice of assessment must be developed—one that is congruent with the theory and practice of authentic reading and writing that is now being developed (Goodman & Goodman, 1981; Harste et al., 1982; Edelsky et al., 1983a; Graves, 1983; Calkins, 1983; Perl, 1983; Lindfors, 1980, 1984; Hudelson, 1984). And research must take the distinction seriously. If it is inauthentic reading and writing that is indeed preferred, then this should be admitted and the pretense should be dropped that it is reading and writing that is being taught, tested, and investigated.

AND NOW TO THE CHILDREN

A year after our data collection ended, I was able to obtain some of the pieces produced by four third graders who had been second-grade subjects in our study. Their third-grade teacher had given some of their work to Bergionni, the Bilingual Program Director. However, I have no idea why certain pieces were saved and not others, why I now have the work of some children but not others. Thus what I can report about the children's writing a year later must be taken as at best a photo with big holes in it.

The gross description of this one-year collection is as follows: there were 43 pieces, 4 from September, 11 from late October through December, 12 from February and March, and 16 from April and May (roughly corresponding to our four collection periods during the study year). Three pieces were in manuscript, 1 partly in manuscript and partly in cursive, and 39 in cursive. Ten were in English, 1 began in Spanish but was completed in English, 32 were in Spanish. The collection contained 10 stories, 3 letters, 26 expository pieces and 4 "others" (a recipe, pages of sentences with spelling or social studies words underlined). All except one looked like they had been assigned. Moreover, almost all seemed to be examples of substitutes for writing rather than of authentic writing. Comparing them to pieces by the same children from the previous year is justified because, as I have already explained, much of the data from the second grade were also inauthentic.

Looking at each piece by itself shows once again, dramatically or subtly, what remarkable hypothesizers these children were regarding written language. This is not a euphemistic way to describe random error; the children continued to produce seemingly deliberate, often stable solutions to orthographic, semantic, and pragmatic problems.

Examining all of these pieces without comparing them with work done the year before provides a picture of some changes over the third-grade year in spelling, handwriting, and punctuation conventions and little change in content. The pieces are interesting on several dimensions. Each child used from one to four different kinds of punctuation markings. Several segmented differently depending on whether they were using manuscript or cursive script. Beginning-of-the-year explorations and "drawings" of cursive forms gave way at year's end to less well-formed but more conventional graphics. English spellings exploited features of English as well as Spanish orthography (silent *e,* double vowels, double consonants, *-ck* clusters, medial *th* for the sound that in Spanish is spelled as *d—lado* in Spanish but *other* in English). The content showed little change over the third-grade year. Almost all pieces appeared to be perfunctory compliances with assignments, offering "acceptable" if fabricated "personal narrative" responses to teachers' questions or topics. For the assignment "what did you do on Christmas," one desert-living child wrote about making a snowman outside. The few personal narratives were chronological reports of surface events rather than focused "stories." There were many signs that children had not re-read their pieces. Another view, however, is provided by comparing the second-, and third-grade work of each of the four individuals.

Perlinda was the child who, in second grade, argued that she didn't want to kill animals because they didn't do anything to bother *her,* who used questions as a stylistic device (examples 2 and 3), and who spelled *clase* as *qlase* when immediately followed by *querimos* and *que* (example 48). She was one of the children who code switched frequently in writing and who we singled out when we tried unsuccessfully to find one obvious characteristic (much code switching? highly conventional spelling? highly unconventional segmentation?) that might predict some broader constellation of characteristics. Perlinda provided details for her second-grade stories and was prone to repeat words (but it must be remembered that her second-grade teacher valued long pieces and many children repeated words in order to turn in a long piece). Recurring themes in her second-grade stories were romance, fighting, and dying.

(95)   Había una vez un hueso chistoso y él, cuando se dormía, él leventaba dormido y comía y se rió. Y un día el hueso chistoso se casó y tenía una esposa que se llamaba huesa chistosa. Y un día el hueso chistoso le dijo a la huesa chistosa—Vamos a agarrar flores—. Y se fueron agarrar flores y estaba un conejo en el zacate y él brincó y la huesa chistosa gritó. Y el hueso chistoso se comenzó a reír y a reír. Y el hueso chistoso se cayó y la huesa chistosa se rió. Y la huesa chistosa tiró al hueso chistoso en el agua. Y él se murió y ella se mató con un cuchillo.

(Once upon a time there was a funny bone and he, when he was sleeping, he would walk in his sleep and eat and laugh. And one day the funny bone got married and he had a wife named (female) funny bone. And one day the male funny bone said to the female funny bone, "Let's gather flowers." And they went out to get flowers and there was a rabbit in the brush and he jumped out. And the female funny bone screamed. And the male funny bone began to laugh and laugh. And the male funny bone fell and the female funny bone laughed. The funny bone got up and they fought. And the female funny bone threw the male funny bone in the water. And he died and she killed herself with a knife.)

In second grade, Perlinda asked questions and provided answers herself as a device for moving her content forward (and do you know what color my totem pole is? It's green and brown and red and . . .). Occasionally, she had characters spouting exclamatory language (Help! Let go!). Her frequent code switching included translation equivalents from each language in the same piece (e.g., *sad* and *triste*). She used the letter *k* in English but not in Spanish. By the end of second grade, she had stopped spelling *que* as *ce* or *cue* and was spelling it conventionally. She spelled *yo* as *yio, llama* as *yama, niño* as *ninio*. Late in second grade, she used a letter name strategy in some spelling inventions (*staba* for *estaba, nojo* for *enojo*). Perlinda made heavy use of *y* to link clauses. She used no punctuation marks in second grade, but except for running together *ami* (a mí), she segmented conventionally. A typical end-of-second-grade expository assignment is (96).

Example 96

(96) Yo juego con mis hermanos y yo juego con mi Teddy Bear porque a mí me gusta mucho mi Teddy Bear y también es grande.

(I play with my brothers and I play with my Teddy Bear because I like my Teddy Bear a lot and also it's big.)

In general, her 15 third-grade pieces were shorter, provided no examples of empathy with characters, and maintained the same second-grade theme of romance, fighting, and death.

(97)   El Pescado Peligroso.
   Un día unos indios fueron a garrar comida en el agua. Pero salió El Pescado Peligroso. Quería matar a una india que se llama María. Pero un indio salió a india María. Pero el pescado mató al indio y se lo comió. La india María lloró mucho hasta cuando se hizo muy mala. La llevaron al medicine man pero se murió de mala. El Fin.

   (The Dangerous Fish.
   One day some Indians went to get food in the water. But The Dangerous Fish came out. He wanted to kill an Indian named Maria but an Indian came out for the Indian Maria. But the fish killed the Indian and ate him all up. The Indian Maria cried till she made herself sick. They took her to the medicine man but she died of the sickness. The End.)

As in the second grade, Perlinda used questions and answers and dialogue in third-grade texts. She stopped using *y* to link so many of her clauses. She continued to code switch in writing more than the other children. *Llamar* was sometimes spelled conventionally; at other times as *yamar*. Letter-name-based inventions continued to appear at the end of third grade (*staba* for *estaba*). As at the end of second grade, her end-of-third-grade segmenting was conventional except for *ami* (*a mí*). In a typical second-grade piece, 82% of the spellings and 98% of the segments were conventional. The respective percentages in a typical third-grade piece were 86 and 100. During third grade she began using accents and a variety of punctuation marks—question marks, exclamation marks, and periods after each prepositional or noun phrase.

Example (98) was written a year after example (96).

Example 98

(98) My Easter Vacation.
Yo fui para California en Easter con mi cousin. Escondimos muchos Easter eggs y me compró un bunny de chocolate. Yo tenía como 15 Easter eggs y me mojé en el beach.

(My Easter Vacation.
I went to California at Easter with my cousin. We hid lots of Easter eggs and he bought me a chocolate bunny. I had around 15 Easter eggs and I got wet at the beach.)

To summarize, there was a change in some local conventions. Perlinda refined some spelling hypotheses, added a new kind of script, wrote smaller, and began to use punctuation. It is hard to argue that there were any great changes in her approach to content.

In second grade, Manuel was the one who addressed his Anglo teacher as *Mrs* and his Chicana teacher's aide as *Sra*. It was Manuel who demanded of his pen pal *porque no me rayaste* (why didn't you write to me?) (example 35). He was the one who tried out a cholo-stylized script; and he was one of the two boys who frequently used the most unconventional segments. In the second-grade assignments concerning social studies material, he contrasted Indian and Anglo relationships to the environment (. . . and the Creek Indians use all of the buffalo and the soldiers only kill the buffalo so that they give them money because they only want to take off the skin to make overcoats so the women who have a lot of money can buy the coats and they only leave the meat and throw everything out). When he wrote personal narratives, he listed events without any particular focus. Throughout the year, his spelling was highly conventional though he consistently spelled *que, quería* and other *qu*'s as *ce* or *cue*. His only punctuation was a period at the end of every piece. At the beginning of second grade, his segments were mostly conventional words. Then in November, he began using what we coded as highly unconventional "anti-phonological" segments—leaving single letters stranded or attaching non-syllabic letters to adjacent words (*meg usta* for *me gusta, pous T ry* for *poster y*). I now believe that for Manuel this was a shift in enscribing rather than segmenting written language. In any case, by the end of the year these segments disappeared except when he wrote in "shape books" (small paper with curvy lines).

Example (99) is one of his second-grade pieces.

(99) Los Ciegos
Los ciegos y los ciegos vivían en una tipi y el mapache les engañó a los hombres ciegos y un hombre ciego hizo mucho carne y hizo ocho pedazos de carne. Y el raccoon cuando los hombres ciegos andaban comiendo, el raccoon andaba agarrando y se llevó cinco y el otro hombre ciego iba a agarrar otra carne y nomás vió dos. Y el hombre fue a agarrar agua y allí también el raccoon puso un lazo y el agua se

Manuel Jueves
los siegos

los siegos y los siegos vivian
En una Tipi y el mapache
le engaño a los hombres
Siegos y un hombre siego
iso mucha carne y iso
hOcho pedasos de carne
y el racun cuando los
hombres siegos andaban comiendo
El racun andaba garandoy
Se llevo sinco y el
OTro hombre siego yva a
Garar otra carNe y nomas
Vio dosy el hombre fue
El garar agua y ai Tambien
El Racun puso un laso y la
Agua se fuey el hombre dijo cue
El racun andava siendoles Tres y ellos se Isieron
Amigos.

Example 99

fue. Y el hombre dijo que el raccoon andaba haciéndoles tres y ellos se hicieron amigos.

(The Blind Men
The blind men and the blind men lived in a teepee and the raccoon tricked the blind men and a blind man made a lot of meat and he made eight pieces of meat. And the raccoon, when the blind men were going along eating, the raccoon went around gathering and he took five and the other blind man was going to get some more meat and he only saw two (pieces). And the man was going to get water and the raccoon also put a lasso there and the water was all gone. And the man said that the raccoon was making three for them and they became friends.)

Among the eight pieces by Manuel from third grade there was one letter; the rest were expositions on assigned topics (If I Were the Principal, What I Remember about the Field Trip, etc.). In the few pieces saved, there were no topics permitting a show of understanding of historical or social issues. His third-grade personal narratives lacked focus. Because some topics in both English and Spanish were contrary to fact Manuel had the opportunity to show his considerable ability to handle complex verb constructions in each language (. . . *and to the ones that say bad words I would go to the principal and borrow his paddle and give him a paddle and then I would put soap in his mouth . . . and if they took the soap out of their mouths I would give him 20 paddles and I would make him wear a hat that said I am a bad boy* . . . and on another occasion in Spanish *si yo era Mr F. yo dejaría a todas las clases que tenieran parties . . ./*(literal translation) if I was Mr F. I would let all the classes that they might have parties . . .).

As in second grade, he continued to connect Spanish clauses with *y* but he did not string English clauses together with *and*. He also continued his second-grade means of punctuation—putting a period at the end of a piece. By the middle of third grade, his already highly conventional spelling became even more so as *cu* and *qu* were sorted out so that *porque, cuando,* and *que* were spelled conventionally and *yo* no longer appeared as *llo*. He also segmented conventionally, showing the slightest return to what we had coded as unconventional segmentation only when he used manuscript script. This confirms my suspicion that his stranded letter segments in second grade had actually been a sign of erratic manuscript handwriting. In a typical second-grade piece, 80% of the words were spelled conventionally; in third grade this figure had risen to 89%. None of his third-grade segments were unconventional; in one second-grade piece 7% were.

Example (100) was written near the end of third grade.

Example 100

(100)   Yo voy a rallar del mineral museum porque a mí me gustó mucho y cuando nos
        metimos nos dieron papeles para hacer field notes y un chavalito acabó primero y
        luego otro muchacho acabó y luego yo acabé y lo llevé para que el hombre me lo
        chequiera y me lo chequió y estaba bien y agarré piedras.

        (I'm going to write about the mineral museum because I liked it a lot and a guy
        finished first and then another boy finished and then I finished and I took it so a
        man could check it and he checked it for me and it was OK and I got rocks.)

In general, already conventional Manuel became somewhat more conventional. However, except for the addition of cursive script (which had implications for his production of written segments) and two definite changes in spelling hypotheses, Manuel's third-grade writing appeared very similar to what he had produced a year earlier.

Rosa was a child who understood all too well the U.S. government's role in the history of some Native American groups (in a report about the Creek Indians. . . . y un día el gobierno les dijo—Váyanse de aquí. Vaya a otra estado que se llama Oklahoma.—Y cuando el gobierno les dijo—Váyanse—y les dijo cuando llegan van a tener todo. Pero el gobierno les estaba hablando mentiras y cuando llegaron no había nada, nomás pura nieve y los soldados no dejaban ir a pararse en ninguna parte. Y cuando sabía el gobierno que allá había gold el gobierno y dijo—Váyanse de aquí. Vayan en otro estado—. . . /. . . And one day the government said to them, "Leave here. Go to another state named Oklahoma." And when the government told them "leave" and told them when they arrived they are going to have everything. But the government was telling lies and when they arrived there wasn't anything, only snow, and the soldiers wouldn't let them go to stop anyway. And when the government found out there was gold there, the government and said, "Leave here. Go to another state" . . .). Rosa was the one who put certain details in an invitation to an outsider (example 18) that she omitted from an invitation to an insider (example 17). She was one of the high *y*-users we singled out to plot the use over time of between-clause links (Child #13 in Figure 3). At first, Rosa wrote long, detailed, but often hard-to-follow stories. By the end of second grade, however, her stories had become coherent, offering both a clear problem and resolution.

(101)   Una vez había un dinosaurio que no tenía con quien jugar y estaba llorando. Y luego llegó un niño y le dijo—¿Porqué estas llorando?—. Y el dinosaurio dijo— Porque no tengo con quien jugar—. Y el niño dijo—Yo jugaré contigo—. Y el dinosaurio y el niño jugaron a kick ball. Y al dinosaurio le gustó mucho y el dinosaurio y el niño eran amigos para siempre.

(One time there was a dinosaur that didn't have anyone to play with and he was crying. And then a little boy came along and said to him, "Why are you crying?" And the dinosaur said, "Because I don't have anyone to play with." And the boy said, "I will play with you." And the dinosaur and the boy played kick ball. And the dinosaur liked it a lot and the dinosaur and the boy were friends forever.)

Rosa used quotations and dialogue in second grade and linked almost all main clauses with *y*. Throughout second grade she used a period to mark the end of some main clauses, then began the next with an *y*. Her spelling inventions frequently omitted letters rather than adding them. A favored hypothesis was to use the letter *y* for all /i/ sounds (*yr* for *ir*, *yso* for *hizo*). Her unconventional segments were either syllable-based or a joining together of *ami* rather than *a mí*.

An example of an end-of-second-grade journal entry is 102.

(102)   Ahora sí me siento bien y cuando llegué a la escuela yo estaba jugando muy contenta. Y yo estaba jugando con mi amigo Veronica y mi hermano está jugando con su amigo.

(Today I do feel well and when I got to school I was playing very happily. And I was playing with my friend Veronica and my brother was playing with his friend.)

There were only six pieces by Rosa in the third-grade batch (two stories, one letter, and three reports). They were full of details. None, however, was on a

*ahora si' me siento
bien. y cuando yege a la
escuela. yo estaba Jugando
muy contenta. y yo estaba
Jugan do con mi amiga
Vero nica. y mi ermano
estaba Jugan do co s a
a migo.*

Example 102

topic that afforded any display of understanding of social studies issues similar to that revealed in some second-grade assignments. At first glance her third-grade stories look disorganized in comparison with those done at the end of second grade. However, some episodes were now developed with details rather than just listed; these may have been the beginning of "chapter stories." Lending some weight to this guess is that on two pages of one five-page story, each new episode (different setting, different time) began with *Un día* (one day), contained several clauses unseparated by periods, but then ended with a very round, fat, dark period. Again, seeming regressions may well have been a step forward. Rosa continued to use dialogue in third grade—only now she had begun to use English-style quotation marks around direct quotes in Spanish. In fact, she attempted various ways to signal direct quotation. One was to use manuscript writing inside the quotation marks embedded in a text written in cursive.

mimama

→ *dijo " yo le voya ayudar a mis Hijos"
ay cuando andavamos fudlando los
Huevos cuando viamos los Huevos*

Example 103

(103)   . . . Mi mamá dijo—Yo le voy a ayudar a mis hijos—. Y cuando andabamos buscando los huevos cuando víamos los huevos . . .

(. . . My mom said, "I'm going to help my children." And when we went looking for the eggs when we saw the eggs . . .).

In a story about a magic horse, for which I think she was trying to write chapters, she also took a first person perspective (. . . *Yo soy una india. Un día fui a buscar unas manzanas para los otros caballos y encontré un caballo bien bonito. Él dijo algo y le dije—¡Tu hablas!—. Él dijo—¡¿Como no?!—. . ./ . . .* I am an Indian. One day I went looking for some apples for the other horses and I found a very pretty horse. He said something and I said to him, "You talk!" He said, "Of course!" . . .).

Though she still relied heavily on *y* to connect clauses, she began to omit explicit connections between some. Throughout third grade, she continued to chunk *ami* (for *a mí*), *aver* (for *a ver*), and other oft-used phrases, and occasionally to segment by syllables. By the end of third grade, she no longer spelled /i/ as *y* (*ir* was spelled *ir*), but *ll* was still depicted as *y* (*yevar* rather than *llevar*). She spelled 81% of the words in one piece conventionally in second grade and produced 96% conventional segments; in third grade she spelled 89% conventionally but her conventional segments dropped to 89%. Like the other children, Rosa added cursive script to her repertoire in third grade. Example 104 shows some features found in several of Rosa's end-of-year third-grade pieces.

Example 104

(104)   A mí me gustó todos los piedras y se miraba el copper como si no fuera. Y también me gustó ir a ver todos los piedras porque se miraban como oro o plata o también copper. Y quise quedarme pero no podía. Me gustó porque mis amigos me llevaron a donde estaba oscuro y se podían a ver piedras.

(I liked all the rocks and the copper looked like it wasn't (copper). And also I liked to go see all the rocks because they looked like gold or silver or also copper. I wanted to stay but I couldn't. I liked it because my friends took me to where it was dark and you could see rocks.)

Overall, Rosa's work revealed some new and more advanced hypotheses regarding punctuation. She supplied more elaborate content and experimented with a new rhetorical device. From the beginning of second grade to the end of third, Rosa seemed to have acquired significantly more control over conveying meanings with written language.

Arturo was one of the "interesting children" presented at the end of Chapter 5 as child #15 (examples 79–82). He was one of those able to explicitly relate to the lives and concerns of others. In examples already shown, he demanded to know what was wrong with a sick principal (example 4) and advised Santa Claus on the easiest way to enter his house (examples 14 and 43). What he wrote about frequently included killing, though these and other pieces projected a clear and sincere "voice." He made heavy use of Spanish orthography in English (in November: *ai joup llu gou*/I hope you go; in April: *dei wa c bi for da fasols was meir*/they walk before the fossils was made). Arturo was the child who, in the middle of second grade, chunked together words from different constituents to produce "anti-syntactic" segments (*para que* + *no* to get *paceno*) and who by the end of the year was very deliberately placing big even spaces, in both Spanish and English, between non-syllabic as well as syllabic letter clusters (*ai la b da ra cs*/ I love the rocks).

Arturo continued to be an interesting third grader. Of the 14 pieces from third grade (5 of which were stories), all were short, most had few details, and many were perfunctory even though they concerned fighting and killing. In several, second-grade-like sincerity reappeared, as for example in Arturo's bewilderment about unjust treatment. Example 105 appeared toward the end of a Halloween story starter about a mysterious hand coming out of a door.

(105)   . . . y le saludé a la mano misteriosa y me dije gracias. Nomás lo saludé y traiga un cuchillo en la mano y me mató cuando lo saludé.

   (. . . and I greeted the mysterious hand and it said thank you. All I did was greet it and it brought a knife in its hand and killed me when I greeted it.)

Example 106 is an after-Christmas-vacation report in which he maintained a sense of responsibility for what happened to him (but I'm going to be good with the teacher) even though he could not account for such punishment (a lack of Christmas presents) with any bad behavior on his part (I never fought with the teacher. She hasn't hit me.).

(106)   Yo estoy triste porque no me regalaron nada. Por eso estoy triste. Tampoco Santa Clos no me regaló nada. Yo nunca pelié con la maestra. Ella no me ha pegado pero yo voy a ser bien bueno con la maestra. Hug us, Teacher, cuando la escuela se acabe.

   (I'm sad because they didn't give me any presents. That's why I'm sad. Santa Claus didn't give me anything either. I never fought with the teacher. She has never hit me, but I'm going to be very good with the teacher. Hug us, Teacher, when school is over.)

At the end of Arturo's second-grade year, we had been worried about his segmentation (see examples 29a and 29b). It appeared to us that he was ignoring the input of conventional published print and was devising increasingly "non-literate" hypotheses. We needn't have worried. The first piece the following year in third grade showed no evidence of his strange segments (*ai la b da ra cs*). Instead, there were explorations in cursive script and syntactically based unconventional segments. (Arturo went from 33% unconventional segments in a second-grade piece to 2% in a late third-grade piece. Conventional spellings constituted 77% and 80%, respectively.)

Example 107 was written a few days before the start of summer vacation. (Segments coded as *sylL* are underlined twice; syllabic-based segments are underlined once.)

Example 107

(107) El dinosaurio es muy triste porque nunca juegan con ellos. Ellos lo escupen a mi dinosaurio porque no les gustó. Él está bueno, es bueno con la gente y la gente la quiere mucho. Él hace protect y él hace protect a la gente y le gusta jugar a las dinosaurios y les gusta correr con él.

(The dinosaur is very sad because they never play with them. They spit at my dinosaur because they don't like him. He is good, he's good with the people and the people like him a lot. He protects and he protects the people and they like to play with the dinosaurs and they like to run with him.)

Example 108, containing no sign of stranded letters or syllable-based segments, was written a few days after summer vacation ended.

(108) Los españoles no dejaron a los indios. No los dejaron aprender en español y los indios no se dejaron . . .

(The Spaniards didn't let the Indians, they didn't let them learn in Spanish and the Indians didn't let . . .)

In third grade, when Arturo used *manuscript* writing in "shape books" with lines he drew by himself to follow the shape of the pumpkin-shaped paper, his

Example 108

segmentation resembled his earlier second-grade work—stranded letters, conjoined words from different constituents, syllabic segments, whole clauses with no internal segments.

Example 109

(109) La bruja cra mágica y estaba volando y se halló un dancing bear y la bruja usó su mágica y la bruja lo hizo una rana y el dancing bear todavía estaba peliando con la bruja y también la bruja usa su escoba para defenderse y la escoba también usa su mágica y la dancing bear los mata con la dagger brillosa.

(The witch was magic and she was flying and she found a dancing bear and the witch used her magic and the witch made him into a frog and the dancing bear still is fighting with the witch and also the witch uses her broom to defend herself and the broom also uses its magic and the dancing bear kills them with the shiny dagger.)

When Arturo wrote on the same kind of pumpkin-shaped, unlined then self-drawn curvy-lined paper—but in *cursive*—his segments were huge syntactic chunks (whole noun or verb phrases).

Example 110

(110) *Un día día este niño* estaba jugando y llegó un niño y *se llamaba Esteban.* Y *el otro se llamaba Georgie.* Y luego un fantasma y *se estaban* peliando el Georgie y *el Stevie* y *el fantasma. Se volvió* loco y empezó a matar gente y *al último se mató el so—.* . . .

> (One day (day) this boy was playing and a boy came up and he was named Steven. And the other was named Georgie. And then a ghost and they were fighting Georgie and Stevie and the ghost. It went crazy and began to kill people and finally it killed the so—. . . .)

This kind of evidence reinforces my belief that some of Arturo's seemingly baseless unconventional segments, coded as *sylL* in second grade, may have been handwriting rather than segmentation phenomena—an unsteady "hand" meeting unlined, round paper that failed to steady the wobbliness. On the other hand, other second-grade segments (*ai la b ra cs*) were more likely true segmentation phenomena. They seemed carefully placed, appeared in connection with all kinds of paper, in two languages, in all types of writing.

I have no guesses about what led Arturo to generate and then abandon that particular segmentation hypothesis. Nor do I have any hunches about the source of the following spelling hypothesis. In the Spring of third grade Arturo suddenly began to invent most peculiar spellings for previously conventionally spelled words. (Words spelled according to this hypothesis are underlined.)

(111) Un día salí de mi casa. Pasaron unos amigos. Me dijeron que si salía con ellos para la tienda. Les dije que la iba a decir a mi mamá. Ella dijo que sí y yo me puse la ropa del Mickey Mouse y nos fuimos. The End.

> (One day I went out of my house. Some friends passed by. They asked me if I could go with them to the store. I told them that I was going to tell my mom. She said yes and I put on the Mickey Mouse outfit and we went. The End.)

un dia   sali de mi   mi casa
pacaron unoc amigos.
me dijieron a si calia
con eioc para la tienda
lec dje a le iba a decir
a mi mama ela djo a
a y yo me puce la ropa
de el mici mauc y
noc juinoc en end

Example 111

Why was Arturo eliminating almost all uses of the letter *s* in favor of using *c* for the sounds of /s/ and /k/? Why was the *ll* avoided (*eioc* instead of *ellos*)? For two years, he had been spelling conventionally such words as *ellos, los, les, unos,* and *salía.* Why, suddenly, such an "un-Spanish" invention as to end words with *c?* To pluralize with a *c?* (English would not be the source of such a hypothesis.) In this third-grade collection, there was only one piece produced after example (111). Because of its neatness and conventional spelling, it looks like a corrected draft—implying coached spelling. That means I have no evidence regarding how long this child used this hypothesis.

Looking at Arturo's work over two years provides confirmation of the view that children create hypotheses regarding written language systems. Arturo's hypotheses were thorough-going enough that we can be sure they were not "performance errors." They were also unusual enough that we can only wonder about their origins. But there is no question that they identify Arturo—and less dramatically, the other children—as hypothesis-generators.

An important question here, of course, in regard to each of these children is: do the end-of-year third-grade pieces also show significant growth in relation to the second-grade pieces? As I answer that question I continue to assume that growth means expanded and reorganized repertoires of possible intentions and means of achieving them. Although these 43 pieces offered some evidence of system-wide reorganization, they provide few signs of greatly expanded repertoires. What they did present was evidence that children learned to write in cursive and became somewhat more adult-like in local conventions such as punctuation and spelling. With the exception of one of Rosa's pieces, there were no other signs of change in global content conventions or intentions, no display of using written language for new purposes and new audiences with new rhetorical means. Where were the benefits of writing as a way of learning, the benefits that were to come from using written language to explore new ideas and find the limits of—or make new connections between—old ideas? *Were* the children using written language for such purposes?

Just what was it that these children met up with in their third-grade classroom?

According to Bergionni and my discussions with the Duncan teachers at workshops that continued through the Spring of 1982, there were few demands that children become *engaged* with children's literature (though there were regular assignments to interact with controlled-vocabulary, written-for-readability "readers"—flawed print without the potential to do its part in the creation of an authentic text, according to the theory in the preceding section). Little was done with published print that concerned authentic text-making. Commercially published print was read aloud, round robin, and was used to answer questions and supply information on book report forms. The print made by children was checked off as completed assignments, put into folders or sent home, but was not treated to frequent content-based conferences, was not put through any process of revising, editing, and publishing, did not become the basis for transformation into other media (e.g., into dramatic production). The children's own writing was almost entirely prompted by assignments that were most likely received as just that—assignments. As the preceding section discussed, some of the assignments were pragmatic "frame-ups" where conditions prevented the ostensible purpose of a piece from being accomplished. With others, little was done to encourage children to adopt the teacher's purpose as their own. Between offering children flawed print, giving them assignments that prevented rather than facilited the use of all cuing systems, and doing little to encourage children to adopt the teacher's purpose in assignments, it seemed the teacher had children engaged in substitutes for writing, not in authentic writing.

If these four children did not show substantial evidence of the advantages that were supposed to result from an in-school emphasis on writing because they were not in fact writing, why did the third graders (or second or first graders, for that matter) the year before look like they had taken giant steps? What I think happened was this: for most of the children in the study, the study year was the first time they had been required, for a significant amount of time each day, to put together anything even resembling a whole text. Even though the normal interactivity of the systems was distorted or severed, the first engagement with orchestrating even some systems was powerful enough to provide an opportunity for dramatic changes in hypotheses and decisions about written language systems. However, after the gains stemming from that first immersion in orchestrating several (though not all) language systems, learners needed experience orchestrating all the systems, undistorted, along with insightful instruction in order to continue to grow significantly. If growth in writing does not come from writing alone (Braddock, 1969) (with no feedback, no reading-like-a-writer (Smith, 1983), no re-visioning), then it certainly did not come from pseudo-writing alone either. Someone has to be responding to, demonstrating for the child as a writer, taking the content seriously, helping with the form when it is appropriate, instructing in what writing is *for*. That did not happen to our second-turned-third graders. Who was at fault? The teacher seems to be the obvious "culprit." But let's look at what else was happening.

THE PROGRAM

In some sense, the most important lesson lies in the tale of the varying fortunes of Duncan's Bilingual Program after the year of the study. The Program's nature and existence had always been integrally related to what was happening in a variety of contexts. As described in Chapter 3, Hispanic parents were firmly behind the idea that their children could be educated in two languages, though most were uninformed about any notions that their children could be educated through something besides drills and exercises. In the years preceding the start of our study, parents participated in District events affecting the Bilingual Program with increased frequency, commitment, and power. Through years of participation with Bergionni in multiple overlapping social networks, they also had affectionate ties and loyalties to the Program Director. Meanwhile, the positions on curriculum and language and literacy development in particular taken by the State Legislature and the State Department of Education (mirroring the general culture's point of view on reading and writing and their instruction) had never been identical with the theoretical position held by Bergionni or her consultants. However, the gap had begun to widen dramatically in the late 1970s. State legislative and State agency actions were effectively closing off opportunities for a kind of classroom practice that was based on anything other than an assumption of separate and discrete oral and written language skills. District administrators had given everything from grudging acceptance to public support for the idea of bilingual education. However, though they expressed pride in the writing children did in the Bilingual Program, they often disapproved of integrating subject matter and of teaching without an emphasis on skill drills. What prevented them from insisting that Bergionni's teachers stop such teaching was the support Bergionni had from the Superintendent. At the start of our study, Bergionni was still able to maintain her push for holistic teaching and a Whole Language approach to literacy by appealing to Superintendent Dearing to exempt the Bilingual Program from the workbook skill programs demanded by the District. She argued for exemption by pointing out that District objectives concerning English spelling and English parts of speech, for example, were inappropriate for children who were being offered instruction first in Spanish literacy and language arts. Despite the fact that she usually won her case with the Superintendent, the teachers were still affected by parents', principals', Program Director's, Curriculum Director's, Superintendent's, School Boards', and State Legislators' positions and moves.

If it was apparent that the shape and content of the day-to-day life in classrooms in the Bilingual Program was intimately connected with all of these various contexts prior to and during the year of our study, it was even more obvious in the years immediately following our last data collection. Before presenting a chronology of District events in those years, two general comments must be made. First, Bergionni owed her power to make Program decisions to several factors: she had strong personal ties to the community; she was trusted and supported by Superintendent Owen Dearing; she was designated as in control of the Title VII monies that funded the Program, enabling her to hire teachers for new slots and to determine the kind and amount of in-service education to be provided for Bilingual Program teachers. Second, while Bilingual Program parents were in favor of bilingual education *per se,* they were not advocates of—many were even unaware of—the theoretical orientation and philosophy we and Bergionni were trying to make a reality. Parents had heard conflicting messages about bilingual education from community religious leaders; the priest urged them to support it; one minister warned that bilingual education was the devil's idea. From many different kinds of evidence, it is fair to say that almost all had resolved that particular conflict in favor of bilingual education before the study began. But they also heard conflicting messages about curriculum in informal talks with the principals and with Bergionni. By 1981, the former had begun to disparage "what goes on in there"; the latter, of course, applauded the gains in literacy and understanding of content. Unfortunately, parent education concerning curriculum was haphazard and almost non-existent (there were only two such sessions with few parents in attendance). The sources of Bergionni's power and the nature of parents' support of the Program featured significantly in the events between 1981 and 1983. What follows is a chronological listing of a few of those events.[3]

Fall 1979–Spring 1980.   Opposition to bilingual education mounts in the retirement community. Arguments over bilingual education appear in newspapers, sermons, farmworker labor organizing meetings. Duncan's Board, surprised by the show of popular support among parents, agrees to the continuation of the Bilingual Program through the following school year. We plan a limited study, thinking the Program would not last beyond the 1981/82 school year.

Fall 1980.   Continued reports in area newspapers of dissension over bilingual education at Duncan. Proposal to renew Title VII funding requires Board approval, thus reopening the debate. Over 100 Bilingual Program parents attend Board meeting, some speak up in Spanish in favor of bilingual education.

Winter 1980–Present (Spring, 1984).   State legislature institutes a variety of mechanisms for upgrading education (e.g., testing for teacher certification, monitoring new teachers, basing student promotions on competency tests). All the mechanisms assume that literacy can and should be assessed with tests based on a "skills" theoretical orientation, that good teaching involves organizing a classroom for the instruction of separate skills. And, of course all the tests assume English language proficiency.

---

[3]I have changed dates and details in some of the events for the sake of privacy.

February 1981.   Local official invites a community leader thought to be a proponent of bilingual education. Proponent turns out to be an opponent, vilifying bilingual education in his speech. Parents protest in Spanish, praise bilingual education.

February 1981.   Principals impress on teachers the importance for all children (including those in the Bilingual Program) to score high on the upcoming standardized tests (given in English). Rumors spread among the faculty that teacher evaluations, tenure decisions, and the like will be tied to students' scores. Bergionni reassures teachers that she, Bergionni, must concur in such decisions regarding Program personnel and that she will not decide on the basis of student scores on English-language tests of skills. When Bergionni is not present at school-building-level teachers' meetings, principals reiterate the importance of high scores.

March 1981.   In an apparent attempt to discourage Bilingual Program parent participation in its meetings, Board changes the location of its meeting to a smaller hall, announces that the meeting will be conducted completely in English. The Board is notified that such a ruling is illegal.

March 1981.   Curriculum Director mandates a new Language Arts Scope and Sequence for the District, requiring all children to be taught a sequence of separate skills in English. Aware that following such a plan would scuttle her holistic, writing-centered Bilingual Program, Bergionni convinces Superintendent Dearing to exempt the Bilingual Program from this requirement. The grounds for her argument are that the Scope and Sequence Statement presumed native-speaker-of-English competence.

April–May 1981.   Bilingual Program parents work with some members of the retirement and ranch owning communities on a petition drive for a special election to redraw the boundaries of Duncan School District.

April 1981.   We collect our final batch of children's writing for our study.

May 1981.   Special election is held regarding redistricting. New boundaries exclude the retirement community, making the Hispanic community the one with the largest number of voters in the District.

July 1981.   Despite his past record of protecting the Bilingual Program, a variety of other factors (including his past association with the retirement community) work against Owen Dearing. The new School Board, elected by those now eligible to vote within the newly drawn District boundaries, offers only lukewarm support to the continuation of Dearing as Superintendent. As he loses favor, others associated with him lose some of their power; Bergionni is one of these.

August 1981.   With the likely prospect that a new Superintendent will be hired who might not protect the Bilingual Program the way Dearing had, and with the Program's existence dependent on year-to-year federal funding, Bergionni initiates a plan to institutionalize bilingual education in the District. She reasons that a Task Force to Investigate the Problem of School Dropouts would surely find that many dropouts did poorly in language- and literacy-related subjects. Such a Task Force would easily realize that a bilingual program, among many other suggestions, would promote greater success for these children and would decrease the number of dropouts. Bergionni approaches Dearing with the plan. He concurs, adding that he will try to persuade the Board to require the Task Force to make recommendations back to the Board, thus giving added weight and authority to those recommendations.

September 1981.   Bergionni and two community leaders convene a Task Force to Investigate the Problem of Dropouts in Duncan District. The Task Force represents Duncan's ethnic groups (Hispanic, Anglo, Black), social class groups (migrant farmworkers, low- and middle-level management, ranch owners, middle-income and middle-status professionals), and program participants (regular program parents, Bilingual Program parents). The Task Force's first response to the figures showing the enormity of the dropout problem is to try to brainstorm ways to raise children's test scores. Some Task Force members and Bergionni together convince the others to go to schools, visit classrooms, talk to principals, counselors, teachers, students—to first take a close look at what children are dropping out of.

September 1981.   Duncan Curriculum Director teaches a District-sponsored course on how to implement the new separate skills Language Arts Statement. The District gives teachers professional growth credits for taking the course.

November 1981.   School Board authorizes the Task Force to make a formal set of recommendations back to the Board, obligating the Board to seriously consider the recommendations.

1981–1982.   We present a series of workshops on writing to Bilingual Program teachers.

1981–1982.   Task Force visits schools, concentrating on the junior and senior high, engaging in what amounts to "consciousness raising." Members express shock at scene after scene of turned-off, tuned-out children, instructional programs with materials that make no contact with students' lives or modes of communication, school procedures (e.g., some concerning showering and dressing) that violate certain cultural norms for some District constituencies. The Task Force wants to narrow school content, bring the expectations down to attaining "minimal skill levels"—an obvious response when set against a background of country-wide, decade-long calls for "back to the basics" as a solution to a wide range of educational and social problems. Bergionni invites a variety of speakers to address the Task Force on the need to expand rather than narrow content, to raise expectations, to have children engaged in whole, complex projects entailing authentic written language use, to have "skills" taught as they are used.

Spring 1982. A second new District-wide Scope and Sequence Statement for Language Arts is written, this time by a committee of teachers. Four teachers per grade (one Bilingual Program teacher and three others) are asked to identify skills they think should be taught for that grade. Bilingual Program teachers are included so that their "perspective" is represented even though the skills listed will be based on the English language. Bilingual Program teachers propose such skills as "varying rhetorical devices for varying audiences," "understanding an author's purpose." The others propose "identifying long and short vowels," "mastering graphemic bases (e.g., -ing, -and, -er)." Each Bilingual Program teacher is outvoted by the other three teachers at that grade level. The net result is that nothing in the Scope and Sequence Statement is congruent with the Whole Language approach Bilingual Program personnel have been urged to work toward. Attached to the Statement is a plan to develop criterion referenced tests to be coordinated with the items listed in the Scope and Sequence Statement.

February 1982. Principals announce at meetings that they will be looking even more closely at student scores on the standardized tests to be given in the Spring. One principal begins to check teachers' lesson plan books to ensure they are teaching what he believes will result in better scores.

April 1982. We send a copy of the final report of our National Institute of Education-funded study on writing in the Bilingual Program to the District Office.

May 1982. Owen Dearing gives principals control over four half-days of in-service for each teacher, including Program teachers, ending what had been one of Bergionni's prerogatives.

May 1982. Knowing his contract would not be renewed, Dearing resigns at Board meeting. Bergionni presents evidence of success of the Bilingual Program—dramatic rise in attendance, drop in discipline problems, rise in quality of children's written work, influx of out-of-District and out-of-State visitors to see an example of "informal education" done bilingually. There are no huge gains in test scores to mention. Her report is received without enthusiasm.

June 1982. Tom Broward is appointed Superintendent.

Fall 1982. Title VII funding ends. One of the budget items lost is funding for in-service education.

September 1982. Principals openly dispute Bergionni's direction. One principal takes one of the upper grade bilingual classrooms out of the Bilingual Program without consulting Bergionni. She appeals to Broward for a reversal. Broward upholds the principal's decision. Parents angrily demand a meeting with the principal. He holds a meeting with 15 parents (but not with Bergionni) at which he denounces the Bilingual Program because it fails to teach children about nouns and verbs. One parent retorts, "They may not know *about* nouns and verbs but they know how to use them!" The principal stays with his decision to "de-bilingualize" the classroom even though Bergionni and parents disagree.

October 1982. With an eye to the direction taken by the State Legislature, the principals begin to apply pressure for higher standardized test scores early in the school year. They warn explicitly that pay raises, tenure, leaves, and other personnel decisions will include considerations of how well each teacher's students score on the test.

October 1982. We present some of the findings of the NIE-funded study at one of the Duncan schools. Invitations are sent to District Office administrators, School Board members, principals, teachers and aides, and Bilingual Parent Advisory Council members. Only teachers and one parent attend. Bergionni notes that no one in the District office can locate the box with the final NIE report we had sent in May.

November 1982. The Task Force on Dropouts makes its report to the Board. Recommendations include a call for better record keeping, more accounting of student histories, a curriculum with more meaningful content, demands for critical thinking, hiring outside consultants to assess all aspects of the Program, and, as expected, continuation and expansion of bilingual education.

November 1982. A new School Board is elected. This Board seems to have great confidence in Superintendent Tom Broward.

January–March 1983. Broward and Task Force have a series of meetings to discuss the findings and recommendations in the Task Force Report.

March 1983.   The Superintendent appeals to the Board. He needs to have people in positions of authority who can work from a clean slate without a history of old alliances. The Board agrees, failing to renew the contracts of two of the principals, the Curriculum Director, and Bergionni.

April 1983.   Bergionni "explains" to people in and out of the District that she will be leaving as Program Director in order to work in a family business in another part of the state.

April 1983.   Broward hires a new Curriculum Director, a woman who had previously worked on the development of many of the District's skills-based scope and sequence statements.

May 1983.   Superintendent Broward sends a memo with his opinion of how to proceed now that he has had meetings throughout the Spring to discuss the Task Force Report. His memo advises the Board to let the Curriculum Director's recommendations take precedence over all others. These either contradict or do not address the same topics included in the Task Force Report. The Board votes to give its attention to the Curriculum Director's recommendations. The Task Force Report is shelved.

May 1983.   In farewell gestures, Bergionni is honored at the local parish church, at fiestas given by various community members, at parties given by Program personnel. Teachers remember the protection, the help with materials, the frequent applause she showered them with. Community members recount with gratitude the years of commitment to their children and all the "extras"— the times she intervened in the court system, her brokering with welfare and clinic bureaucrats.

June 1983.   A new Bilingual Program Director is hired. A former high school Spanish teacher, she has no prior experience in elementary education, no experience in elementary bilingual education. One of her first actions is to order a series of phonics workbooks for each classroom.

Now let us return to the third-grade teacher of the four children whose work was analyzed in the preceding section. This was the teacher whose children did not show the advantages of a curriculum centered on writing as a way of knowing and learning because they had, in fact, not participated in such a curriculum. Instead, they had taken part in a program full of simulations of writing. What was happening in the various embedded contexts of school, Program, and District administration (let alone the wider contexts of increasing unemployment among community members, salary setbacks for teachers, and renewed rumblings about the failure of American education)? What would have impinged on a teacher who might not have understood or accepted a Whole Language theoretical approach to literacy development in the first place even though she might have tried out a few more holistic techniques or assignments?

Prior to 1981 we consultants had not offered enough opportunity for teachers to see living examples of instruction based on the worldview we were arguing for. Our on-site visits to demonstrate and help teachers in their own classrooms as a means of both showing and converting had been too infrequent. And certainly we had been unable to provide the safe environment needed for cognitively risky ideology-switching. This teacher, then, along with other Program teachers, had been left out on a limb with a radically new idea. She might well have scheduled some of the activities Bergionni was advocating because of the pull of personal loyalty to the Program Director. But it would not have been likely that she would have shifted profoundly to adopt the theoretical worldview underlying those activities. Instead, with Bergionni's authority diminishing (as shown in the preceding chronology)—and with it her former ability to deflect the pressures on teachers—the teacher would have been pushed from all other sides to hold on to her existing views.

Her usual fears about tests and scores would have been given fertile ground to grow. Not only would they have been fed by her own beliefs that low scores say something real about literacy, but now she was being encouraged to tie her anxieties about her own abilities as a teacher and her fears for her own job security to the tests. She was beginning to have to justify lesson plans that included project work, the reading of whole books, the writing of stories—but she did not have to justify lesson plans that consisted of notations such as "Book 3, #2–17." The wonder is not why, after years of in-service, the teacher was still not having children really write, but why, with so much harassment, she tried to have children do anything that even *looked* like writing!

The sophisticate nods and says that education is always political. Political in the sense of daily maneuverings over who would control what decisions and activities. Political in the sense of supporting the power of one set of global interests over another. (These two senses might be directly or indirectly related to each other.) The political becomes especially obvious in settings where language, ethnicity, and social class are implicated in the agenda of both daily maneuverings and global interests—settings like bilingual education programs. None of the administrative "main characters"—principals, Superintendents, Curriculum Director, Board members, Program Director—could opt out of the political maneuvering. Bergionni's moves may have been consciously and explicitly grounded in education and language policy issues, but she too had to be deeply involved in power struggles if she wanted any of her ideas to be put into practice. In the end, it wasn't flaws in her educational ideas that were the cause of the fundamental change in direction of the Bilingual Program; it was that Bergionni either made the wrong moves or, more likely, ran out of cards to play.

A case can certainly be made then that the fortunes of Duncan's Bilingual

Program were determined more by struggles over who was to hold power than over educational ideas, by concern over who would win at the top than over who would learn at the bottom. But that would not be the whole story. The "sides" fighting for power were also divided ideologically over what would be won, what would be learned—that is, over language arts curricula. At one time, they were also divided over policies of language choice. Bergionni had won that one, however—a success that still endures for now at least. Moreover, she had educated the parents so that they too had some educational and linguistic reasons (along with their social and political ones) to offer for why they supported initial literacy instruction in Spanish, why they wanted biliteracy maintained in the higher grades, why they wanted some content offered bilingually and some offered in each language throughout the school years. In the few-year struggle presented chronologically above, then, policy over language choice was not an issue. What *was* being contested (in addition to whose decisions would prevail) was whether the two languages would be used for teaching children how to do workbook exercises or for teaching them to use oral and written language more effectively, for learning facts or for learning new ways of thinking.

The Board, uneducated about language and literacy, held the prevailing underlying theoretical orientation to literacy and operated with traditional notions about what school should be like—even if many of their own family and friends had failed in just those kinds of schools. District Office personnel (Title I Director, Migrant Program Director, Curriculum Director, Language Arts Coordinator) and school principals shared the Board's underlying assumptions. Moreover, they had the credentials, they were in step with the State legislature and popular opinion, they knew the jargon, and, as I have indicated, they had gained the power within the District that lent even more legitimacy to the popular view. Teachers too held a skills theory of language and literacy, but some were beginning to question parts of that theory; some were beginning to revise underlying assumptions in a holistic direction. All envisioned schooling as far less traditional, less subject-segregated, and less textbook-oriented than their principals. Bergionni, of course, was squarely in the Whole Language camp, as were her consultants. But neither she nor the consulting staff spent large enough blocks of time (e.g., all day for several weeks) or made frequent enough follow-up visits (i.e., weekly) to the classroom to work with the individual teachers, side by side, socializing them into a new worldview as well as a new practice. So there they were—District administration and Board on one theoretical and curricular side; Bergionni and consultants on another; teachers somewhere in between on some issues, lined up with the District administration on others, with Bergionni on still others.

Unfortunately—and typically, I think—the curricular and theoretical issues were never aired in any detail. From the outside, it looked like nothing more than political in-fighting. All the complex and contradictory ideas about the nature of learning, language, and literacy, though always implicitly part of the struggle, were never given a hearing. Bergionni's decision to leave with dignity, to refuse to let the community know that she had been fired, was significant in helping her cope with the private turmoil engendered by this professional defeat. However, that decision also had the unforeseen effect of closing off one opportunity for bringing the theoretical dispute into the open. Not that a debate between a "skills" view of reading/writing and language arts and a "whole language" view would have resulted in District or community support for Bergionni's position. It would have been a most unbalanced contest. On one side would have been the weight of tradition, deep and pervasive beliefs that reading and writing consist of separate skills, and a major institution with a closed system of interlocking parts (testing, materials, instructional program, teacher preparation programs) based on and reinforcing a skills view. On the other side would have been some highly respectable empirical data to support a holistic view, a relatively small number of people to support it—people with high standing in the research community (but unknown elsewhere) along with a handful of educators able to disentangle the typical from the inherent in order to even perceive a Whole Language view. Still, even a lost debate would have made the "whole language" position less strange in future discussions. But that never happened.

If the teachers were caught in the middle as influence over curriculum and instruction was part of what was being fought over, the children were on the receiving end. And, as it turned out, from my perspective what they received was the short end. By the Fall of 1983, they were again taking part in an instructional program many of their older siblings had failed at or dropped out of—only now the program was offered in two languages. True, that is somewhat of an improvement. But from the problems monolingual English speakers have with instruction based on a skills orientation to monolingual English literacy (and similar problems for native Spanish speakers in regard to monolingual Spanish literacy instruction, described by Ferreiro & Teberosky, 1982), there seems little reason to hope that the use of Spanish alone will prevent school failure.

As a researcher, I must acknowledge that there is no definitive proof from this study that these particular children would have sustained their initial school success if they had been offered a curriculum based on authentic reading and writing. Although we did see how children blossomed at first with an introduction to *in*authentic journals and *simulations* of writing instead of workbooks and blatant exercises, we never did have the opportunity to see the impact over time of frequent authentic writing on written language development. (Such opportunity has been offered in other studies, however—(Edelsky et al., 1983a; Calkins, 1983; Graves, 1983.) The opportunity was not denied us because authentic writing was tried, failed, and then scuttled, or because it is such an inherently difficult idea that it was impossible to put it into practice. It was not tried because it is not a matter of "try and see and then go back to the other if it doesn't work." "Trial" in relation to Whole Language means a change in underlying worldview regarding literacy and language as well as instructing (choosing materials, providing information, evaluating) according to that worldview. Once a shift in worldview occurs, one does not revert to the old one if trouble arises. (The new worldview becomes a given, as the old one was. When practice falters, the cognitive tinkering is with less fundamental analyses, but not with the worldview itself [Kuhn, 1970].) Teachers would have had to have shifted *paradigms* (not just techniques) from "skills" to "whole language" if we were to have seen *writing* (not "writing") develop.

The urgings, suggestions, and demonstrations of one Program Director and a few consultants did not provide enough contextual support to effect this change in fundamental beliefs and practices. Regardless of the theoretical strengths of the idea, regardless of the various markers of success that went along with even surface shifts in practice, without active support (and certainly absence of punishment) from various other contexts, teachers could not establish the classroom contexts required for authentic written language use.

We began this research optimistically, having great faith in the children's ability to succeed in school when school meant reading and writing that incorporated "skills" into authentic use rather than when it meant "skills" by themselves. We also began it pessimistically, worrying, knowing that the ax was soon to fall on the Bilingual Program. And we began with a strong theoretical stance that contexts matter, that what is going on in the classroom, the school, the District, the community is important to the production of a piece of writing. Analyses of data from the study year confirmed our optimism. They also elaborated and refined our stance on contexts. It became clear that contexts were not background settings; they were vehicles through which development occurred. Unfortunately, the years following the data collection year justified the pessimism. The ax did fall, though not at the time, in the manner, or with the outcomes we had predicted. Those years, too, further illuminated the centrality of contexts—the extent to which they are implicated in a theory of reading and writing, the impact they had on the daily practices in classrooms, and the shape they gave to the life history of one small Bilingual Program in the Southwest.

QUESTIONS USED IN INTERVIEWS WITH TEACHERS AND AIDES

1. When does writing occur in your classroom? (Talk about time, what counts as ''writing''?)
2. What is the writing time like?
3. What benefits do you expect from doing writing in school?
4. What changes do you expect to see in the writing over the course of the year?
5. What relationships do you see between writing in the first language and writing in the second language?
6. Do children have to complete their writing? When? Which pieces?
7. What do you consider good/bad writing?
8. How are the journals done? The invented stories? Where do the topics come from?
9. What material is used in your reading program?
10. How much time do you devote to reading?
11. When and from what material do you read aloud to the children?
12. What other reading do the children do in Spanish?

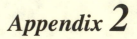

Appendix 2

CATEGORIES FOR CODING THE WRITING DATA

Aspect	Category and Coding Abbreviation		Example
Code switching	(*wcs*)	word code switch (if the same switched word or phrase occurred several times in one piece it was only counted once)	
	Number of switched words		
	Orthography of switched item		
	(*orth S*)	Spanish	mi pari (party)
	(*orth E*)	English	Mr.
	(*both +*)	used in each language	muy sad/muy triste[a]
	(*wcls*)	word class of the switch	
		(*n+*) noun agreeing in gender/number	un pari
		(*n−*) noun not agreeing in gender/number	Ias cowboy están (the cowboy are)
		(*add*) address term	Mr.
		(*adj*) adjective	es muy crazy (he's very crazy)
		(*art*) article	la teacher
		(*exc*) exclamation	Popeye dijo yay (Popeye said yay)
		(*prep*) preposition	de Mario (by Mario)
		(*v*) verb	el hace protect (he protects)
	(*phcs*)	phrase code switch	

Appendix 2 (*Continued*)

Aspect	Category and Coding Abbreviation	Example
	(phrase = 2 or more adjacent words in one constituent)	
	number of switched phrases	
	(*frm* +) formulaic	fioltrip (field trip)
	(*frm* −) non-formulaic	bear in the woods
	orthography of the switch	
	(*orth* S) Spanish	estic bol (stick ball)
	(*orth* E) English	little black sambo
(*sent* +)	phrase is a sentence	I hope you go again to school
(*sent* −)	phrase is not a sentence	me gusta *el low rider* (I like the low rider)
(*fit*)	switch fits into "flow"	
	(+) yes	se llama Little Black Sambo (his name is LBS)
	(−) no	el Christmas tree Christmas
(*REAS*)	Inferred reason for switch	
	(*cl*) clarity	miramos cactus de christmas cactus de Navidad (we saw Christmas cactus, Christmas cactus)
	(*egi*) ethnic group identity	Querido *Mr.* Adler (Dear Mr. Adler)
	(*ll*) learned in that language	hicimos popcorn (we made popcorn)
	(*lv*) lexical variation (synonym instead of repetition?)	triste. . . . . . .sad (in same piece)
	(*tpt*) teacher provided phrase/word in that language	Bear in the Woods (title)
Spelling Inventions	(a maximum of 3 pages per piece were analyzed for spelling to make the task manageable—the first and last pages and one in the middle)	
	(*INV*) Inventive treatment of multiple instances of same word	

(*continued*)

Appendix 2 (*Continued*)

Aspect	Category and Coding Abbreviation		Example
	(*dif*)	different invention each time	mayestra . . . maeyestra . . . mallestra (maestra/teacher)
	(*rtdif*)	some spellings conventional, others different	vamos . . . bamos . . . bmos (vamos/we go)
	(*rtsta*)	some spellings conventional, others stable inventions	vamos . . . bamos . . . bamos (vamos/we go)
	(*sta*)	stable inventions	jimos . . . jimos (fuimos/we went)
(*VINV*)	number of vowel inventions		
(*CINV*)	number of consonant inventions (a vowel or consonant invention in a word appearing more than once and spelled the same way in each appearance was counted only once regardless of the number of times the word appeared in that piece)		
			via (había, there was) = 1 vowel invention, 2 consonant inventions
			tene (tiene, she has) = 1 vowel invention
(*RINV*)	reason for invention		
	(*ell*)	elision (deletions occurring when 2 words are run together in flow of speech)	enthen (and then), van agarar (van a agarrar/they're going to get)
	(*lenm*)	letter name (uses sound of letter name rather than sound represented by letter)	staba (estaba/she was)
	(*norm*)	speech community norm (spelling corresponds to community's pronunciation)[b]	muncho (mucho, much), patras (para atrás/back)
	(*phft*)	phonetic feature (uses phonetic rather than phonics categories, such as place or manner of articulation, voicing, sound perceptibility)[c]	tanbien (manner of articulation) (también/also)

Appendix 2 (*Continued*)

Aspect	Category and Coding Abbreviation		Example
	(*phgen*)	phonic generalization (uses "rules" from phonics lessons, or pronunciation corresponds to anticipated spelling)	vien (*bien*/well), ciero (*quiero*/I want)
	(*sorth*)	use of Spanish orthography for English words	ceimar (K Mart), joup (hope)
	(*spst*)	spelling strategy (inferred prolonged pronunciation *within* a word, resulting in added letters)	ma*l*estra (maestra/teacher)
	(*x*)	we don't know	dlahimales (animales/animals)
	(*xL1, xL2*)	incomplete first or second language acquisition (spelling influenced by developmental level)	sabo (sé/1 know), motocico (motorcycle)

Non-Spelling Conventions

(*SEG*) Segmentation

	Category and Coding Abbreviation		Example
	(*conv*)	any conventional (+) yes (−) no	
	(*xconv*)	unconventional	
	(*conj*)	no space between conjunction and adjacent words or within a string of function words from same constituent	y*llo* voy (y yo voy/and I go), a*la* tienda (a la tienda/to the store)
	(*frm*)	no space within a formulaic chunk	ELFIN (El fin/The end)
	(*nm*)	no space within a name	Misdaton (Miss Dalton)
	(*none*)	no space within or between propositions	jimosaltendacomprsoda (Fuimos a la tienda. Compré soda./We went to the store. I bought soda.)
	(*not adj*)	no space between adverb and adjective	*muybonitas* (muy bonitas/very pretty)
	(*not cp*)	no space between words from contiguous	*paraceno* (para que no/so that + NEG)

(*continued*)

Appendix 2 (*Continued*)

Aspect	Category and Coding Abbreviation		Example
		different constituents or phrases	
	(*not NP*)	no space within an NP	*micasa* es bonita (mi casa es bonita/my house is pretty)
	(*not PP*)	no space within a prepositional phrase or between *a* and IO pronoun	*alatienda* (a la tienda/to the store), *ami* me gusta (a mí me gusta/I like)
	(*not VP*)	no space within a VP	*megusta* la flor (me gusta la flor/I like the flower)
	(*NPVP*)	space between but not within an NP and a VP	losreyes-letrajeron . . . (los reyes le trajeron . . ./the kings brought him . . .)
	(*syl*)	spaces between syllables	me *gus ta ba* (me gustaba/I liked)
	(*sylL*)	single letter stands by itself	stauor pous *T* ry (Star Wars poster y/Star Wars poster and)
	(*sylw*)	spaces between syllables within a word and one syllable is attached to adjacent word	es tamala (está mala/she's sick)
	(*xprop*)	no space within a proposition	jimosalcine (Fuimos al cine/we went to the movies)
(*PUNC*) Punctuation			
	(*com ap*)	appropriate use of comma	
	(*com nap*)	inappropriate use of comma	yo tengo, siete, anos (yo tengo siete años/I'm seven years old)
	(*cpend ex*)	number of expected complete sets	
	(*cpend ob*)	number of observed complete sets	
	(*hyp*)	used hyphen (anywhere)	
	(*invde*)	invented designs on letters	
	(*invend*)	invented end marks (stars, logos, etc.)	
	(*obc*)	number of observed capital letters (anywhere in piece)	
	(*obe*)	number of observed end marks	
	(*pcl*)	pattern, unconventional use of	

Appendix 2 (*Continued*)

Aspect	Category and Coding Abbreviation	Example
		capital at start of each line
	(*pcle*)	pattern, unconventional use of capitals for certain letters
	(*pcp*)	capitals to start each page of a piece but no other punctuation
	(*pmsf*)	capital to start and period at finish but no internal punctuation
	(*pnol*)	pattern, unconventional use of a number on each line
	(*ppe*)	period at end of piece but no other punctuation
	(*ppl*)	pattern, unconventional use of period at end of each line
	(*ppp*)	period at end of each page of a piece with no other punctuation
	(*ppw*)	pattern, unconventional use of period after certain words
	(*Q*)	used question mark (anywhere)
	(*unt*)	underlined the title
(*TILD*) Tildes		
	(−)	none required, none appear
	(+)	required and appear
	(∅)	required but missing	nino (niño/child)
	(*ap*)	used on appropriate letter
	(*napn*)	appears over the wrong nasal	ñino (niño/child)
	(*napv*)	appears over a vowel	una vẽs (una vez/one time)
(*ACNT*) Accent Marks		
	(*ap diph*)	used appropriately, to diphthongize	río (river)
	(*apstr*)	used appropriately, to maintain stress	mamá
	(*nap*)	used inappropriately	
	(*nr*) not required		sé fue (se fue/he left)
	(*onc*) on a consonant		eśa (esa/that)
	(*onxv*) on wrong vowel		diá (día/day)
(*HWT*) Handwriting		
	(*allcur*)	all in cursive	
	(*licur*)	some is in cursive	
	(*mocur*)	almost all in cursive (e.g., only child's name is in manuscript)	
	(*sccur*)	"scribbles" in cursive	
	(*cc*)	color of writing tool matches meaning of word	*rojo* is written with red marker

(*continued*)

Appendix 2 (*Continued*)

Aspect	Category and Coding Abbreviation		Example
	(*cnc*)	color of tool doesn't match meaning of word, but child uses different colors for different words	*rojo* is written with brown marker
	(*ex*)	explores (tries out different shapes for letters)	
	(*L*)	makes lines on unlined paper	

STYLISTIC DEVICES

(*SET*) Setting   takes place in or concerns:

	(*com*)	immediate community	See example (33), Chapter 4
	(*hom*)	home	Mi casa es rojo y el color rojo está bonito y muchas gracias mi mama está bonita. Yo tengo naranjas y manzanas y una bandera y me gusta muchísimo. (My house is red and the color red is pretty and thankfully my mother is pretty. I have oranges and apples and a flag and I like it very much.)
	(*imag*)	imaginary	See example (1), Chapter 4
	(*lcom*)	larger community	See example (73), Chapter 5
	(*outcom*)	outside the community	En mis vacaciones fuimos a Magdalena. Y en Magdalena fuimos a la Isla del Padre y en la Isla del Padre es un mar bien grande y allí te puedes bañar y será muy divertido. Y leugo fuimos a Reynosa. Fuimos a ver una tía mía y a mí me compraron un juego de lotería. Bueno, es todo. Gracias. (On my

Appendix 2 (*Continued*)

Aspect	Category and Coding Abbreviation		Example
			vacation we went to Magdalena. And at Magdalena we went to Padre Island. And on Padre Island it's a really big sea and there you can bathe and it'll be a lot of fun. And later we went to Reynosa. We went to see an aunt of mine and they bought me a lottery game. OK, that's all. Thank you.)
	(*rex*)	real but unknown setting	See example (47), Chapter 4
	(*sch*)	school	See example (26), Chapter 4
(*CHAR*) Characters Mentioned			
	(*an*)	animal	See example, (22), Chapter 4
	(*comad*)	community adult	See example (8), Chapter 4
	(*fam*)	family	See example (7), Chapter 4
	(*fant*)	fantasy	Hoy es jueves. Fantasma Espantoso (Today is Thursday. Frightening ghosts)
	(*hist*)	historical	See example (15), Chapter 4
	(*peer*)	peer	See example (20), Chapter 4
	(*perf*)	performers	See example (86), Chapter 5
	(*rel*)	religious figures	Hoy es jueves. Me gusta el niño de Dios y los reyes le trajeron regalos, muchos regalos. Estaban bonitos y los reyes le trajeron muchos regalos. Estamos haciendo un

(*continued*)

Appendix 2 (*Continued*)

Aspect	Category and Coding Abbreviation		Example
			libro y está bonito el libro de Jesús. (Today is Thursday. I like the Son of God and the kings brought him presents, many presents. They were pretty and the kings brought him many presents. We're making a book and it's nice, the book of Jesus.)
	(*schad*)	school adult	See example (16), Chapter 4
	(*self*)	self	See example (80), Chapter 5
	(*self +*)	self + unidentified others	See example (82), Chapter 5
(*DIAL*) Dialogue			
	(*dir*)	direct	See example (7), Chapter 4
	(*ind*)	indirect	Mi mamá dijo que se le quemó a mi tía y se le quemó la ropa. (My mother said that my aunt got burned and her clothes got burned.)
(*STSENS*) Sense of Story			
	(*pr*)	problem + resolution	See example (101), Chapter 7
	(*p*)	problem but no resolution	See example (70), Chapter 5
(*STYSYN*) Syntax That "Adds Style"			
	(*full*)	full or extended form	See example (83), Chapter 5
	(*rep*)	repeat of a pattern	See example (5), Chapter 4
	(*rev*)	reversal	Había una vez una princesa que estaba llorando todo el tiempo. *Estaba*

Appendix 2 (*Continued*)

Aspect	Category and Coding Abbreviation	Example
		llorando la princesa. La princesa estaba llorando. Está feliz porque tenía regalos. (Once upon a time there was a princess who was crying all the time. She was crying, the princess. The princess was crying. She's happy because she had presents.)
	(*incon*) inconsistent tense usage	See example (88), Chapter 5
	(*conpr*) consistent present	See example (16), Chapter 4
	(*conpt*) tense, consistent past	See example (39), Chapter 4
	(*1p*) consistent 1st person	See example (6), Chapter 4
	(*3p*) consistent 3rd person	See example (9), Chapter 4
	(*mxp*) mixed person	See example (10), Chapter 4

STRUCTURAL FEATURES

(*TP*) Type

	Category and Coding Abbreviation	Example
(*s*)	signature	
	(*s*) single	JOSÉ
	(*r*) repeated	Davíd (26 times)
(*c*)	caption (under a picture)	esta es una flor/this is a flower
(*j*)	journal	
	(*dscp*) description	Hoy es miércoles. Yo sé leer. Tenemos un cocono. (Today is Wednesday. I know how to read. I have a coconut.)
	(*ex*) exploring	faces drawn in letters, stylized letters
	(*h*) heading only	Hoy es lunes (Today is Monday)
	(*pl*) plans	Hoy es martes. Vamos en la montaña tener

(*continued*)

Appendix 2 (*Continued*)

Aspect	Category and Coding Abbreviation		Example
			vacaciones y 25 enero nos vamos a Texas. (Today is Tuesday. We're going to the mountain to take a vacation and the 25th of January we're going to Texas.)
	(*pos*)	position on one major topic	See example (84), Chapter 5
	(*r*)	reports	See example (20), Chapter 4
(*L*)	letter		
	(*grt*)	greeting (birthday or Christmas)	See example (12), Chapter 4
	(*gw*)	get well	See example (13), Chapter 4
	(*inf*)	informing (all about X)	See example (15), Chapter 4
	(*intr*)	introduction (to pen pal)	See example (16), Chapter 4
	(*inv*)	invitation	See example (18), Chapter 4
	(*r*)	news and chit-chat	See example (3), Chapter 4
	(*of*)	offer of help	Queridos Señores, Yo te quiero ayudar con los animales porque están en danger y se están muriendo muchos animales y una gente los matan y nomás los dejan tirados y una gente los matan y se comen la carne porque la necesitan. Tu querida amiga, P. (Dear Sirs, I want to help you with the animals because they're in danger and many animals are dying and some people kill them and leave them

Appendix 2 (*Continued*)

Aspect	Category and Coding Abbreviation	Example
		thrown around and some people kill them and eat the meat because they need it. Your dear friend, P.)
	(*rq*) request	See example (14), Chapter 4
	(*th*) thank you	See example (29a&b), Chapter 4
(*E*)	Expository	
	(*cd*) partially copied or dictated	Santa Clos trae presentes. Santa Clos trae muñecas. Santa Clos sale en la noche. Santa Clos trae carros. Los enanos ayudan a Santa Clos. Santa Clos trae juguetes. Santa Clos trae bolsas. (Santa Claus brings presents. Santa Claus brings dolls. Santa Claus goes out at night. Santa Clause brings cars. The dwarfs help Santa Claus. Santa Claus brings toys. Santa Clause brings bags.)
	(*dscp*) description	See example (1), Chapter 4
	(*Ilk*) "I like"	me gusta Carlos, me gusta Jorge, me gusta Juan (I like Carl, I like George, I like Juan)
	(*inf*) all about X	See example (86), Chapter 5
	(*pl*) plans	Yo voy a ser más grande y yo quiero trabajar en un restaurante y manejar los cocineros.

(*continued*)

Appendix 2 *(Continued)*

Aspect	Category and Coding Abbreviation	Example
		(I'm going to be bigger and I want to work in a restaurant and manage the cooks.)
	(*pos*) position on/reaction to non-media	See example (100), Chapter 7
	(*prj*) projecting into unlikely future	See example (10), Chapter 4
	(*r*) report	See example (75), Chapter 5
	(*srm*) summary of or reaction to media	See example (94), Chapter 5
(*st*) story		
	(*in*) invented	See example (97), Chapter 7
	(*re*) retelling of known story	Este es un cuento de un muchachito y se llamaba Little Black Sambo, etc. (This is a story of a little boy and his name was Little Black Sambo, etc.)
(*B*) book		
	(*c*) captions only (1 caption per picture per page)	
	(*st*) with story line	See example (95), Chapter 7
(*p*) poetry		
	(*nr*) non-rhyming	Carrito Tiene motor Corre como conejo Me gusta el carro Lowrider (Little car It has a motor It runs like a rabbit I like the car Lowrider)
	(*r*) rhyming	Los pajaritos son bonitos. A mí me gustan los pajaritos. Son muy bonitos y me gusta como vuelan. (The little birds are pretty.

Appendix 2 (*Continued*)

Aspect	Category and Coding Abbreviation		Example
			I like the little birds. They're very pretty And I like how they fly.)
	(*o*)	other (disconnected/random words)	Yo las . . . a . . . yo porque ya si ser y em a la . . . (I the to I because already if to be and [?] to the . . .)
(*LG*) Language			
	(*S*)	Spanish (though there may be isolated words or phrases in English)	
	(*E*)	English (though there may be isolated words or phrases in Spanish)	
	(*eS*)	begins in English, mostly in Spanish	
	(*ES*)	part English, part Spanish	
	(*Se*)	most in Spanish, ends in English	
	(*Es*)	most in English, ends in Spanish	
(*UN*) Unassigned			
	(+)	yes, child wrote spontaneously	
	(−)	no, child wrote as an assignment	
(*WD*) Words			
	(number, not counting "hoy es" in journals or signatures or heading in letter)		
(*CTP*) Culturally Specific Items			
	(part of culture of this community but not shared with Anglo community)		cebollas, lowrider, piñata, chicharrones, etc.
(*BT*) "Bootlegged" Topics			
	(parenthetically inserted into piece—child is tattling or being outrageous)		other children's or own misbehavior, drugs, blowing nose on mother, etc.
(*AUD*) Intended Reader			
	(*anonad*)	anonymous adult	See example under Type, letter offer

(*continued*)

Appendix 2 (*Continued*)

Aspect		Category and Coding Abbreviation	Example
	(*gen*)	general (a default category; when no one reader was named and when teacher had not directed child to write)	See example (9), Chapter 4
	(*in*)	child/animal in class	Estimado Loro, Me gusta el nombre Chiflo para tí y ayer sí escribí una carta para tí pero mi nombre estaba atrás del papel. C. (Esteemed Parrot, I like the name Chiflo for you and yesterday I *did* write a letter for you but my name was on the back of the paper. C.)
	(*inad*)	in-school adult	See example (13), Chapter 4
	(*out*)	child out of class	See example (16), Chapter 4
	(*outad*)	out-of-school, named adult	See example (18), Chapter 4
	(*Tdg*)	teacher in role of direction-giver (whenever the writing was prompted by the teacher's assignment and had no other named audience, the intended reader was inferred to be the teacher as giver of assignments/directions)	See example (75), Chapter 5
(*ACT*) Signals Knowledge That There is a Reader			
	(*aQ*)	answers remembered question posed by intended reader (e.g., teacher as direction-giver asked Q and child responded)	Me gusta mucho y estaba jugando con mis amigas . . . (I like it a lot and I was playing with my friends . . .) (no mention of what she likes)
	(*cl*)	clarifies an earlier statement	. . . una tía mía se casó con mi tío. Quiero a mi tía mía. Comí arroz y frijoles

Appendix 2 (*Continued*)

Aspect	Category and Coding Abbreviation	Example
		y cominmos carne y estaba rico. *Es Olivia C.* (. . . an aunt of mine got married to my uncle. I like my aunt. I ate rice and beans and we ate meat and it was delicious. She is Olivia C.)
(*cl PRO*)	closing pronoun in letter refers to reader	Tu amigo, F (Your friend, F)
(*cmpt*)	compliments intended reader	. . . y Ud. esta bonita . . . (. . . and you are pretty . . .)
(*dirSA*)	specific speech act directed to reader (e.g., a promise, request, question of information, order, etc.—compliments treated separately)	Querido Mr. F, ¿Cuánto cumpliste ahora? (Dear Mr. F, How old are you now?)
(*h*)	names intended reader in the heading	Querida Mrs. B (Dear Mrs. B)
(*mk*)	uses marks or arrows for reader (directing reader to turn page or to look up/down/sideways to find next words)	
(*nm*)	names intended reader in the text	Santa Clos, yo quiero que me traiga una bicicleta . . . (Santa Claus, I want you to bring me a bicycle . . .)
(*pinf*)	gives precise information about time or place	See example (18), Chapter 4
(*pol*)	politeness terms	. . . Es todo. Gracias (. . . That's all. Thank you)
(*pr*)	makes asides/parenthetical remarks	Ellos no querían a tomar agua del mar porque *yo no sé que pasa* ellos sabían que el agua tenía mucha sal. (They didn't want to drink the sea water because I don't

(continued)

Appendix 2 (*Continued*)

Aspect	Category and Coding Abbreviation		Example
			know what might happen, they knew that the water had a lot of salt.)
	(*ref2p*)	refers to intended reader in 2nd person	. . . y gracias a Ud., Mrs. S, porque nos dió paletas y le doy gracias otra y una vez . . . (. . . and thank you, Mrs. S, because you gave us popsicles and I thank you again and again . . .)
	(*ref3p*)	refers to intended reader in the 3rd person	. . . La maestra trajo sus niños . . . (. . . The teacher brought her children . . .)
	(*rlt*)	related own experiences to intended reader's experiences	See example (12), Chapter 4
	(*rhQ*)	rhetorical question	¿Y qúe para si mi hermano está así? (And what if my brother was like that?)
(*BEG*) Beginnings			
	(*char*)	introduces character	Este es el cuento de unos hombres que estaban ciegos y el mapache que les haciá males . . . (This is the story of some men who were blind and the raccoon that was doing them wrong . . .)
	(*frm*)	formula	Hoy es _____ (on journals) (Today is _____)
	(*1pt*)	first part of event	Yo me subí en el avión con mi hermana y miré al carnaval y miré muchas cosas y comí quequis . . . (I

Appendix 2 (*Continued*)

Aspect	Category and Coding Abbreviation	Example
		went up in an airplane with my sister and I looked at the carnival and I looked at a lot of things and I ate cakes . . .)
(*2pp*)	second pair part (second slot in a two-part sequence, such as *answer* in a question/answer sequence)	See example under Signals Knowledge That There is a Reader, answers remembered question
(*item*)	first item in an assortment or list	See example (73), Chapter 5
(*pos*)	position on topic or purpose of the piece	Me gusta el programa . . . (I like the program . . .)
(*prj*)	projecting into a contrary-to-fact situation (teacher has *not* provided the opening for all to write about)	Si yo no tenía un brazo, iba a ser muy triste . . . (If I didn't have an arm I was going to be very sad . . .)
(*reas*)	gives reason for writing	La clase está estudiando los Indios Creek y yo me dijo la maestra que tú sabes de los Navajos y no de Creek y me dijo que te mandábamos un cuento de los Indios Creek . . . (The class is studying the Creek Indians and the teacher just told me that you know about the Navajos and not about Creek and she told me that we should send you a story about the Creek Indians . . .) (goes on to tell about the Creek Indians)

(*continued*)

Appendix 2 (*Continued*)

Aspect	Category and Coding Abbreviation		Example
	(*rej*)	explicit rejection of teacher's topic	See example (15), Chapter 4
	(*stg*)	setting (establishing time or place)	Era oscuro y estaba lloviendo y tenía mucho miedo . . . (It was dark and it was raining and I was very afraid . . .)
	(*to*)	teacher-provided opening	Una noche iba yo manejando mi carro en camino para la casa de mi amigo. De repente se reventó una llanta. Cuanda me bajé de mi carro, oí un ruído espantoso . . . (One night I was driving my car along the road to my friend's house. Suddenly a tire blew. When I got out of my car, I heard a terrifying noise . . .) (children were to finish the piece)
	(*tpc*)	names topic	yo hice un totem pole . . . (I made a totem pole) (rest of piece is about the totem pole)
	(*ttl*)	title	How To Escape From The Pirates
	(*typ*)	states type	yo le mando esta *carta* con mucho cariño y . . . (I send you this letter with much affection and . . .)
(*END*) Endings			
	(*byn*)	by + name	. . . de María M.C. (. . . by María M.C.)
	(*dt*)	date	
	(*end*)	explicit end	Es todo. (That's all.), El Fin (The End)

Appendix 2 (*Continued*)

Aspect	Category and Coding Abbreviation		Example
	(*frm*)	formula	. . . feliz como siempre, tu amigo, M. (. . . happily ever after, your friend, M.)
	(*nc*)	no closure	lists, "I like."
	(*nice*)	something "nice"	. . . y estan bonitos. (. . . and they're nice.)
	(*nml*)	first name	
	(*nml+2*)	first and last name	
	(*pol*)	politeness	. . . y gracias maestra (. . . and thank you, Teacher)
	(*pos*)	position on the topic or purpose of the piece	See example (84), Chapter 5
	(*refbg*)	refers back to beginning	See example (9), Chapter 4
	(*sall*)	summary of the whole/total wrap-up	See example (85), Chapter 5
	(*spt*)	summary of or comment on a part	See example (44), Chapter 4
	(*x*)	unfinished (stopped mid-word or mid-sentence)	
	(*xnxt*)	more complex structure or more elaborate, longer, or emphatic wording for last lines or clauses	See example (83), Chapter 5
(*OP*) Organizational Principle			

(Categorizing a piece as organized according to time, space, associative, or classificatory principles was not done simply by looking at linking words such as *because* or *then*, since such words did not always signal causal or temporal relations between clauses. It was these relations, inferred by the adult reader, that were used for coding organizational principles.)

	(*ass*)	associative (loosely connected ideas, no apparent hierarchy)	See example (24), Chapter 4
	(*bs*)	big shift in topic, type, or intended reader	See example (17), Chapter 4
	(*cd*)	dictated or copied	See example below under Organizational Principle, repetition of a frame
	(*clas*)	classificatory (a hierarchy of ideas)	See example (84), Chapter 5
	(*f*)	repetition of a frame	Santa Clos trae presentes. Santa Clos

(*continued*)

Appendix 2 (*Continued*)

Aspect	Category and Coding Abbreviation	Example
		trae muñecas. Santa Clos sale en la noche. Santa Clos trae carros. Los enanos le ayudan al Santa Clos. Santa Clos trae juguetes. Santa Clos trae dulces. (Santa Claus brings presents. Santa Claus brings dolls. Santa Claus goes out at night. Santa Claus brings cars. The dwarfs help Santa Claus. Santa Claus brings toys. Santa Claus brings candy.)
	(*frm*) uses known formula and fills in slots	Habían 10 conejitos. Uno se fue. Habían 9 conejitos . . . (There were 10 little rabbits. One left, there were 9 little rabbits. . . . Completes the structure borrowed from "Ten Little Indians.")
	(*rdm*) random words or phrases	See example under Type, Other
	(*rep*) repetition/duplication of clauses	Totem poles protect you. They have faces of animals. My totem pole has a lion on it. Totem poles are big and they have wings and they are too big and they are too big and they are too big and they are from the Navajos.
	(*sp*) space (co-occurring attributes or events)	See example (20), Chapter 4
	(*ti*) time	See example (6), Chapter 4

Appendix 2 (*Continued*)

Aspect	Category and Coding Abbreviation		Example
(*COH*) Cohesion (*EXO*) Exophoric Reference			
	(*goth*)	general other(s) (child probably does not know who "they" are)	See example under Type, letter, offer of help
	(*poth*)	particular other(s)	See example (41), Chapter 4
	(*rdr*)	reader	See example (2), Chapter 4
	(*ttl*)	title	See example (93), Chapter 4
	(*w*)	writer	See example (44), Chapter 4
	(*w+*)	writer + others	See example (39), Chapter 4
(*LINK*) Links Between Clauses			
	(*and*)	additive	y (and), y también (and also), 4 others
	(*but*)	adversative	pero (but), 4 others
	(*so*)	causative	porque (because), por eso (therefore), 20 others
	(*then*)	temporal	cuando (when), luego (later), 14 others
	(*other*)	other	que (that), donde (where), 7 others
	(∅)	no links	See example (19a), Chapter 4
(*QATT*) Quality Attributes in the Content			
	(*apa*)	awareness of audience or purpose	
	(*can*)	candor (also realism)	
	(*coh*)	coherent (understandable to adult reader)	
	(*exl*)	expressive language (uses analogy, metaphor, dialogue, onomatopeia)	
	(*inf*)	informative (descriptive, detailed)	
	(*ins*)	insight (below-the-surface perspective)	
	(*iow*)	involvement of the writer (shows personal feelings, sincerity, genuineness, tries to convince, advises reader)	

(*continued*)

Appendix 2 (*Continued*)

Aspect	Category and Coding Abbreviation		Example
	(*org*)	organization (sequential, complete, closure included)	
	(*ori*)	originality (tackles a problem, uses fantasy or humor, seems unique)	
	(*voc*)	unique or varied vocabulary	

[a]Wherever segmentation and spelling are not at issue, adult conventions have been used for the examples provided.

[b]To help in determining the category of community norms of Spanish, we turned to: Sanchez, R. Nuestra circunstancia linguistica. *El Grito 6:* 45–74, 1972.

[c]Two sources were used to help determined place and/or manner of articulation for this category. These were: Stockwell, R. & Bowen, J.D. *The Sounds of English and Spanish.* Chicago: University of Chicago Press, 1965; and Quilis, A. & Fernandez, J. *Curso de Fonética y Fonología Española.* Madrid: Consejo Superior de Investigaciones Científicas, Instituto Miguel de Cervantes, 1969.

REFERENCES

Amastae, J. Investigating bilingualism on the border: A review. In F. Barkin, E. Brandt, & J. Ornstein-Galicia (eds.), *Multilingualism: Languages in contact in the borderlands*. New York: Teachers College Press, 1982.

Anderson, A., Teale, W., & Estrada, E. Low income children's pre-school literacy experiences: Some naturalistic observations. *Quarterly Newsletter of the Laboratory of Comparative Human Cognition 2:3:*59–66, 1980.

Barkin, F. Personal communication, 1981.

Barrera, R. Reading in Spanish: Insights from children's miscues. In S. Hudelson (ed.), *Learning to read in different languages*. Arlington, VA: Center for Applied Linguistics, 1981.

Bereiter, C. Development in writing. In L. Gregg & E. Steinberg (eds.), *Processes in writing*. Hillsdale, NJ: Erlbaum, 1979.

Birnbaum, J. Why should I write: Environmental influences on children's views of writing. *Theory Into Practice 19:3:*202–210, 1980.

Bissex, B. Patterns of development in writing: A case study. *Theory Into Practice 19:3:*197–201, 1980.

_____. Seeing writing: Acts of re-vision. Paper presented at annual meeting of The National Council of Teachers of English, Boston, 1981.

Boiarsky, C. Learning to write by writing. *Educational Leadership 38:6:*463–464, 1981.

Braddock, R. English composition. In R. Ebel (ed.), *Encyclopedia of educational research, 4th Ed*. Toronto, Canada: MacMillan, 1969.

Calkins, L. Children learn the writer's craft. *Language Arts 57:2:*207–213, 1980.

_____. *Lessons from a child*. Exeter, NH: Heinemann, 1983.

Carter, R. & Cuscoe-Lanasa, B. A study of a compilation and analysis of writing vocabulary in Spanish of Mexican American children. *AILA*, 1978.

Clay, M. Reading errors and self-correction behavior. *British Journal of Educational Psychology 39:*47–56, 1969.

_____. *What did I write?* Auckland, New Zealand: Heinemann Educational Books, 1975.

_____. *Write now, read later: An evaluation*. Auckland, New Zealand: Auckland Council of The IRA, 1977.

Cole, M. Introduction. In U. Bronfenbrenner, *The ecology of human development*. Cambridge, MA: Harvard University Press, 1979.

Coles, R. & Goodman, Y. Do we really need those oversized pencils to write with? *Theory Into Practice 19:3:*194–196, 1980.

Cronbach, L. Beyond the two disciplines of scientific psychology. *American Psychologist 30:*116–127, 1975.

Cronnell, B. Black English and spelling. *Research in the Teaching of English 13:*81-90, 1979.

Cummins, J. Linguistic interdependence and the educational development of bilingual children. *Review of Educational Research 49:*222-251, 1979.

Davison, A. & Kantor, B. On the failure of readability formulas to define readable texts: A case study from adaptations. *Reading Research Quarterly 17:2:*187-209, 1982.

DeFord, D. Young children and their writing. *Theory Into Practice 19:3:*157–162, 1980.

————. Literacy: Reading, writing and other essentials. *Language Arts 58:6:*652–658, 1981.

Donnelly, C. & Stevens, G. Streams and puddles: A comparison of two writers. *Language Arts 57:7:*735–741, 1980.

Dyson, A. Teachers and young children: Missed connections in teaching/learning to write. *Language Arts 59:7:*674–680, 1982.

————. The role of oral language in early writing processes. *Research in the Teaching of*

Edelsky, C. The child as sociolinguist. ED 179 977, 1980.

————. Development of writing in a bilingual program. Final report, Project NIE G-81-0051, 1982.

————. A critique of several versions of popular theory: Plus ça change, plus c'est la même chose. In H. Trueba & B. Blair (eds.), *Advances in second language literacy.* San Diego: Center for Ethnographic Research, San Diego State University, 1983a.

————. SEGMENTATIONANDPUNC·TU·A·TION: Developmental data from a study of young children's writing. *Research in the Teaching of English 17:2:*135–156, 1983b.

Edelsky, C. & Draper, K. Reading/"reading"; writing/"writing"; text/"text." In A. Petrosky (ed.), *Reading and writing: Theory and research.* Norwood, NJ: Ablex, in press.

Edelsky, C., Draper, K., & Smith, K. Hookin' 'em in at the start of school in a "whole language" classroom. *Anthropology and Education Quarterly 14:4:*257–281, 1983a.

Edelsky, C., Hudelson, S., Flores, B., Barkin, F., Altwerger, B., & Jilbert, K. Semi-lingualism and language deficit. *Applied Linguistics 4:1:*1–22, 1983b.

Edelsky, C. & Smith, K. Is that writing—or are those marks just a figment of your curriculum? *Language Arts 61:1:*24–32, 1984.

Emig, J. Non-magical thinking. In C. Frederickson, M. Whiteman, & J. Dominic (eds.), *The nature, development, and teaching of written communication,* vol. 2. Hillsdale, NJ: Erlbaum, 1982.

Ervin-Tripp, S. & Mitchell-Kernan, C. ⌐hild discourse. New York: Academic Press, 1977.

Ferreiro, E. What is written in a written sentence? A developmental answer. *Journal of Education 160:*25–39, 19⁷ ⁾

————. The relation between oral and written language: The children's viewpoints. Paper presented at annual meeting of International Reading Association, St. Louis, 1980.

Ferreiro, E. & Teberosky, A. *Literacy before schooling* (Translated by K. Castro). Exeter, NH: Heinemann, 1982.

Fillmore, L. W. The second time around: Cognitive and social strategies in second language acquisition. Doctoral dissertation, Stanford University, 1976.

Fishman, J. Lecture under the stars, Summer lecture series. University of New Mexico, Albuquerque, July, 1980.

Flores, B. Bilingual reading instructional practices: The three views of the reading process as they relate to the concept of language interference. *California Journal of Teacher Education 8:3:*98–122, 1981.

Flower, L. & Hayes, J. A cognitive process theory of writing. Paper presented at Conference on College Composition and Communication, March, 1980.

Giacobbe, M. E. Who says that children can't write the first week of school? Unpublished manuscript, n.d.

Glaser, B. *Theoretical sensitivity*. Mill Valley, CA: Sociology Press, 1978.

Goodman, K. Analysis of oral reading miscues: Applied psycho-linguistics. *Reading Research Quarterly 5:*9–30, 1969.

———. The reading process: Theory and practice. In R. Hodges & E. Rudorf (eds.), *Language and learning to read*. New York: Houghton Mifflin, 1972.

———. Acquiring literacy is natural: Who skilled Cock Robin? *Theory Into Practice 16:*309–314, 1977.

Goodman, K. & Goodman, Y. Reading of American children whose language is a stable rural dialect of English or a language other than English. Final report, Project NIE C-00-3-0087, 1978.

———. Learning to read is natural. In L. Resnick & P. Weaver (eds.), *Theory and practice of early reading*. Hillsdale, NJ: Erlbaum, 1979.

———. A whole-language comprehension-centered view of reading development. Manuscript prepared for NIE, 1981.

Goodman K., Goodman, Y., & Flores, B. *Reading in the bilingual classroom: Literacy and biliteracy*. Rosslyn, VA: National Clearinghouse for Bilingual Education, 1979.

Gottesman, J. & Schilling, M. *A common ground for assessing competence in written expression*. Office of the Los Angeles County Superintendent of Schools, 1979.

Graves, D. An examination of the writing processes of seven year old children. *Research in the Teaching of English 9:*227–241, 1975.

———. Andrea learns to make writing hard. *Language Arts 56:5:*569–576, 1979a.

———. Growth and development of first grade writers. Paper presented at annual meeting of Canadian Council of Teachers of English, Ottawa, 1979b.

———. Let children show us how to help them write. Unpublished manuscript, 1979c.

———. Research doesn't have to be boring. *Language Arts 56:1:*76–80, 1979d.

———. A new look at writing research. *Language Arts 57:8:*913–919, 1980.

———. *Writing: Teachers and children at work*. Exeter, NH: Heinemann, 1983.

Griffin, P. Untitled, unpublished manuscript. Arlington, VA: Center for Applied Linguistics, n.d.

Halliday, M. A. K. *Language as social semiotic: The social interpretation of language and meaning*. Baltimore: University Park Press, 1978.

Halliday, M. A. K. & Hasan, R. *Cohesion in English*. London: Longman, 1976.

Harste, J. Language as social event. Paper presented at annual meeting of American Educational Research Association, Boston, 1980a.

———. Written language development: A natural concern. Paper presented at NIE-FIPSE Grantee Workshop, Los Angeles, 1980b.

————. Personal communication, 1981.

Harste, J. & Burke, C. A new hypothesis for reading teacher research: Both teaching and learning of reading are theoretically based. In P. D. Pearson (ed.), *Reading: Theory, research and practice. Twenty-sixth yearbook of the National Reading Conference*. St. Paul, MN: Mason Publishing Company, 1977.

————. Examining instructional assumptions: The child as informant. *Theory Into Practice 19:3*:170–178, 1980.

Harste, J., Burke, C., & Woodward, V. Children's language and world: Initial encounters with print. In J. Langer and M. Smith-Burke (eds.), *Bridging the gap: Reader meets author*. Newark, DE: IRA, 1981.

————. Children, their language and world: Initial encounters with print. Final report, Project NIE G-79-0132, 1982.

————. The young child as writer-reader and informant. Final report, Project NIE G-80-0121, 1983.

Harste, J. & Carey, R. Comprehension as setting. In J. Harste & R. Carey (eds.), *New Perspectives on comprehension, Monograph in language and reading studies, no. 3*. Bloomington, IN: Indiana University, 1979.

Hatch, E. *Second language acquisition*. Rowley, MA: Newbury House, 1978.

Heath, S. B. Oral and literate traditions—endless linkages. In A. Humes (ed.), *Moving between practice and research in writing*. Los Alamitos, CA: SWRL, 1981.

————. What no bedtime story means: Narrative skills at home and at school. *Language in Society 11:1*:49–76, 1982.

Hudelson, S. Kan yu ret an rayt en ingles: Children become literate in English as a second language. *TESOL Quarterly 18:2*:221–238, 1984.

————. An examination of children's invented spellings in Spanish. Unpublished manuscript, n.d.

Humes, A. A method for evaluating writing samples. SWRL Technical Note TN 2-80/02, Los Alamitos, CA, 1980.

Hymes, S. The ethnography of speaking. In J. Fishman (ed.), *Readings in the sociology of language*. The Hague: Mouton, 1970.

————. *Language in education: Ethnolinguistic essays, Language and ethnography series*. Arlington, VA: Center for Applied Linguistics, 1980.

Kamler, B. One child, one teacher, one classroom: The story of one piece of writing. *Language Arts 57:6*:680–693, 1980.

King, M. & Rentel, V. Quarterly report for NIE, Projects 8-0555 and 790137, Cognitive processes of contextual features produced by children in three modes of discourse, June 1, 1980–September 1, 1980.

Kjolseth, R. Bilingual education programs in the U.S.: For assimilation or pluralism? In B. Spolsky (ed.), *The language education of minority children*. Rowley, MA: Newbury House, 1972.

Krashen, S. Second language acquisition lecture notes. Summer Institute of Linguistics, University of New Mexico, Albuquerque, 1980.

Kroll, B. Developing a sense of audience. *Language Arts 55:7*:828–831, 1978.

Kuhn, T. *The structure of scientific revolutions*. Chicago: University of Chicago Press, 1970.

Laboratory for Comparative Human Cognition. A model system for the study of learning disabilities. *Quarterly Newsletter of the Laboratory for Comparative Human Cognition 4:3*:39–66, 1982.

Labov, W. The logic of non-standard English. In F. Williams (ed.), *Language and poverty*. Chicago: Markham, 1970.

Lindfors, J. *Children's language and learning*. Englewood Cliffs, NJ: Prentice Hall, 1980.

————. Grant proposal, Mina Shaughnessy Scholars Program, Fund for the Improvement of Post-Secondary Education, 1984.

McDermott, R. Social relations as contexts for learning in school. *Harvard Educational Review 47:2*:198–213, 1977.

Mejías, H. Errors and variants in Spanish composition. *Proceedings of SWALLOW VII*: 88–112, 1978.

Milz, V. First graders can write: Focus on communication. *Theory Into Practice 19:3*: 179–185, 1980.

Moffett, J. & Wagner, B. J. *Student centered language arts and reading, K-13*. New York: Houghton-Mifflin, 1976.

Natalicio, D. Reading and the bilingual child. In L. Resnick & P. Weaver (eds.), *Theory and practice of early reading, vol. 3*. Hillsdale NJ: Erlbaum, 1979.

Newkirk, T. Cognition and writing. *Harvard Educational Review 52:1*:84–89, 1982.

Odell, L. Writing in non-academic settings. Paper presented at The Colloquium Series on Qualitative Research, Arizona State University, Tempe, AZ, 1982.

Ogbu, J. School ethnography: A multilevel approach. *Anthropology and Education Quarterly 12:1*:3–29, 1981.

Oksaar, E. Multilingualism and multiculturalism from the linguist's point of view. In T. Husen & S. Opper (eds.), *Multilingual and multicultural education in immigrant countries*. Oxford: Pergamon Press, 1983.

Perl, S. How teachers teach the writing process. *Elementary School Journal 84:1*:19–44, 1983.

Peters, A. The units of language acquisition. *Working Papers in Linguistics 12:1*, University of Hawaii, 1980.

Poplack, S. 'Sometimes I'll start a sentence in English y termino en español': Toward a typology of code switching. Language Policy Task Force #4. New York: Centro de Estudios Puertorriquenos, 1979.

Pratt, M. L. *Toward a speech act theory of literary discourse*. Bloomington, IN: Indiana University Press, 1977.

Quillis, A. & Fernandez, J. *Curso de fonética y fonología Española*. Madrid: Consejo Superior de Investigaciones Científicas, Instituto Miguel de Cervantes, 1969.

Raimes, A. Tradition and revolution. *TESOL Quarterly 17:4*:535–552, 1983.

Read, C. *Children's categorizations of speech sounds in English*. Urbana, IL: NCTE, 1975.

Rentel, V. A longitudinal study of children's planning and cohesion in three modes of discourse: Interactive speech, dictation, and writing. In A. Humes (ed.), *Moving between practice and research in writing*. Los Alamitos, CA: SWRL, 1981.

Rosenblatt, L. *The reader, the text, the poem*. Carbondale, IL: Southern Illinois University Press, 1978.

Rosier, P. & Farella, M. Bilingual education at Rock Point: Some early results. *TESOL Quarterly 10:4*:379–388, 1976.

Sanchez, R. Nuestra circunstancia linguistica. *El Grito 6*:45–74, 1972.

Scribner, S. & Cole, M. Unpackaging literacy. In M. Whiteman (ed.), *Writing: The nature, development and teaching of written communication, Vol. 1, Variation in writing.* Hillsdale, NJ: Erlbaum, 1981.

Shanklin, N. Relating reading and writing: Developing a transactional theory of the writing process. Unpublished doctoral dissertation, Indiana University, 1981.

Shuy, R. Relating research on oral language functions to research on written discourse. Paper presented at annual meeting of American Educational Research Association, Los Angeles, 1981.

Skutnabb-Kangas, T. & Toukomaa, P. *Teaching migrant children's mother tongue and learning the language of the host country in the context of the sociocultural situation of the migrant family.* Helsinki: The Finnish National Commission for UNESCO, 1976.

Smith, F. *Comprehension and learning.* New York: Holt, Rinehart & Winston, 1975.

_____. *Understanding reading,* 2d edition. New York: Holt, Rinehart & Winston, 1978.

_____. The language arts and the learner's mind. In R. Farr & D. Strickler (eds.), *Reading comprehension: Resource guide.* Bloomington, IN: Indiana University Reading Programs, 1980.

_____. *Writing and the writer.* New York: Holt, Rinehart & Winston, 1982.

_____. Reading like a writer. *Language Arts 60:5:*558–567, 1983.

Sowers, S. A six year old's writing process: The first half of first grade. *Language Arts 56:7:*829–835, 1979.

_____. KDS CN RIT SUNR THN WE THINGK. *Learning,* in press.

Staton, J., Shuy, R., Kreeft, J., & Reed, L. *Interactive writing in dialogue journals: Linguistic, social and cognitive views.* Norwood, NJ: Ablex (in press).

Stein, N. & Glenn, C. An analysis of story comprehension in elementary school children. In R. Freedle (ed.), *New directions in discourse processing.* Norwood, NJ: Ablex, 1979.

Stockwell, R. & Bowen, J. D. *The sounds of English and Spanish.* Chicago: University of Chicago Press, 1965.

Szwed, J. The ethnography of literacy. In M. Whiteman (ed.), *Writing: The nature, development and teaching of written communication, Vol. 1, Variation in writing.* Hillsdale, NJ: Erlbaum, 1981.

Temple, C. Spelling errors in Spanish. Doctoral dissertation, University of Virginia, 1978.

Temple, C., Nathan, R., & Burris, N. *The beginnings of writing.* Boston: Allyn & Bacon, 1982.

Urzúa, C. A language learning environment for all children. *Language Arts 57:1:*38–44, 1980.

Vygotsky, L. *Mind in Society.* Edited by M. Cole, V. John-Steiner, S. Scribner, & E. Souberman. Cambridge, MA: Harvard University Press, 1978.

Wellmeier, N. Personal communication, 1981.

Whiteman, M. What we can learn from writing research. *Theory Into Practice 19:3:*150–156, 1980.

Woodward, V. On confusing product for process. Paper presented at annual meeting of National Council of Teachers of English, Cincinnati, 1980.

Zappert, L. & Cruz, B. *Bilingual education: An appraisal of empirical research.* Berkeley, CA: BABEL/Lau Center, 1977.

AUTHOR INDEX

Italics indicate bibliographic citations

SUBJECT INDEX